PRAISE FOR *ASK*

"I am delighted to provide a few opening thoughts for this remarkable new book about the challenge of learning what we most need to know from the people around us.... In this readable, compassionate, intelligent, and useful book, Jeff Wetzler teaches us how to do just that... And learning how to ask others what they truly think, know, and feel has never been more important." [Excerpted from Foreword]

—Amy Edmondson, HBS professor and author of *The Fearless Organization* and *Right Kind of Wrong*

"In *Ask*, Jeff Wetzler goes deep on the first step in the Radical Candor order of operations: solicit candor. The book provides an invaluable, highly actionable method for drawing out the real thoughts, feelings, and experiences of those around you. If you want to build relationships and organizations rooted in honesty and openness—improving learning, innovation, and results in the process—this book is required reading. *Ask* gets to the heart of what it takes to invite the full humanity of those around you."

—Kim Scott, bestselling author of *Radical Candor* and *Radical Respect*

"Most people see value in sharpening their listening skills, but few know where to start. This book is an actionable guide to improving at inquiry—and to learning more and bonding more with the people around you."

—Adam Grant, #1 *New York Times* bestselling author of *Hidden Potential* and *Think Again*, and host of the podcast *Re:Thinking*

"Asking and listening are at the heart of what it means to be a human being in relationship with others. In *Ask*, Jeff Wetzler presents a practical framework for uncovering the wisdom inside in the hearts and minds of those around you. The tools in this book offer an antidote to our age of disconnection, taking seriously the potential for creativity, collaboration, and courage within us and between us. Here's a book that points the way to a larger life."

—Parker J. Palmer, author of *Let Your Life Speak, Healing the Heart of Democracy,* and *On the Brink of Everything*

"In *Ask,* Jeff Wetzler demystifies the art and science of asking the right questions to move beyond perfunctory responses. The tools offered in this book, which Jeff models better than anyone I know, provide a practical road map to a more productive, collaborative, and effective approach to both personal and professional interactions."

—Irene Rosenfeld, former chair and CEO of Kraft Foods and Mondelēz International

"Jeff Wetzler's breakthrough book, *Ask,* unlocks the key to building authentic relationships by asking deeply personal and intimate questions. Jeff's unique framework, illustrated through moving stories, shows us how to move from judgment to authenticity in our relationships, and lights the way to our personal growth."

—Bill George, former chair and CEO of Medtronic, executive fellow at Harvard Business School, and bestselling author of *True North*

"The greatest resource for anyone passionate about making a big impact is the wisdom of the people around us—from those closest to the issues being addressed to our team members, partners, and investors. *Ask* is an inviting and easy guide for unlocking this wisdom and elevating the voices we most need to hear. This book is essential reading for anyone looking to make positive change in the world."

—Wendy Kopp, founder of Teach For America and CEO of Teach For All

"Moving, inspiring, thoroughly researched, and deeply practical, this book shows that we all have the power to change the world, simply by cultivating our own and others' curiosity and nurturing the learning and connection it creates. An engaging must-read for leaders, teammates, parents, educators, and even students—everyone!

—Bruce Patton, coauthor of mega-bestsellers *Getting to YES* and *Difficult Conversations*, and cofounder of the Harvard Negotiation Project and the Rebuild Congress Initiative

"From a young age, I learned the wonders of asking one good question after another. And when we pose good questions to others around us, we open whole worlds of discovery and authentic connection. *Ask* provides an astonishingly practical yet profound method for cultivating this kind of curiosity, listening, and reflection that is deeply needed in today's organizations and communities."

—Rhonda Broussard, CEO of Beloved Community and author of *One Good Question*

"Jeff Wetzler teaches a profoundly useful truth: questions can be better than answers. Even more, he has deep practical insight about how to ask great questions, both as an art form and a systematic discipline. If people everywhere increased their questions to statements ratio, replacing self-certainty with genuine curiosity, the world would be a better place—and I hope Jeff's book inspires people to do exactly that."

—Jim Collins, bestselling author of *Good to Great*

"Listening is the new 'superpower.' Never has it been more important—or more challenging—for leaders to access key information and perspectives from those around them. In this fascinating, engaging, and insightful book, Jeff Wetzler draws from science and practice to offer a much-needed solution to this pervasive challenge. In these highly uncertain times, *Ask* provides an essential compass for leaders and organizations alike."

—Benjamin Finzi, managing director and global CEO program leader, Deloitte

"*Ask* is a great primer for leaders to improve the quality of their conversations with their teams and support deeper learning and relationships. Through compelling stories, it vividly exemplifies key concepts while equipping you with practical, hands-on tools to enhance your collaborative efforts with colleagues."

—Susana Córdova, commissioner of education, State of Colorado

"From research to relationships, no tool is more powerful than a good question—and yet so few of us are ever taught how to design or pose one. *Ask* demystifies this process, offering a deeply researched and widely applicable approach to getting to the heart of what other people really know, believe, and feel. The tools and methods in book will transform the way we learn from and with one another."

—Shereen El Mallah, assistant professor, University of Virginia

"Now more than ever, we must overcome the barriers so many face to realizing their full potential. Our future depends on our collective ability to bring forth the best talent, the brightest ideas, and the most innovative solutions. *Ask* teaches leaders how to tap into the diversity of perspectives, experiences, and ideas that organizations need to thrive in the twenty-first century and beyond."

—John Rice, CEO and founder of Management Leadership for Tomorrow

"At the root of all transformative change is our ability to bring curiosity, questions, and deep listening to connect with one another—especially with those different from us. In *Ask*, Jeff Wetzler breaks down this deceptively difficult task into incredibly practical steps, opening up new possibilities for leadership, love, and liberation."

—Thaly Germain, CEO of Onward and managing director of transformation and culture at Berlin Rosen

"In an increasingly global and multipolar world, *Ask* is an essential book. It places curiosity, inquiry, and close listening at the heart of effective leadership. I would encourage every leader, aspiring leader, and change-maker to read this book as it might just bring us one step closer to addressing some of humanity's most pressing problems."

—Asheesh Advani, president and CEO, Junior Achievement (JA) Worldwide

"Jeff has worked alongside some of the foremost experts on group dynamics, including Chris Argyris, David Kantor, and Diana Smith. He has not only applied the insights he gained from these thought leaders in his own leadership across multiple organizations but also integrated them to develop his own distinctive point of view. This book does a masterful job of bridging theory and practice, offering invaluable guidance to any leader who seeks to build a culture of curiosity, creativity, and continuous learning."

—Sameer B. Srivastava, professor of business administration and public policy, Haas School of Business, UC Berkeley

"In a toxically divided world, getting and staying curious about each other—especially when we're so different—is an act of courage and defiance. Jeff Wetzler gives us a step-by-step method for building the skills we need to actually hear each other. *Ask* offers a well-researched and widely applicable approach for turning our assumptions into questions that unlock the world around us. I'm keeping it close by as a reference, and so should you."

—Mónica Guzmán, senior fellow for public practice at Braver Angels and podcast host of *A Braver Way*

"*Ask* offers both a practical how-to guide and a compelling why-to narrative on the art of inquiry as a tool for team building and collaborative learning. Using stories, studies, data, and heaps of humility, Wetzler makes the case that curiosity is both the bridge to understanding our time's complex problems and the missing skill we need to connect to one another across the divisions and distrust that too often stand in the way of true learning and partnership."

—Debby Irving, author of *Waking Up White* and *Finding Myself in the Story of Race*

"Effective twenty-first-century leadership is all about collaboration and connection. In *Ask*, Jeff Wetzler offers a concrete, actionable framework for making the critical shift from 'me' to 'we' that our time demands. This is a call to action for all of us—from corporate CEOs to social entrepreneurs to world leaders—to tap into our true collective potential."

—Jeffrey C. Walker, former vice chair of JP Morgan Chase & Co., and coauthor of *The Generosity Network*

"This book offers you the wisdom of nearly thirty years of practice in the field of how to utilize the *Ask* Approach to tap into the hidden power of the relationships around you. We know that well-constructed questions, asked in proper environments can benefit you and your team greatly. But Jeff Wetzler goes well beyond that. In *Ask*, Jeff provides systematic models and exercises for how to utilize that skill into action, thereby changing the way you lead, and dare I say, live."

—Topaz Adizes, Emmy Award–winning director, founder of The Skin Deep, and author of *12 Questions for Love*

"As a journalist, I know that few tools are more powerful than good questions. This authentic, deeply researched, and wildly entertaining book doesn't just make the case for why asking matters, but how to do it well. At a time when we can't seem to agree on the color of the sky, the skills of asking and listening deeply are more critical than ever. The world is in dire need of this book right now."

—Jenny Anderson, author, contributing columnist at *TIME*, and former *New York Times* journalist

"Curiosity leads to conversations, and conversations unlock the understanding we need to find and reach our mutual goals. We can all learn to do this better, and Jeff's book is a great place to begin."

—Seth Godin, bestselling author of *This Is Marketing*

"There is a growing movement afoot in today's world and it is being led by the questioners—the people who have figured out that the best way for us to live, learn, grow, and connect with one another is to lead with curiosity and thoughtful, beautiful questions. Jeff Wetzler's invaluable book shows you how to embrace this way of being and interacting. A must-read for any aspiring 'questionologist' (which should be all of us)."

—Warren Berger, bestselling author of *A More Beautiful Question*

"In an incurious world where everyone wants to talk but no one wants to listen, Jeff Wetzler's book *Ask* is a breath of fresh air. He compellingly and eloquently underscores the urgent need given our global crisis of connection to focus on learning about the thoughts, feelings, and experiences of others by asking them questions rather than just sharing our own. He also provides concrete steps using our natural capacity for curiosity, including the interpersonal type which has been empirically proven to be essential for genuine human connection. His book offers us, in other words, a concrete solution to our crisis that is leading to our soaring rates of loneliness, suicide and mass violence. Read it now!"

—Niobe Way, professor of developmental psychology at NYU, past president of the Society for Research on Adolescence, author of *Deep Secrets: Boys' Friendships and the Crisis of Connection* and the upcoming *Rebels with a Cause: Reimagining Boys, Ourselves, and Our Culture*

ASK

TAP INTO THE HIDDEN WISDOM OF PEOPLE AROUND YOU FOR UNEXPECTED BREAKTHROUGHS IN LEADERSHIP AND LIFE

JEFF WETZLER

NEW YORK BOSTON

Interior illustrations by Kendal Dooley

Balance
Hachette Book Group
1290 Avenue of the Americas
New York, NY 10104
GCP-Balance.com
@GCPBalance

Originally published in hardcover and ebook by Hachette Go in May 2024
First Balance trade paperback edition: May 2026

Balance is an imprint of Grand Central Publishing. The Balance name and logo are registered trademarks of Hachette Book Group, Inc.

Print book interior design by Marie Mundaca

Library of Congress Control Number: 2023044404

ISBNs: 9780306832673 (trade paperback), 9780306832680 (ebook)

Printed in the United States of America

LSC-C

Printing 1, 2026

To my mentors.

*My greatest hope is that
this book can channel, amplify, and pay forward
the most important wisdom and love that
I have been so fortunate to receive from you.*

Who is wise?
One who learns from every person,
as it is said:
From all who taught me, I have gained understanding.

—Pirkei Avot 4:1

CONTENTS

AUTHOR'S NOTE

THE NAMES AND STORIES MENTIONED THROUGHOUT THE BOOK vary in whether they are real or disguised. When first and last names are used, the stories appear either with the permission of those referenced or are already in the public domain. When first names only are used, I have adjusted the stories by changing names and key details to protect anonymity, and in some cases I have aggregated multiple examples into one composite story to optimally bring out the point being made.

FOREWORD

I AM DELIGHTED TO PROVIDE A FEW OPENING THOUGHTS FOR THIS remarkable new book about the challenge of learning what we most need to know from the people around us. I believe that the future success of today's organizations—public and private sector alike—will depend upon our willingness to tackle this challenge, both individually and collectively. In sum, this book is about why this challenge matters, why it persists, and how we can do better.

In my research and teaching at Harvard Business School, I have discovered that countless executive and MBA students are stuck in ways of communicating that prevent them from achieving the goals they care about most. The majority of them have succeeded in the past by knowing the right answers. Unfortunately, this has trained them in a habit of thinking that is deeply incurious, which in turn shapes their interactions with others in subtle but problematic ways. To move forward, they must renew their innate curiosity and focus it on new questions, while also learning how to listen deeply to the answers their questions generate. In short, they, and all of us, need to understand how to *really* learn from the people with whom we work and live. In this readable, compassionate, intelligent, and useful book, Jeff Wetzler teaches us how to do just that.

In the pages ahead, you will be introduced to a practical, learnable skill set that will help you practice the humble, inquiry-based leadership that you and your organization desperately need. Where I've emphasized academic research over the past three decades, in a remarkably similar domain, Jeff has devoted his considerable talents to discovering the best ways to help people master the art of learning with and from others. I am very glad that he has done this. The resulting work, captured in the pages that lie ahead, manages to be both timeless and timely.

Let's start with timeless. Both Jeff and I had the benefit of studying from master thinkers and practitioners, most notably one of my Harvard PhD advisers, Chris Argyris, who—in a long and productive intellectual journey that began over six decades ago—first uncovered and analyzed the thinking patterns and skills elucidated in this book. Jeff and I also each had the pleasure of learning from Chris's most dogged student, my longtime friend and onetime coauthor Diana Smith, whose work has brilliantly explicated the persistence of the individual and team non-learning dynamics that get us in trouble, while also simplifying the ideas and skills we need to get unstuck. This tutelage gave Jeff (and me) the confidence to say that interpersonal learning in teams and organizations has always determined the extent to which people cooperate, problem solve, and accomplish impressive goals together. And yet, as Argyris documented, our social conditioning gets in the way of practicing the learning we need to do to thrive in this way. These robust discoveries make for timeless challenges.

Why is it timely, then? Because the problems we are encountering today—in companies, schools, nonprofits, and politics—have never been thornier, nor more consequential. We live in uncertain times, with competing—often polarizing—views found everywhere. The modern world—with its ever-increasing speed, its overwhelming information density, and the sheer complexity of our organizations and the environments in which they operate—presents unique challenges to communication.

It comes down to this: Our ability to make the best-possible decisions in the face of conflict, with a lack of easy answers, depends on whether we engage in high-quality conversations—conversations driven by a genuine intent to learn and problem solve together. To replace mindsets and habits of unilateral control with those of mutual discovery. In my experience, the mindsets and habits of mutual discovery are excruciatingly rare, but fortunately these skills can be learned. And that is why this book is both important and timely.

Finally, my own research has explored how psychologically safe environments enable learning, experimentation, teamwork, and innovation in organizations. One thing is clear from this body of research: psychological safety at work is by no means the norm. The instinct for self-protection can overwhelm the instinct to learn, grow, and contribute. But when people practice curiosity, caring, and commitment to making a difference, they do help build psychologically safe environments that foster candor and mutual learning. This is why I agree so strongly with Jeff that leaders, teams, and organizations who commit to *practicing the art of asking* will have a competitive advantage over those who remain closed off to this type of learning. This book can help you learn how to learn from those who matter most in your life and your work, and in so doing learn to solve problems together.

Ask does a remarkable job in bridging the often-wide chasm between the theory in this domain (captured in a half century of research ideas and data on interpersonal learning that people like me have played a role in developing) and practice. The value of the knowledge that comes out of business schools like mine depends on the extent to which it can be translated into concrete actions that all of us can practice. Jeff's gift lies in translating important research insights into concrete, learnable steps. And learning how to ask others what they truly think, know, and feel has never been more important.

Enjoy reading about it.

Amy Edmondson
Novartis Professor of Leadership and Management
Harvard Business School
Author of *Right Kind of Wrong: The Science of Failing Well*[1]

Introduction

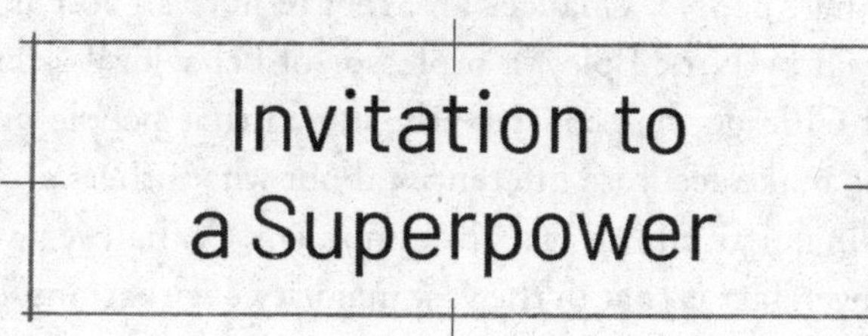

Invitation to a Superpower

IF YOU COULD HAVE ANY SUPERPOWER YOU WANTED, WHAT WOULD you pick?

When pollsters asked Americans this question, two answers tied for the number one spot: *reading other people's minds*[1] and *time travel*.[2]

You can probably guess that this book isn't about time travel. It *is* a book about our desire to find out what other people really think, feel, and know, and a road map for how to build this superpower that so many of us—including me and, presumably, *you*, since you bought this book—long to have.

You sense that there's a wealth of knowledge all around you. You might have a gut sense that there are things people aren't telling you, or that they are sugarcoating what they really think (hint: you're probably right). Maybe you feel stuck, repeating the same mistakes or the same frustrating relationship patterns again and again. You may suspect, correctly, that discovering what people are holding back from sharing would unlock valuable growth, learning, and connection for both of you. You want to gain critical perspective, improve your relationships, come up with smarter solutions, and make better, faster decisions, all while lightening the burden of having to make them by yourself. If any of the above describes you, you are far from alone. It's why so many of us, myself included, want the ability to learn what's in others' hearts and minds.

Why might some respondents to the poll *not* have prioritized mind reading as their superpower of choice? Perhaps they think they're already great at "reading" people. Chances are, they're not as good at it as they think. Research by Nick Epley, a professor of behavioral science at the University of Chicago, has consistently shown that people *overestimate* their ability to make accurate inferences about what others around them are really feeling or thinking at a given moment.[3] Whatever we tell ourselves, the proven fact is that in the vast majority of situations, our ability to guess correctly is only barely more accurate than a coin flip, *regardless* of how well we think we know the other person.[4]

Epley points out that the most common advice on how to peer into other people's minds just doesn't work. *Read their body language.* Nope—turns out people are pretty bad at that.[5] *Try walking in their shoes.* Nope—as Epley, along with his colleagues Tal Eyal and Mary Steffel, discovered through a series of twenty-five experiments—trying to take someone else's perspective does little to improve our accuracy in reading others.[6]

In fact, there's only *one* thing research has shown consistently and accurately allows us to discover what others know, think, and feel: **asking them.** "The only thing that we've ever found in our research that allows you to understand what's on another person's mind better is just asking them," says Epley.[7]

But "just asking them" is easier said than done, particularly when the stakes are high. In those situations, asking can feel as out of reach as mind reading or time travel or turning invisible (also high on the list of Americans' most desired superpowers). Many of us fear that asking a question will somehow discomfit us or the other person. That fear might be readily overcome if it weren't due to the unfortunate fact that few of us are ever *taught* the art and science of asking. While many books exist to encourage and teach us to better share what *we* know, think, and feel with others—great books like *Radical Candor* and Brené Brown's fantastic body of work—less has been written about how we can best *draw out* what *others* know, think, and feel. Couple this dearth of knowledge with social norms that emphasize self-reliance, competition, and conflict avoidance, and you begin to understand why so many of us avoid asking.

With this book, I want to change that. I want to offer the number one desired superpower to anyone who's willing to learn: not just to ask the best questions, but to engage in such a way that your questions are welcomed and the answers you get are honest and rewarding for everyone involved.

I fundamentally, passionately believe three things:

1. When we all have this superpower, we'll be more informed, more creative, and more connected. The world will be a better place.
2. This is a *learnable* kind of superpower—not like shooting spider webs from your fingers or flying over buildings. You just have to master some specific practices.
3. Most people haven't learned these practices. And herein lies an incredible opportunity.

I've spent the past twenty-five years helping people work and learn together in all sorts of environments. I've consulted to top executives at Fortune 500 companies around the world, overseen the training of thousands of teachers, managed teams of people with diverse backgrounds and skill sets, even built a thriving organization from the ground up. Throughout it all, I've seen the same pattern show up over and over again. No matter the context, no matter the role, *people too often fail to learn vitally important information from others who are right around them.*

MY PATH TO *ASK*

This book probably wouldn't exist if I hadn't met Chris Argyris, a renowned Harvard Business School professor. Chris was simultaneously a director at the business consulting firm Monitor Group, which I joined right out of college. A brilliant Greek American man with receding white hair, thick dark eyebrows, and a curious smile, Chris spent most days at Monitor tucked away in his windowless office, reading and writing. Since his reputation as one of the world's leading experts on organizational learning and communication was the reason I had joined the firm, one day I mustered up the courage to knock on his door and introduce myself. This kicked off an ongoing dialogue that would turn out to be life-changing. The fruits of Chris's lifelong pursuit to discover why people don't learn more from one another have become imprinted in my understanding of myself and those around me. Starting in Chapter 1, you'll get a deeper dive into Chris's most compelling methods.

Entranced by Chris's theories, I quickly started applying them in my own work as a manager and consultant. My early efforts were, at best, a bit awkward. The first time I remember putting Chris's ideas into practice was with a direct report named James. After giving him some guidance, I took a deep breath and said, "James, what's your reaction to what I just shared?" He replied, "Um, actually . . . I found it extremely demotivating." I was shocked. He had shown no outward sign of this reaction. If I hadn't asked him that simple question, I would have walked away not realizing I had just weakened our relationship and left him questioning his future working with me on this project. Further, we would not have had the subsequent conversation about the project, which revealed some information that each of us held but hadn't shared with the other—a miscommunication that could have really been damaging to the project, not to mention our relationship. I left the interaction thinking, *Wow, that was awkward and uncomfortable—but ultimately awesome learning, for both of us. Who's next?*

With time and continued practice, my initially awkward attempts began to feel more natural. I was given more responsibility at the firm to ensure that Monitor's consultants around the world—as well as key clients—learned and applied the methods that Chris had pioneered. This gave me the opportunity to work with leaders from New York to LA, Milan to Munich, Seoul to Tokyo, at organizations ranging from Fortune 500 companies to major NGOs like the World Bank. Over the years, I evolved my tool kit substantially through working with incredible mentors at Monitor, including two other legends in the fields of family systems and organizational dynamics: David Kantor and Diana Smith.

I consistently observed three patterns in the leaders I worked with, regardless of the kind of organization or the continent on which it sat. First, people again and again reported with amazement that this was *the most powerful material they'd ever learned professionally.* Deceptively hard, but worth every drop of effort. Second, they became aware, often for the first time, of how their own actions blocked the results they most wanted, stunted their relationships, and cut off learning. But the most important pattern I observed was the third: once they started working with these concepts, they got better very quickly and immediately opened new possibilities for themselves and those around them. These experiences confirmed what I had suspected as a young college graduate: I had stumbled upon pure gold, a simple set of ideas and tools that could unlock learning, better decisions, and stronger relationships all around the world.

When I left business consulting to join the educational nonprofit Teach For America (TFA), I arrived as a fish out of water. I was the "corporate guy," brought in to help the organization develop thousands of new teachers across the country, while improving the quality of their performance. It was a wild transition, and I had plenty of colleagues who were initially skeptical of a business wonk with little background in the education industry. Suffice it to say, the experience was humbling, with many lessons learned the hard way. If I hadn't spent the prior decade learning the practices put forth in this book, I undoubtedly would have crashed and burned. Instead, I stayed for ten rewarding years, during which I was able to help TFA grow, innovate, and affect the education of millions of students nationwide.

Which brings us to my present. Since 2015, I have been the co-founder and co-CEO of Transcend, alongside a close colleague and friend, Aylon Samouha. Transcend is dedicated to reinventing and modernizing every facet of K–12 education. As a cornerstone of our work, we listen to and learn from students, teachers, parents, and employers in designing schools of the future. This is an organization and a model that would not exist without the superpowers of *Ask*. They have enabled me to recruit, lead, and retain top, diverse talent; to raise tens of millions of dollars from investors; to support the most visionary leaders and cutting-edge communities across the country; and to constantly learn and grow as a leader. But most important, they enable me to connect at a human level with people—often across many lines of difference—by better understanding where they're coming, who they are, and what matters to them in life.

THE SHARED REWARDS OF ASKING

As you'll see throughout the book, people don't always give you the whole story right up front. There's almost always a backstory, which won't come out unless you ask in the right ways. And that deeper story is even more interesting and important than the first one you get.

What's the deeper story behind why I became so drawn to asking and listening?

It goes back to my childhood, and how it shaped the way I engage with the world. In my town while I was growing up, I was one of very few Jewish kids. Explicit actions and subtle cues around me left me feeling like an outsider who was not safe. I thought that staying safe meant staying quiet, so I learned to observe and listen. A lot. And when I did engage, asking questions felt safer than announcing my own opinion; luckily, I was a curious kid, with plenty of questions. When you draw upon a survival strategy day in and day out, it starts to become the way you operate.

By high school I had become less shy—by performing onstage, as a magician, which was a serious hobby in my family's lineage for many generations. But magic is also a discipline that trains you to hold your cards close to your chest; that's what makes the illusion work. I carried that tendency into adulthood, in the form of a default instinct to hold back.

What all this meant was that, for much of my life, I was a person bursting with ideas and knowledge and opinions—even secrets—that stayed *inside* my head. I dreamed of being asked by someone—a friend, colleague, or party guest—"What do *you* think, Jeff?" If I'm really honest, I'm sometimes *still* that person, sitting quietly until someone gives me "permission" to speak. Maybe you can relate.

All that to say: I grew up knowing firsthand how much great stuff others could be finding out from me if only they'd ask me more questions. At some point of maturation, that lonely yearning transformed into a much more meaningful insight: *if I'm holding back so much, maybe others are too.* Multiplied across the many thousands of people I had crossed paths with in my life, how much had I missed? How many insights, stories, and solutions were bobbing silently along in other people's heads, lost forever because the world had conspired to make them feel that their thoughts didn't have value, or that the value would be unrecognized by others?

These days, I'm even more aware of how true this is, and how it disproportionately affects some groups and individuals more than others. For example, American history continues to demonstrate that speaking candidly while Black is a riskier business than it is for white people. Many underrepresented groups confront this painful reality in some form or another—and suffer further because self-silencing is a heavy burden. Data from one famous study, the Framingham Offspring Study, showed that women who silenced themselves in their marriages were four times more likely to die in the ten years following the initial study, even after controlling for other known risk factors, such as smoking, blood pressure, and age.[8]

Framing the issue in terms of life and death may seem extreme, but the fact is that carrying the burden of constantly withholding can take a real toll on people's mental and physical health. Further, when people silence themselves, they deprive their colleagues, teams, and communities of the tremendous value of their point of view. Both as a consultant and a leader of my own teams and organizations, I've seen firsthand how much hidden wisdom lies dormant inside the heads of colleagues, staff, customers, even bosses.

The good news is that, when you truly adopt the approaches in this book, it doesn't just help you, it benefits the people you seek to learn from. Those who felt wary to speak learn that when they're with you, they're in a safe harbor. They can express what they know, feel, and believe. In this way, asking is more than just a tool for learning; it's an act of caring that connects us deeply to those around us.

In other cases, your questions can awaken someone to their own wisdom. Not everyone has had the empowering experience of being recognized as an expert, or as a valued teacher. When you can do that for someone, you're apt to see them step into their own potential and contribute in ways neither of you may have seen coming.

When we give others the chance to share openly and honestly, we are offering them a gift. An invitation to authenticity. And in fact, research shows that when people share more honestly, it has all kinds of benefits for them, including improved mental and physical health and more rewarding personal relationships.[9]

And the benefits don't stop with you and the other person. Imagine what could become possible if we could fully unlock the collective genius that resides in each of our teams and organizations. What would it look like to raise a generation of kids connected by a shared desire to learn from one another? How might this help to heal the growing polarization all around us? What could become possible in the world if we approached everyone we met—even those with whom we vehemently disagree—as if we could learn something from them?

THE *ASK* APPROACH™

Now, over a quarter century after walking into Chris's office at Monitor, I have synthesized everything I learned, taught, and experienced into the ***Ask* Approach**: a research-based, practice-tested methodology that can be mastered and applied step-by-step.

Your education in asking begins in **Section I**, where you'll learn *why* people don't share—the specific barriers that lead them to clamp down and stay silent. You'll also learn what kinds of information people are *least likely* to share with you. (Hint: It's the stuff you most need to know!)

In **Section II**, you'll learn the five-step ***Ask* Approach** that you can use to unlock learning, growth, and connection in any area of your life:

Step 1: Choose curiosity. I'll guide you through a powerful mindset shift that will prevent you from making the quick assumptions that limit learning and damage our relationships.

Step 2: Make it safe. Lots of people withhold, even if you do ask them questions. This is a seminar on how you can support others to open up and say what they're afraid or unwilling to say by making it more comfortable, easy, and appealing to share.

Step 3: Pose quality questions. Discover the highest-impact questions you should be asking, but aren't—complete with scripts, workarounds, and follow-up ideas.

Step 4: Listen to learn. We all know it's important to listen to what people are saying, but this practice triples the information you'll be able to *hear* and ensures you've got the right takeaways.

Step 5: Reflect and reconnect. You'll learn how to evaluate which insights have real value—and then you'll translate that value into action and take steps to keep the learning momentum going and deepen your relationships along the way.

Finally, in **Section III**, you'll learn how to build your newfound skills into your entire life: at work, home, and in the world.

This book is meant to be dog-eared, highlighted, and read together with friends and colleagues. Then I hope you'll pull it back off your shelf whenever you encounter situations where learning from others around you really matters. When you come across exercises, I encourage you to take the time to really engage with them, as these will make the difference between knowing the content and actually being able to implement it. For easy access to the core tools and frameworks of the book all in one place, go to www.AskApproach.com.

A WORTHWHILE RISK

Learning a deeper, more humble way of interacting with the important people in your world isn't without risk. It takes hard work and bravery on your part, along with a fair share of emotional investment. It is almost impossible to open yourself to learning without sometimes feeling vulnerable and exposed. That's one reason so few people take this work on—but the more of us who do, the easier it becomes. This is an opportunity to lead, wherever you are in life.

Having seen so many people succeed using these practices, I know anyone can do it—and here's why it's worth the effort. **You will see at least three benefits when you use the *Ask* Approach:**

1. **You'll create better results.** You'll make smarter decisions based on a more full and accurate range of insights that you'll discover. You'll co-create more innovative solutions. You'll

also get unstuck from conflicts more quickly and spend more of your time being productive and creative.

2. **You'll forge stronger relationships.** You'll connect more deeply with people, whether or not they look like you, talk like you, or think like you. You and others around you will be rewarded by unblocking the flow of information. Greater trust and connection will flourish.
3. **You'll grow and improve faster.** You'll hear more honest feedback, you'll get helpful suggestions, and you'll become aware of your blind spots. When learning becomes your way of operating, it feels much safer to experiment and even falter. Relieve yourself of the burden of pretending you have all the answers, and you'll grow in profound, even unexpected, ways.

As I write this book, the world has awakened to the immense power of artificial intelligence through the advent of chatbots powered by large language models. While AI is changing so many aspects of life, it seems unlikely that it will ever fully replace the uniquely human skill of connecting with other human beings in ways that produce deep, mutual learning. Said otherwise, technology alone will never be sufficient to produce these benefits. However, as you'll see from the sidebars in Chapters 3, 5, and 6, there are some exciting new ways that technology may be able to enhance your efforts to learn and apply the *Ask* Approach.

Whether you get support from AI or just do it the old-fashioned way, here are some more "real-life" benefits I've personally experienced—and seen others gain—through using the *Ask* Approach. Are any of these results you'd like to see in your own work or life?

- Discover where you *really* stand in a critical relationship... and what you need to do to make things right
- Break out of a persistent conflict through finding better, more mutually satisfying outcomes than either of you could have imagined
- Identify the fatal flaws in your plan *before* you waste a ton of time and resources implementing it

- Gain insight into why people treat you the way they do . . . *and* how you are affecting them
- Help and support others you care about (teammates, family, friends) in whatever ways that *they* really need, even if they're hesitant to ask for it
- Unite people with diverse perspectives, to create deeper connections, accomplish amazing things, and draw strength from everyone's differences

LET'S GO

I hope, by now, you are starting to see why I believe asking is nothing short of a superpower. While *Ask* is full of practical tips—even specific phrases—you can use to discover what you most need to find out from others, more important, it's a set of practices for lifetime learning. By asking more and better questions—of ourselves and of those around us—we set ourselves up for continuous growth and renewal.

Toni Morrison once said, "If there's a book that you want to read, but it hasn't been written yet, then you must write it."[10] Well, this is a book that I myself *need* to read, and reread. As you'll see in the chapters that follow, I *still* have experiences where I discover that people knew or believed important things that I didn't find out until too late. I continue to have moments when I jump to conclusions and forget to be curious. I have many blind spots that get in the way of learning from others across various kinds of differences. The act of researching and writing this book helped me remind myself of the importance of curiosity and asking questions, especially in my all-too-human moments of feeling certain, judgmental, and righteous. I haven't shied away from sharing those moments here, because I believe you'll take away as much from my shortcomings, gaps, and failures as you will from my skills and successes.

My greatest hope is that this book will open all our minds to the power and possibility of learning from all those we encounter—to change our relationships, our organizations, and our communities for the better.

SECTION I

The Invisible Problem That Plagues Relationships Everywhere

IN SECTION I, WE'LL DIVE INTO A PHENOMENON I CALL "THE UNSPOKEN." This refers to the thoughts, feelings, and ideas that others around us hold but too often don't share.

In Chapter 1, we'll explore the most important things people keep in their heads and hearts but never tell us, and we'll examine the consequences of our not finding out.

In Chapter 2, we'll look at the reasons people withhold, including the four biggest barriers to their sharing.

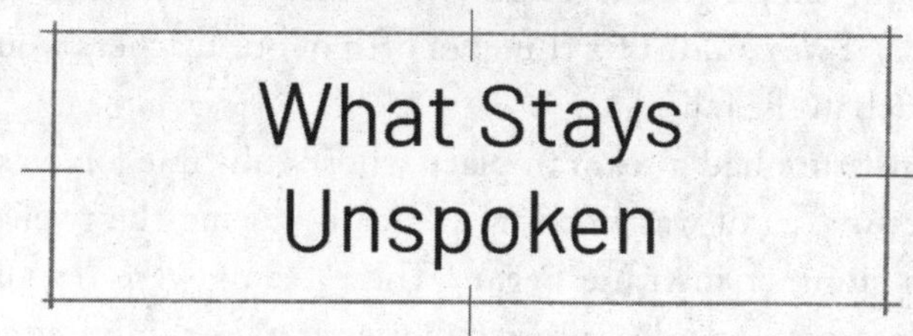

Chapter 1

What Stays Unspoken

Essential question: What do you most *need to know that people are* least *likely to tell you?*

HAVE YOU EVER HAD AN EXPERIENCE WHERE YOU WERE *THE LAST* to learn something vital in a situation that was important to you—and did you further discover that there were people who could have clued you in, but didn't? I've seen this happen to people I've coached more times than I can count—but was still completely gobsmacked when it happened to me.

Teach For America is a nationwide nonprofit that recruits and trains recent college graduates to teach in low-income schools while building a movement of leaders who work for educational equity. After nearly a decade in management consulting, I was the organization's chief learning officer, charged with helping them scale and improve the training and performance of teachers across the country. My tenure there had a regrettably rocky start.

Less than a year into the job, I received an urgent phone call. Jade, a key leader on my team, was calling to inform me that our Northwest Summer Institute—one of our five summer training sites—was facing major challenges, just a few months before it was scheduled to begin. These institutes provided our newly minted college graduates with much of the training they'd get before they were face-to-face with students. In other words, if we couldn't fix things, a fifth of our teachers would not be ready to teach in the fall.

Each institute had a team in place whose full-time job was to make sure that every detail was lined up perfectly during the twelve months *before* each summer institute began. These teams were responsible for securing classroom and dormitory facilities at a host university, partnering with local school systems for summer school teaching practicums, and hiring and training a hundred local staff tasked with everything from instruction and coaching to serving meals to transporting our teachers to and from the various activities. And who was ultimately in charge of these teams? Me. I'd been in contact with them and their leaders consistently throughout the year and believed I had done everything possible to ensure their success.

And yet, here was Jade, calling to tell me that major elements of one entire summer institute were not in place. The classrooms at the host university were not available at the times when we were scheduled to teach in them. Local schools that had agreed to let our teachers train within their summer school program had decided at the last minute not to hold summer school, and the schools that were holding it were now using a totally different curriculum than we'd expected. Key members of the summer staff responsible for supervising and instructing our new teachers did not have the experience or skill needed to carry out the high caliber of training we required, and some of them had already quit.

My pulse raced as I disconnected the call. I stared down at the screen in my hands in stunned silence, a new reality slowly sinking in. I pictured five hundred new teachers at the Northwest Institute rising up in protest. More important, I pictured five hundred classrooms in the fall without the well-trained teachers that their students deserved.

After my moment of panic, I became mystified as to why all year long, I'd remained so unaware of the problems brewing, despite the many conversations I'd had with my team all along the way. According to what Jade uncovered, things had been unraveling for months. Why was I just learning about it now, when it might be too late to turn the ship around?

Thankfully, Jade stepped up in a heroic way. She relocated across the country to the local training site and worked intensively with the team on the ground, who sprinted day and night to rectify every problem in the weeks before the program began. In the end, the Institute ran smoothly, and thankfully, the teachers were prepared. But had Jade not been able to perform this minor miracle, redoing months of planning in a few short weeks, the program would have totally failed.

How could I have been so blindsided? All along the way, I had checked in on how things were going and what help the team needed, and I consistently left with the impression that, despite some minor hiccups, things were generally on track. It turns out, the team was scrambling to fix things as best they could, but they didn't let me in on the full extent of the challenges, nor did they request my help. Bottom line, I was unaware of what multiple people on the team knew about how bad things were but never told me. And while I'm sure I had asked a number of questions during our meetings, the approach I'd taken clearly hadn't encouraged my colleagues to feel safe giving me "real talk" about the challenging but absolutely critical information I needed to know *before* the point of crisis.

Up until that moment, I had believed that we had strong working relationships where we could speak openly and directly. But clearly there was something that stopped people from speaking up in a moment when it really mattered.

What's worse, I started to wonder: If they didn't share information this time, despite the stakes, what other thoughts, beliefs, and feelings might they, or others for that matter, be withholding?

THE LEFT-HAND COLUMN

Earlier in my career, I learned a name for this painful and pervasive pattern of withholding. It was during my first job out of college, at Monitor Group. As a consulting firm, Monitor's success hinged on our ability to find information and insights that produced the best solutions for our client organizations. To develop quality recommendations, information of all kinds needed to flow continuously throughout the organization, to our clients, and from our clients back to us.

Because of this, Monitor invested heavily in understanding what might block people's ability to learn from one another and what they could do about it. Chris Argyris, the professor you met in the Introduction, provided the driving intellectual leadership required to set the effort into motion. With a joint appointment to Harvard's Business School and Graduate School of Education, Chris's life mission was to understand and overcome the obstacles to people learning in organizations.

Chris's work with leaders of companies all around the world often started the same way, with *the two-column case*. He would ask someone to draw a vertical line down the middle of a blank sheet of paper. The right-hand column would contain lines from the actual dialogue of a recent challenging interaction, as best as the case writer could recall. In the left-hand column, the case writer would write the unspoken thoughts and feelings they experienced throughout the interaction.

To give you a sense of what this looked like, here's a simple example. The "case writer" was a new project manager within the consulting firm, interacting with a client they found to be difficult:

CONSULTANT'S UNSPOKEN THOUGHTS AND FEELINGS	ACTUAL DIALOGUE
You've got to be kidding! We met three times last week alone! Every time we have to prep for a meeting with you, it stops the research process, creating delays.	Client: I'd like to set up a meeting with you to discuss the research your team is doing.
Let me see if I can hold her off so we can actually get some work done.	Me (Consultant): Okay, we're always happy to meet. The team is in the midst of gathering the data right now. It might be best if we meet once we've crunched the numbers.

I know you're concerned about the timeline. Me too! We're delayed because *YOU* keep changing the direction every time we meet. If I make any more changes, this project will run way over budget and we'll miss our deadline. Then the team members will get pulled off this project and we'll both be stuck.	Client: Actually, I'd rather meet sooner because I'm getting concerned about the timeline, and I have a presentation to our board where I need some data. I also have some new ideas and information for you.
	Me (Consultant): Sure, we're happy to squeeze in a meeting at your convenience.

Notice how much the case writer is holding back from sharing with the client and the dissonance between the message that gets across and what this consultant really thinks.

At the end of this chapter, you'll get a chance to try this exercise yourself by writing your own two-column case. If you're like most people—myself included—your left-hand column might turn out to be pretty colorful. You might be thinking (but not voicing) things like,

Why doesn't she get that this is a terrible idea?

or

You have no idea where your team is coming from. Why don't you be quiet and listen to us?

or

I feel so let down by you.

or

Does he really think this is my fault? Doesn't he realize all that went wrong before I got involved?

Whatever you're thinking or feeling and not saying, one thing is true: because it's in your left-hand column, it's unspoken. That means the other person doesn't get access to it. And that's a problem, because behind any colorful language or harsh judgments you may be making is often a treasure trove of important thoughts and feelings and information that the other person never finds out.

Guess what else is true? The other person you're interacting with also has a left-hand column. That means *they* have a gold mine of insights, experiences, feelings, and ideas that *you* are not getting access to.

Now, I should note that not *everything* in another person's left-hand column is useful or necessary for us to know. Some of what we might find in there is the result of their own inner dialogue, insecurities, or petty judgments (we all have them!). For example, we definitely do *not* need to know if they think our new haircut makes our forehead look too big or how they rate our intelligence. But buried within the muck of others' left-hand columns are often gems of wisdom waiting to be discovered. By practicing the approach in this book, you will learn how to invite other people to share their *most* useful, relevant insights and experiences and to distinguish which information is useful for you to integrate into your own understanding.

Throughout my time at Monitor and in subsequent leadership roles, I've used this two-column-case format to help myself and others—whether consultants, clients, senior leaders, employees, or colleagues—reflect on their interactions and grow their skills at communicating more productively.[1] Reading the left-hand columns of their two-column cases is like looking through a secret window into a gold mine of important information, views, and feelings that live locked away in the heads and hearts of other people. The people interacting with them never get access to this priceless information.

Seeing the breakdown of learning in the people I work with—and in the day-to-day lives of friends and family—is heartbreaking. It's like watching avoidable train wrecks in slow motion, waiting for what often feels like an inevitable collision. And despite seeing this in the people I was working to help and studying the pattern closely over the course of my career, I myself can still fall into the very same traps in my interactions, in my roles as a leader, a parent, a community member.

When we fail to recognize and overcome the barriers that lead the people around us to hold back, we miss out on enormous learning and insights, which are right there in front of our noses! And when we remain in the dark about this valuable information, *we* suffer the consequences. We make worse decisions. We miss out on creative solutions to pressing problems. Our relationships stay surface level or even deteriorate. Our professional and personal growth stagnates. We fail to reach our potential and to nurture it in others. Everyone suffers.

The *Ask* Approach, as you'll see throughout this book, is how we help the people around us shift more of the useful but unspoken stuff that's in their left-hand column over to the right, where they can voice it for the benefit of everyone.

THE GOLD MINE IN *OTHERS'* LEFT-HAND COLUMNS

One of the things I've learned in observing this phenomenon across many different contexts is that there are predictable patterns to *what kinds of information* people tend to keep locked away. By knowing what hidden gems to look for, we can begin to open the door to learning. Based on the hundreds of two-column cases that I have read over the years, my lived experience and coaching of others, and the social science research, I've identified the **four most important things that people around you tend to withhold:**

What People Withhold

1. Their struggles and frustrations...and what help they need
2. What they *really* believe or feel about an issue...and where their views come from
3. Their honest feedback for you...and suggestions for how you can improve
4. Their most audacious ideas and dreams... which they fear might sound crazy

I want to share a story to illustrate how this pattern of withholding plays out.

Allison, a hard-charging and successful manager in a midsize marketing company, prides herself on getting things done and exceeding her goals while also caring for all the people who work for her. When she recently hired Dahlia to be a project manager supporting her and others across the organization, she was sure she had found the perfect fit. Dahlia had thrived in her previous job, where she had earned a reputation as an expert in project management.

During the first three months, everything seemed to be going well. Dahlia quickly built up her company knowledge, asked great questions, and fit right into the culture. As time went on, however, Dahlia began missing deadlines and dropping balls, a real problem for a project manager. At first, Allison didn't think much of it. Dahlia's son had recently gotten strep throat; perhaps she was just catching up on things. But over time, the pattern persisted, then worsened. She kept missing deadlines and failed to appear in several meetings with no explanation. Soon, colleagues across the organization were calling Allison, complaining that Dahlia was failing to follow through.

Allison's heart sank. Was this new hire that she'd been so excited about not going to work out after all?

Feeling anxious, Allison messaged Dahlia and asked for a meeting the next day.

As Allison approached the small conference room where they would meet, Dahlia was already there, shifting nervously in her chair. Her shoulders were rigid. Allison could see bags under Dahlia's eyes from what surely was a long night—probably a combination of work and taking care of her family. Allison felt for her. She had a family of her own and understood firsthand how stressful and disruptive it was when a child was sick. She didn't want to create stress for Dahlia, but she also knew that for the sake of the business and her own sanity, she couldn't let this go on any longer. So, after some awkward pleasantries, she took a deep breath and started in.

"Dahlia," Allison began, trying her best to meet Dahlia's eyes, "I'd like to share some observations and concerns I have. I see you dropping balls, and I'm worried that we are really starting to fall behind on the work."

"I know," Dahlia replied quickly; "I really apologize. It's been a hard time with my son getting sick. But I am in the process of catching up and should be back on track soon."

This was what Allison expected her to say and so Allison was already prepared with a response. "I'm sorry your son has been sick. I really am. But as I think about it, we were falling behind even before that happened."

At this point Allison noticed a slight shift in Dahlia. Her jaw set a bit harder, she sat up a bit straighter. Was she going to get defensive? In case she needed to supply more evidence to drive home the point, Allison mentally ran through some concrete examples of Dahlia's dropped balls that she had prepared earlier.

"It's true. There's a lot to do, but I know I can get it done," Dahlia replied. "Two weeks, tops." She opened her mouth to say more but appeared to stop herself. Allison thought Dahlia was about to make excuses, but when Dahlia closed her mouth, Allison didn't push.

"I'm glad to hear that," Allison jumped in, "because others on the team are counting on you."

When Allison left the room, she felt relieved. She'd had the hard conversation, and Dahlia had agreed to step up. She was cautiously optimistic that things would get back on track now. One more problem off her overcrowded plate, she hoped.

Dahlia, however, walked away feeling dismissed and deflated, and with a totally different perspective. A panic rose in her chest as she realized that she'd agreed to something she couldn't possibly achieve. What was she going to do? She feared disappointing Allison again, but also felt resentful at Allison's seeming disinterest in hearing *why* she had gotten so behind. The biggest problem wasn't that her son had been sick, although that had certainly made things more difficult. In Dahlia's view, the real problem was how workflow was structured in the organization. Allison had no idea how disorganized and overwhelming things were, nor did she seem to care.

While Dahlia outwardly apologized for falling behind and agreed to do better, she kept unspoken a wealth of useful information. If we were reading a two-column case written by Dahlia, we would see the following *unspoken* thoughts and feelings in Dahlia's left-hand column:

DAHLIA'S UNSPOKEN THOUGHTS AND FEELINGS	WHAT EACH PERSON SAID
Allison seems really stressed. I know she's a hard-charger and never lets balls drop.	Allison: Dahlia, I'd like to share some observations and concerns I have. I see you dropping balls, and I'm worried that we are really starting to fall behind on the work.
It's clear I have no choice but to just say I'll do it. That's what she wants to hear. I don't want her to think I'm incompetent.	Dahlia: I know. I really apologize. It's been a hard time with my son getting sick. But I am in the process of catching up and should be back on track soon.
I've done project management for over a decade! I know in my bones that it's literally impossible for me, or anyone, to complete all that's on my plate. Allison is clueless about all the things that people from other divisions are asking me to do. And of course, I'll say yes because I'm new and want to make a good impression. I don't want to lose this job.	Allison: I'm sorry your son has been sick. I really am. But as I think about it, we were falling behind even before that happened.
And another thing Allison is clueless about: there are a ton of inefficiencies in this company. The requests I get from across three different divisions are all for slightly different versions of the same exact work. People are duplicating one another's efforts, but they don't even know it. What a waste of time and money—and she's making such a big deal about being a couple weeks behind?!?	Dahlia: It's true. There's a lot to do, but I know I can get it done. Two weeks, tops.
If Allison would let me, I could come up with a project-tracking system just like what I built in my last organization—it would help us prioritize projects and save the company time and money. And it would actually let Allison and her VP look across all the projects and see what I see, not just the redundancies but also that some projects seem pretty misaligned to our strategy, at least in my opinion. Too bad all she cares about is that my stupid to-do list is up to date.	Allison: I'm glad to hear that because others on the team are counting on you.

As we saw when we listened in on their dialogue, none of Dahlia's left-hand column came through in the conversation with Allison. It all stayed unspoken. Allison walked away thinking she had done the hard work of "managing" the problem. Instead, the way she led the meeting cut her off from the very expertise that she had been so excited to get by hiring Dahlia. She left the room knowing no more than when she entered. Allison also had no idea how Dahlia experienced her—as a hard-charging manager to whom the only acceptable answer is "I got it, boss."

All of this would have been extremely useful for Allison to know. She could have gained critical insight into the dysfunction in her organization, information she could address together with the division's president. Further, she could have enlisted Dahlia's expertise to improve the workflow design and project management systems, all while making Dahlia's role actually manageable. Learning about the impact of her hard-driving style might have led to Allison taking measures to help people feel more comfortable to open up. All of this could have made Allison more successful as a leader and made her relationship with Dahlia far more productive, trusting, and honest. Without this information, the conversation became a bandage over an infected wound instead of a remedy to a deeper set of issues within the relationship and organization.

Even though we only looked at Dahlia's left-hand column, Allison, of course, had her own set of unspoken thoughts and feelings. Her left-hand column was filled with concerns about the pressures she felt to deliver on time, her hopes for how Dahlia would have ultimately brought her ideas about improving the workflow systems, and observations she'd been hearing from others across the organization about how Dahlia was showing up. Imagine how Dahlia—and their relationship—could have benefited if she'd gotten access to Allison's unspoken thoughts and feelings. In every interaction, both people have left-hand columns, and when important insights get withheld, everyone suffers.

WITHHOLDING IS INVISIBLE BUT ALL AROUND US

The unspoken gulf between Allison and Dahlia is all too common. The pervasiveness of the pattern is well documented in studies of organizations around the world. In one study of managers from industries that ranged from pharmaceuticals to advertising to financial services, **over 85 percent of people** interviewed admitted to remaining silent with their bosses about a concern on at least one occasion, even though they felt the issue was important. What's more, **nearly three-quarters (74%)** of those people said that their colleagues were also aware of the issue and also felt uncomfortable speaking up.[2] And when asked if they felt comfortable speaking up *in general* about issues of concern, **nearly half (49%)** of employees said that they did not.[3] Imagine the cost to an organization when half the people don't share information or opinions about what concerns them!

It's also not limited to interactions that happen inside organizations or "vertical" relationships between managers and the staff who work for them. While the examples in this book focus more on interactions that occur in the workplace, the phenomenon exists in every area of our lives. Every human being has a left-hand column running in every interaction they have throughout their day. That means these same patterns of unspoken thoughts and feelings—and therefore missed opportunities to learn and connect—can happen in any kind of relationship. Imagine the doctor who fails to discover that her patient wasn't taking the prescribed medicine because the patient didn't want to disclose her underlying fears of the side effects. Or the father who doesn't find out that his teenage daughter is suffering from anxiety but doesn't want to talk about it because she doesn't want to be judged. Or the adult sibling who doesn't realize that her estranged brother no longer talks to her because of a resentment from long ago that he harbors but never shared. As you read through the following chapters, I encourage you to consider the ways in which this phenomenon plays out across a range of relationships in your life. I'd wager that you'll find more examples than you'd initially imagined. As we'll explore in the next chapter, dynamics of difference—whether power, culture, gender, race, operating style, or many others—exacerbate the problem of people missing out on learning from one another.

Despite how pervasive and costly this problem is, I have found that we can overcome it. It *is* possible to consistently learn from those around us in a way that is effective, transformative, and, perhaps most important, *mutually* beneficial. When the many people I've worked with begin to take the right steps, a whole world of possibilities opens up. What they learn from their clients, colleagues, friends, and family members transforms their decisions, teams, and relationships. It radically reduces the fear, anxiety, and awkwardness so many people experience heading into otherwise-tense conversations. It puts them on the same side of the table instead of seeing the other person as a potential adversary. It leads them to discover and co-create amazing new ideas. The benefits can be immediate *and* lasting.

All of this is possible, and the bulk of this book (starting in Section II) is dedicated to outlining the concrete steps of the *Ask* Approach, so you can find out what you most need to learn from the people around you. But before you can learn how to reap these rewards, you need to understand the answer to one deceptively simple question:

Why don't people tell you what's most important for you to learn?

This is the essential question we'll tackle in Chapter 2. To get the most out of it, and to deepen your learning from this chapter, try the exercises below before you go further.

SUMMARY OF KEY POINTS

Essential question: What do you *most* need to know that people are *least* likely to tell you?

1. In every interaction, people keep much of what they really think and feel hidden away in their *left-hand column*—a gold mine of information and insights. This includes:

    - What they struggle with . . . and what help they need
    - What they really think or feel about an issue . . . and where their views come from

   - Their honest feedback for you... and suggestions for how you can improve
   - Their most audacious ideas and dreams... which they fear might sound crazy

2. Unfortunately, more often than not, people fail to learn this information from one another. This comes at a great cost to decisions, solutions, relationships, and effectiveness.
3. This invisible problem is everywhere—in our organizations, families, communities, and close relationships.

EXERCISES

1A. Identify two important relationships in your life—whether with your boss, colleagues, employees, friends, community members, clients, family, and so on. For each relationship, ask yourself how confident you are that you are truly learning each of the following kinds of insights from the other person. In each cell of the following table, write: "high" if you're very confident, "low" if you're not, and "medium" in between (or "N/A" if it doesn't apply). You can use this as a "heatmap" of sorts, to help you see where you might have more to learn.

How confident are you that you are truly learning...	Relationship #1: ________	Relationship #2: ________
What they struggle with... and what help they need?		
What they really believe or feel about an issue... and where that comes from?		
Their honest feedback for you... and suggestions for how you can improve?		

Their most audacious ideas and dreams . . . which they fear might sound crazy?		

1B. The next time you have a challenging interaction, write your own two-column case about it soon after it's over. You can use the following format, or find a more detailed template at AskApproach.com.

MY UNSPOKEN THOUGHTS AND FEELINGS	WHAT WE EACH SAID

Examine your left-hand column, and consider: What did the other person miss out on learning from you? Now, imagine if the other person were writing a two-column case about the very same interaction. What might their left-hand column look like? What might they have been thinking and feeling that they didn't share with you?

Chapter 2

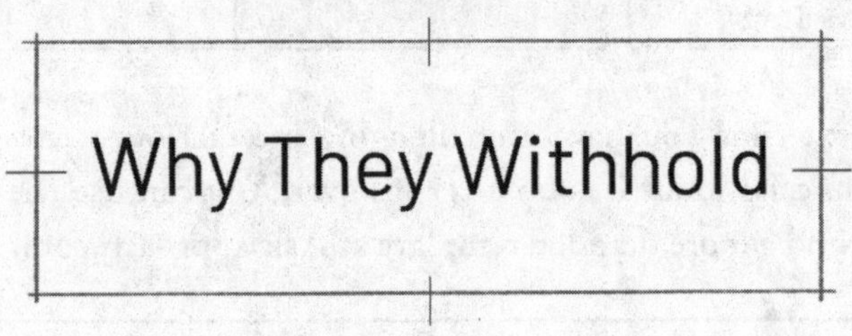

Why They Withhold

Essential question: Why don't people tell you what's most important for you to find out?

NOW YOU KNOW: THE THINGS PEOPLE AREN'T TELLING YOU ARE incredibly important. If you're anything like me, you may be anxious to dive into the steps of the *Ask* Approach right away. Whether you're feeling enthusiastic or wary, I want to encourage you to first dwell in this chapter's essential question.

If you want to engage others in the brave habit of speaking up, you first have to understand *why* it's so difficult for them to share with you. They have their reasons. Developing empathy and awareness of what those reasons may be is where the work must begin.

One of my favorite bosses at Monitor was Jim Cutler. With a baritone voice and a wry but raucous sense of humor, Jim had an unusual talent for working well with all kinds of people.

Several years after I arrived at Monitor, Jim was charged with building Monitor's new Human Capital business, his first time running a large commercial division. A few years in, the group had brought in millions of dollars in revenue, and demand was growing strong. While satisfied with the growth of the business, Jim was curious to see what he could learn from his colleagues that would help him continue to grow as a leader. He asked Amelia, a staff member within his division, to conduct for him an anonymous 360-degree review (a method of collecting feedback) from his colleagues and employees.

When Amelia returned with the feedback, however, it was not at all what Jim had expected. While his colleagues had many complimentary things to say about his leadership and the ideas that his team produced, they said in no uncertain terms that Jim was not doing as much as he should be to grow the revenue of the business. In their view, he lacked the commercial drive that someone in his role needed to have—a message that was delivered most forcefully by his peers who ran other divisions of the company.

Jim was stunned. Flabbergasted.

These were close colleagues, several of whom Jim considered to be personal friends—so close that their spouses were also friends. They went to each other's houses to gather socially. They went on trips together. They went to each other's weddings. How could they have held back on sharing with Jim the serious concerns they'd been harboring about his leadership? Jim felt hurt and betrayed, and more than a little embarrassed.

Why had Jim's friends and colleagues held back, despite clearly caring about him? Despite knowing he valued direct feedback? Despite operating inside an organizational culture that had placed a high premium on direct communication and learning?

This brings us to the essential question that you must answer if you want to learn more from others: *Why don't people tell you what's most important for you to find out?*

FOUR MAJOR BARRIERS

To tackle this question, we'll explore four powerful barriers that prevent others from sharing with you what's really in their heads and hearts.

As we work through each of these barriers, I encourage you to consider the ways in which each may be at play in the examples you identified during the exercises at the end of Chapter 1. By actively applying the

Why People Withhold

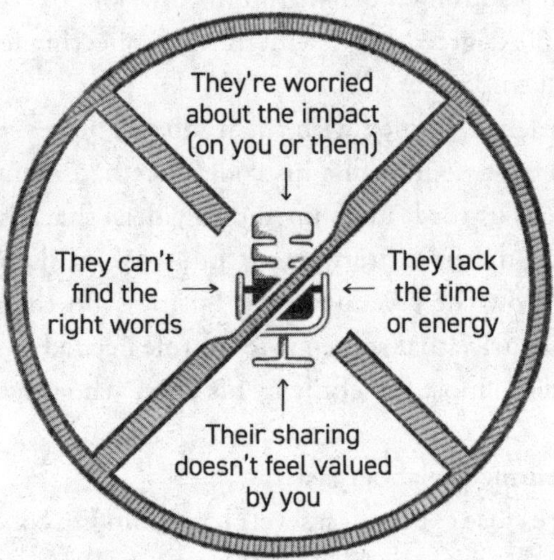

information in this chapter to your own experience, you will be able to access an even deeper level of empathy and understanding, which will be incredibly valuable throughout the how-to part of this book (Section II).

Context, Power, and Identity Matter

One final point before we dive in: a person's decision to share or withhold is inextricably linked to their surrounding environment. This includes organizational cultures, societal forces, and their associated norms, expectations, and power structures—all of which play out differently for everyone, depending on roles, identities, and life experiences. Your interactions with others exist inside these many layers of context, which profoundly shape how people relate to you. As you'll see in this chapter and throughout the book, communicating across lines of difference both enrich and complicate the act of asking and sharing, regardless of where you sit.

Of course, it is far beyond the scope of this book to examine every dimension of difference that can occur when two or more people interact. The examples in this chapter are not meant to cover the full spectrum of human differences, but to illustrate how just a few of them—race, gender, and power—may show up when you are trying to learn from another person. The more you understand potential fault lines, the better you will become at leaping across them—which is incredibly important, because some of the richest learning comes from the people who are most different from you.

With all this in mind, let's dig into the factors that influence why those around you often don't share what could benefit you to find out.

Barrier 1: They Are Worried About the Impact of Sharing

This is, by far, the biggest and most common reason that people decide to hold back from sharing what they really think, know, or feel, even when it would be incredibly valuable for you to hear. They could be worried that what they have to say will irritate, upset, discourage, burden, or embarrass you. They might worry about the consequences for themselves—what if you judge or shame them, or even punish them for sharing? They could also worry about the potential harm that could be done to their relationship with you, from creating unnecessary awkwardness to damaging it irreparably.

Worries About the Potential Impact on You

Ninety-seven percent of people who notice a smudge on the face of someone near them won't mention it, according to one study.[1] And the number one reason people stayed silent? They felt bad about how saying something might affect the person with the smudge—they didn't want to embarrass them. How ironic that in trying to be kind and help the other person avoid embarrassment, they let them walk around with a potentially embarrassing smudge on their face! Many cultures, both in organizations and throughout society more broadly, place a high value on people "saving face," so it's not surprising that people hold back to avoid embarrassing others.

I was recently meeting with a mentor of mine, Harriet, and we were talking about a prominent organization in our field. She mentioned that she'd recently stepped off the board of this organization after many years because she felt like both the organization and the leader were growing out of touch with reality. I asked if she'd told the CEO this, and she replied,

"Jeff, you know usually I'm a direct person, but in this case I didn't tell the CEO the real reasons why I left the board. I knew she would take it hard, and I didn't want to upset her." Harriet prized protecting the CEO from feeling hurt over sharing her real reasons for stepping off the board. While understandable, it didn't do any favors for this CEO, especially since others around her also harbored the same concerns that led Harriet to step away.

Does it help if you have a good, trusting relationship? While trust can help assuage these types of worries by creating more of what Harvard Business School professor Amy Edmondson has termed *psychological safety* in the interaction (more on this in Chapter 4), the closeness of your relationship can also work in the opposite direction. The more someone cares about you and your opinion of them, the higher the stakes they may feel in sharing something that might land badly with you. Think of a time when you needed to share some hard feedback with your partner or a close friend. You probably didn't want to hurt them, and the last thing you wanted was to jeopardize a relationship that matters so much to you. This helps to explain what Amelia found out when she asked Jim's colleagues what had stopped them from ever sharing their observations and feedback directly with him. They told her that in past situations when they gave Jim feedback, they sensed that it might have hurt him or touched a nerve. As people who cared so much about Jim, why would they want to do that to their good friend? It felt better, and safer, to stay quiet.

Part of the problem is that—on average—people tend to *overestimate* the harm they will cause you by sharing feedback, and they *underestimate* the benefits. Researcher Nicole Abi-Esber and her colleagues who did the earlier-described "smudge study" kept on digging to figure out why so many people fail to give feedback even when it would be incredibly useful. In a follow-up study, they asked people to give one another unsolicited feedback.[2] By comparing participant surveys rating how uncomfortable they believed feedback would make their partner versus how uncomfortable the partner actually self-reported feeling, the researchers found a consistent mismatch between people's perceptions of their impact, and how the partner really received it. Others hold back sharing valuable information based on a well-intentioned but overblown desire to protect you, even though your not knowing may end up harming you more in the end.[3]

Worries About the Consequences for Themselves

People have enough stress in their lives; they aren't looking to add more by telling you something that they fear could make you judge or, worse, punish them. When I spoke to former Medtronic CEO Bill George, author of the management classic *True North* and a world expert on authentic leadership, he told me that the number one reason people hold back from sharing with others is the fear of being judged or rejected.

These fears can exist in any type of relationship. We all want to feel safe, accepted, and held in positive regard by other people. Nearly all of us can point to a moment growing up when we were shamed or punished for saying what we really thought or felt. These experiences stick with us, carrying into our relationships with friends, partners, and colleagues. I have seen this dynamic play out time and again in my own work. For example, when my colleague Andrew came to me complaining about a decision made by his manager, Kathleen, I naturally asked him if he had shared his concerns with her. "Are you crazy?" he said vehemently. "She'd never get where I'm coming from, and she'd think I'm not a team player." For a species whose survival hinges on one's place by the fire, the fear of being rejected or judged is a powerful factor in one's decision not to take the risk of sharing their true thoughts or feelings.

But someone needn't have personally experienced judgment or punishment to fear these consequences of speaking up. People in groups and organizations take cues from one another, and especially from their leaders, about whether it is safe or dangerous to share honestly. Someone might witness something happen to a peer or hear a story about someone getting yelled at or fired for speaking their mind. In this way, silence can quickly become endemic in an organization or culture, even if leadership or policy changes. These fears tend to compound the lower one sits in the hierarchy, such that those who possess the least power in the group or organization (the same people who sometimes have the most direct access to highly valuable information, by the way) are more likely to withhold because they are worried about the stakes of being judged or punished. Even if someone is only temporarily in a position of less power, their fears of judgment and rejection can become activated. In my own work, when

I'm presenting to potential investors who I really hope will fund Transcend, I can feel my fear of saying the wrong thing increase.

Power imbalance can lead to withholding outside of organizations as well. In a survey of 4,510 Americans, somewhere between 60 and 80 percent admitted to withholding from their doctor information that could be relevant to their health. When asked why they didn't share, the majority said that they feared being judged by the doctor, they felt embarrassed, or they didn't want to be seen as "difficult" or wasting the doctor's time. (Women, younger people, and those in poorer health were significantly more likely to withhold information.)[4] If people won't share what's on their minds in service of *their own health*, you can imagine how strongly a similar dynamic plays out in the workplace, where the personal benefit of speaking truth to power may be nebulous compared to the risks that can feel huge.

This fear is all the more potent for those who have personally experienced bias or bullying or who belong to a group that has historically been (or is still today) punished for speaking up. While sharing what we really think, feel, and know is always a risk to some degree, the stakes of sharing are not distributed evenly. Humanity has no shortage of examples of marginalized groups being silenced, imprisoned, and even murdered for speaking their truth to power. To this point, Shay Stewart-Bouley and Debby Irving, educators on effective communication in relationships between Black and white people, explained to me that while both parties often experience fear while engaging in cross-racial conversations, it's important to recognize that the stakes playing out in each person's left-hand column are not the same.[5] While white people may worry about offending the other person or being perceived as racist, Black people may be contending with fears of serious retaliation, material punishment, or worse.

Worries About the Consequences for Everyone

Often these worries occur simultaneously: people worry that sharing what they really think will offend or upset you, *and* they fear the consequences to themselves. For instance, research shows that white leaders may withhold sharing clear, critical feedback to employees of color because they are worried they will offend them and be perceived as racist.[6] A related phenomenon has been found between male leaders and female employees.[7] It's not that the feedback they provide is untrue, but it is less substantial and more likely to be vague or sugarcoated. But because regular and specific feedback is essential to personal and career development, not receiving it can stunt growth and leave the other person in the dark. There's actually a term for this—*protective hesitation*—first coined by management scholar and Morehouse College president David A. Thomas to describe relationships in which both parties hold back from bringing up sensitive issues.[8] Thomas's research, which focused on cross-racial relationships between mentors and protégés, illustrates how this instinct to protect the feelings of the other person can be particularly harmful for the protégé, who misses out on important feedback that could spur further career growth.

The hit HBO show *Insecure,* based on the experiences of the show's Black creator, Issa Rae, spotlighted this same dynamic in an episode focused on Issa's job as the sole Black employee of a nonprofit youth organization. In a team meeting, she pitches an idea for a youth field trip to the beach; however, instead of giving her honest feedback about their concerns with her idea, her colleagues all just pitch alternative ideas. She goes ahead with her plan, a beach day, and only later learns about their actual concerns when she overhears two coworkers griping about the overwhelming logistical challenges. She then finds out that her colleagues have actually been emailing one another and their boss about their concerns, in addition to having meetings behind her back in the break room. "They didn't want to seem like they were questioning your judgment," a friendly white coworker explains nervously, "and they weren't sure how you'd react."

I've talked with white leaders across multiple sectors who report trepidation about giving feedback to colleagues of color, for fear of it being perceived as racist or biased. I myself have occasionally withheld fully direct feedback based on second-guessing whether my critiques were indeed biased and thereby perpetuating oppression. There are real and complex issues here, but avoiding hard and direct conversations entirely is rarely a good move when it comes to everyone's learning.

For those with marginalized identities, the combination of these barriers represents a triple bind. They are less likely to receive direct feedback *and* less likely to feel safe sharing their true thoughts and feelings openly. What's more, whatever feedback they do receive *is* more likely to contain bias, burdening them with the additional task of sifting through what's legitimate and what's not (more on this in Chapter 7).

Barrier 2: They Can't Find the Right Words

Another reason people hold back from telling us what they really feel, think, or know is that they simply can't find the right words to express themselves.

Their Mind Moves Faster Than Their Lips

Research by neuroscientist Ned Sahin and others has revealed that the human brain thinks at around 900 words per minute. That's pretty fast, especially considering that the average person can only spit out about 125 words during the same amount of time.[9] Think about it: that means *you are only hearing about 14 percent of what a person is really thinking*— not because they are intentionally withholding what's in their brain, but because the pipe of the spoken word is just too narrow to get out all the thoughts that are occurring to them!

They Haven't Built the Skills

There is a reason that an entire industry's worth of consultants and coaches and trainers are teaching people how to communicate hard things to one another: it's not easy to do! Finding the right words to express what we are thinking or feeling is a skill, particularly when what we have to say isn't all glowing. When others aren't sure how to say what they want to say well, staying quiet can feel like the easier and safer choice.

As *Bambi*'s Thumper once told us, "If you don't have anything nice to say, don't say nothing at all." Many people take a look at the slew of critical judgments in their own left-hand columns and conclude, quite reasonably, that sharing these raw reactions would likely cause more harm than good. Part of the problem is that few of us are ever taught how to express ourselves in ways that are both kind and constructive. We fluctuate between not-the-whole-truth pleasantries ("It's fine!") and unfiltered outbursts ("What's wrong with you!?") that do little to help us be heard or really understood. For this reason, someone might know they have something important to share with you, but if they just can't figure out how to say it in a productive way, they'll likely keep it to themselves.

They're Worried Their Words Aren't Acceptable

Many cultures, especially those in the corporate world, place a high value on traditional forms of analysis and data and tend to dismiss intuitive modes of emotional expression as irrational or untrustworthy. The same goes for personal experience. The actual or perceived requirement for "proof" can lead many people, particularly those whose lived experience has been questioned or even denied, to withhold sharing these very valuable types of information.

This is unfortunate because so many essential insights occur first at the intuitive level—someone just has a gut feeling that something is wrong with your suggestion, or that something important is missing from their team's upcoming product launch, even though they can't point to concrete evidence. Or, sometimes, what they really need to share is emotional. Maybe they want to tell you that the real reason they have been missing deadlines recently is that they are struggling with crippling anxiety, or they feel angry and hurt about something you said last week, but they think you'll only hear them if they translate their experience through rational words that just escape them.

One common example of this is the valid fear of *tone policing* experienced by many women and people of color, who worry that if they don't express themselves the "correct" way, they will be dismissed or criticized.[10] Writer and researcher Maura Cheeks provides a lens into the kind of calculations that have led her, a Black woman, to hold back. In a powerful *Harvard Business Review* article,[11] she writes, "I tend to wait until everyone else has spoken before choosing to weigh in. Part of that is simply because I'm an introvert. But another part is because I've been conditioned by society and its predominantly white institutions to feel that as a Black woman I come across as aggressive, bossy, and selfish when I speak my mind compared to a man or white woman making the same statements. Many people feel as though they can't be their true selves in the workplace at the risk of seeming unprofessional."

Sometimes, cultural differences in what constitutes "acceptable" speech leads people to withhold things that their culture marks inappropriate but that you might actually want to know. Or they do tell you, but the message gets lost along cross-cultural airwaves. I have a colleague, Jenee Henry Wood, who was raised in a southern state. She is incredibly tactful and gentle in how she delivers feedback—so much so that those of us from regions that emphasize a more direct, confrontational communication style at times miss the point entirely! Recently, after seeing me put a few sparse comments in a draft report that she sent to me, Jenee sent me a note saying, "Jeff, have you finished reviewing the memo I sent you, or do you plan to spend more time on it tomorrow?" I thought she was asking me a factual question, but I later learned that this was her polite, southern way of telling me that she was craving more in-depth feedback than she'd seen me give her so far! Meanwhile, someone from a culture that emphasizes face-saving and politeness might perceive the characteristic directness of a stereotypical New Yorker as a harsh personal attack.

They're Still Working Out What They Really Think or Feel

Another reason people may not have the right words is that they aren't yet sure what they actually think or feel. Sometimes, people need to process more internally, while other times, they may not know what they think until it's drawn out of them. Writers Joan Didion, Flannery O'Connor, and Stephen King have all acknowledged that they often don't know what they really want to say about something until they put words on the page.[12] When asked about his views on a human rights crisis in Africa during his tenure, Henry Kissinger reportedly replied, "I do not yet know what I think about the situation in Mauritania, because I have yet to hear what I have to say about the situation in Mauritania."[13] While secretaries of state have advisers to help them develop their opinions, all that most people need is a little prompting. In these situations, a good question and some deep listening can actually help the person discover what they really think or feel, a gift to both the asker and the sharer (more on this in Chapter 6).

Introverts present a special case here. A lot of their knowledge, thoughts, and feelings simply play out inside their heads. It's not that they're deliberately withholding anything. As Susan Cain points out in *Quiet: The Power of Introverts in a World That Can't Stop Talking*, somewhere between one-third and one-half of Americans are introverted, meaning that they listen more than they talk and think more before speaking than extroverted people do.[14] Yet Cain reminds us that some of the world's greatest ideas have come from those who prefer to keep their internal worlds internal, such as Vincent van Gogh, Bill Gates, and Eleanor Roosevelt. Just because they aren't apt to broadcast their thoughts and ideas or because they prefer to take more time to really think things through before sharing doesn't mean their ideas aren't valuable. They simply need time and space (and, as we will get to, perhaps an invitation) in order to share with others.

Barrier 3: They Lack the Time or Energy

Sometimes people hold back because **they don't have the time or energy to share**, or they feel that sharing will draw them more deeply into the situation than they are mentally or emotionally prepared to go. This could be because of overwhelm from the stress and pace of life, from burnout at home or work, or from the exhaustion of feeling like they aren't fully accepted.

They're Too Busy or Overwhelmed

As is the case with so many leaders, my day-to-day work reality is one meeting after another. During each meeting, incoming emails, direct messages, and texts pile up, which I try my best to return before it's too late. I'm lucky if I can keep up with the urgent ones before the next thing hits. So, if at the end of a meeting, I'm thinking, *What that person said felt kind of off*, or *They're missing some information*, or *They might not be aware of this other thing that happened*, there's barely any time for me to say it to them directly before I'm onto the next thing. When I'm at my very best, or if the thing is really a big deal, of course I'll find the time to say it. But lots of small to medium-size things can slip through the cracks and build up.

As I've become aware of this, I let the people around me know about this tendency. I explain that it's not that I'm uninterested in their development, I'm just juggling so much. Because I really do want to contribute to their growth, I encourage them to pause me and ask for feedback and input—at which point, without fail, I will slow down and offer any and all contributions I can make.

Some people take me up on this and regularly ask me for guidance. However, if they don't, I'm liable to skip over a lot of moments when I could have been helpful to them but am too rushed to think about it.

I know I'm not alone in this. So many people spend their days rushing from one thing to the next, squeezing in emails between meetings and appointments and a seemingly endless list of errands. It's easy (and understandable) for them to feel that they can't afford the time to slow down and share with us what they're really thinking or feeling, especially if doing so feels like it might add another thing to their already overflowing plates. Other times, they are moving so fast that they simply forget that their input might be valuable.

They're Too Depleted to Share

Nowadays, it seems, we're all just on the edge of barely making it. Juggling work and life and health and children and finances and parents and friends and community adds up to way more than a full-time job. Add to that worries about the world around us—from politics to climate to a range of other issues, including the lingering effects of a global pandemic and the additional burdens and loss that created for so many. All of this adds up in the workplace, where demands haven't let up, and people are being asked to grind out more productivity than ever. A 2022 external poll by Deloitte of one thousand US professionals revealed that 77 percent of employees surveyed are experiencing burnout.[15] Now, layer onto this the burdens of trying to stay afloat economically or living with discrimination, microaggressions, or even fear for safety. The American Psychological Association has linked discrimination-related stress to a number of mental and physical health issues, as well as work and financial challenges, all of which compound and leave those experiencing discrimination with very little energy left over to tell us what we really need to hear from them.[16]

Researchers in Australia found that in medicine, a profession prone to stress and exhaustion, the more that nurses experienced burnout, the less they spoke up (and the less responsive their managers were). The relationship between burnout and choosing to stay quiet is compounded by the fact that holding in one's thoughts, emotions, and desires can actually add to the emotional exhaustion that, in turn, makes us less likely to have the energy to speak up.[17] This then becomes a vicious cycle: the more cognitive and emotional resources people expend withholding what is really in their hearts or minds, the less likely they are to have the energy to share when it's crucial.

Regardless of who they are, if their gas tank is near empty, it's a rational choice to keep their mouths shut instead of enduring the cognitive and emotional labor, and sleepless nights, often associated with offering input or ideas, let alone sharing tough feedback. It's understandable. Yet when people around you make this understandable choice, you miss a valuable opportunity to learn, your relationship with them suffers, and the organization loses out.

Barrier 4: Their Sharing Doesn't Feel Valued by You

Whether accurate or not, people often believe you aren't really interested in what they have to say. How do they develop this belief? Let's take an extreme case—a friend of mine, Michael, had just completed a four-month project as a junior analyst that entailed a lot of unexpected evening and weekend fire drills, work that he thought could have been avoided with some specific changes in how the partner in charge managed the project. So, when it was over, he typed up some constructive feedback, printed it out, and hand delivered it to his boss Doug, saying, "I put together some feedback for you about your leadership of the project." Doug had never seen a junior person do anything like this. He stood up, took the paper, and said, "Thank you, Michael"—simultaneously ripping it in half and letting the pieces fall into his trash can.

Michael's willingness to volunteer detailed feedback on his boss's performance is . . . let's just say, unusual, and his typewritten memo was a quite assertive way to go about it. But his boss's extreme reaction left no doubt in Michael's mind—and in the minds of everyone at the accounting firm who later heard the story—that his boss was completely uninterested in his input. Most people aren't as intrepid as Michael; they just *assume* from the start that you don't want to hear their input. If they don't know for sure that their voice is valued, chances are they will choose to stay silent.

Past Experiences Have Led Them to Believe You Don't Care—or You Can't or Won't Act On—What They Have to Say

People largely base predictions about how you will respond in the future on how they've seen you react to similar situations in the past. If someone has tried to tell you something before and felt that you didn't listen, didn't care, or didn't act on the information, they are less likely to share again in the future. But they need not have had a bad experience with *you specifically* to be wary of sharing again—even having a bad experience sharing with someone like you (another boss or direct report, another person of your race, another doctor, another manager, to name some examples) can spill over into their interactions with you.

This effect can occur on the collective level as well. For example, the #MeToo movement was like a dam bursting forth with long-withheld information, with women all over the world sharing their stories of sexual harassment and assault publicly for the first time. Many men were baffled by this outpouring of information by the women in their lives and all around them. How could they not have known? Why didn't the women speak up sooner? Women responded: Why would I take the risk of sharing when all the evidence suggests I won't be believed? A long history of men not believing women's stories and failing to take action against perpetrators shaped women's predictions about whether the risk and vulnerability of trying to share again is worthwhile.

Prior attempts to share, which have repeatedly resulted in nothing changing, can easily produce an "it's hopeless" mentality. People are not going to continue to invest energy in ways that have borne little fruit in the past. This is one of the reasons why how you handle the period *after* their sharing has occurred matters so much; we'll come back to that in Chapter 7.

The Culture Leads Them to Question Whether *Anyone* Is Interested in What They Have to Say

I have a teammate, José, who recently told me that he frequently struggles with self-doubt when it comes to sharing his ideas at work. Even though he has great instincts, he holds himself back from speaking up because he fears that what he has to say isn't actually valued. Further, he fears that if he says something out loud and he's wrong, it will confirm his worst fear—that others will find out he doesn't really know what he's doing or deserve to be at the organization. José is someone I hold in incredibly high regard, but that has nothing to do with his inner experience of himself, which is what keeps him silent. There's a term for this particular brand of self-doubt—*impostor syndrome*—and it is just one example of the ways in which people can become conditioned to believe that their thoughts, views, emotions, or experiences are not valid or valued.[18]

People receive cultural messages all the time about whose input is valued and whose is not. Traditionally, the majority of those sharing their opinions in our newspapers and on our screens have been straight white men. When people don't see themselves reflected in the culture as the type of person whose knowledge, ideas, and experience are valued by the collective, they are likely to feel their sharing is unwelcome. By contrast, those who see people like them speaking openly all around them are more likely to feel empowered to share and to assume that they will be listened to.

In a pivotal study on the relationship between gender and speaking up, Victoria Brescoll, a professor of organizational behavior at the Yale School of Management, studied how often US senators took the floor and how much time they spent talking while there.[19] She found that male senators consistently spoke more often and for longer periods than their female colleagues, who, Brescoll found, believed that talking a lot would result in negative reaction. This was true regardless of how powerful a woman was: while seniority (power) for men had the effect of increasing their speaking time, seniority had no effect on the women senators' speaking time.

Were the female senators' patterns of holding back valid? Brescoll decided to explore that question too. In a follow-up experiment, she tested people's perceptions of fictitious CEOs, who were described as talking more or less than others in power. Both male and female participants rated female CEOs who spoke more as less competent and less suitable as leaders, suggesting the female senators' hesitancy was justified. But even when the punishment is less common than is feared or expected, the mere perception can tilt the scales powerfully toward staying quiet.

WITHHOLDING IS RARELY MALICIOUS

What about people who withhold because they're not interested in helping you, or in order to create an advantage for themselves? It would be naive to think this doesn't happen in some cutthroat organizations and toxic cultures. However, in my experience, this motivation for withholding is far less common than all the other ones listed previously. And while this is not a book about game theory or power plays, the *Ask* Approach will give you the greatest chance of creating a more cooperative dynamic with someone who may have a competitive—or even negative—orientation to you. If that fails, at least you will be able to rule out all the other reasons they could be withholding. And if you give them a fair test but ultimately conclude that they are truly out to get you, then you may want to put down this book and pick up Machiavelli's *The Prince* or Robert Greene's *The 48 Laws of Power.*

MOVING BEYOND THE BARRIERS

Remember Nick Epley's key finding in the Introduction—that the best way to find out what someone else really thinks, feels, or knows is to ask them? Many of the barriers described in this chapter can be immediately overcome *simply by asking.* Asking questions signals interest, provides encouragement, and acts as permission for a person to share what's on their mind that they might not otherwise feel entitled to express. Other barriers need more than just the invitation of a question. They require safety, personal connection, patient follow-up, and thoughtful listening, to name just a few. All these conditions are covered in the *Ask* Approach, which will allow you to overcome most, if not all, of the barriers we've discussed.

If I didn't believe it were possible, I wouldn't have written this book. Over and over again, I have experienced the magnificent learning, growth, and connection for all involved when having conversations using the *Ask* Approach. You only need the right set of tools. That is exactly what Section II is all about.

SUMMARY OF KEY POINTS

Essential question: *Why* don't people tell you what's most important for you to find out?

1. If you want to learn what people really think, know, and feel, it's important to first develop empathy and awareness around the barriers that stop them from sharing what might be useful for you to know.
2. People tend to hold back sharing due to one or more of four powerful barriers:
    - They're worried about how what they have to say could negatively affect you, them, or your relationship.
    - They can't find the right words because they lack the skills or language to express themselves in ways that feel acceptable, or because they are still processing internally.
    - They don't have the time or energy to share.
    - They think you're not truly interested in hearing from them.
3. Differences in culture, identity, power, and styles of expression can intensify each of these barriers or could lead you to miss hearing what they actually *are trying* to express.

EXERCISES

2A. Think about a relationship or interaction where someone didn't share with you something important they knew, thought, or felt. Which of the four barriers might have held them back?

- They were worried about the impact of sharing (on you or them or the relationship).
- They couldn't find the right words to say it.
- They lacked the time or energy to share.
- They didn't think you were truly interested.

Take a moment to consider more deeply:

- What might have been going on for them that made this barrier stop them from sharing with you?
- If it was an interaction across a line of difference (e.g., power, gender, race, style, etc.), how might the dynamics of difference have exacerbated the barrier?

2B. Think about whether or how (if at all) you might have inadvertently contributed to them feeling stopped by any of these barriers. If so, what might you have done differently to reduce the barriers? This will prime you for learning the steps of the *Ask* Approach in Section II!

SECTION II

The *Ask* Approach

EXPERTS AGREE ON ONE THING: THE BEST AND MOST ACCURATE way to find out what others around us think, feel, and know is...to ask them. *How* to ask is the focus of this section.

The *Ask* Approach is a set of steps that cultivate mutually beneficial learning, leading to smarter decisions, more creative solutions, and deeper connections. Each chapter in this section dives deeply into one of the five steps depicted in the following diagram—weaving together stories, frameworks, scientific research, and most important, practical strategies you can immediately apply.

The *Ask* Approach

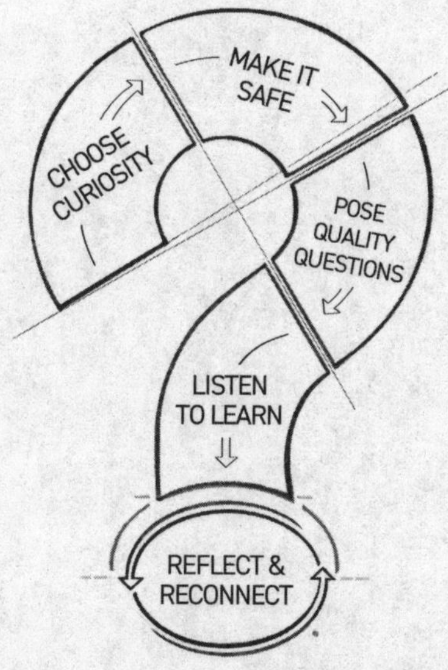

I encourage you to take your time exploring each step. The *Ask* Approach is neither a cookbook recipe nor a script to follow blindly. Rather, each step contains a set of deep practices for human connection. That means you'll need to use your judgment when you apply them in your own life. In some cases, you may choose to have multiple conversations with someone before you can make it all the way through the steps. In other cases, you may double back through some of the steps before you complete the *Ask* Approach. All of that is not only okay, it's to be expected. Human relationships are messier in real life than any framework can depict on paper.

So get curious about relationships where you could benefit from applying the *Ask* Approach, and then customize how you apply it to each one. The goal here is learning and connection.

Now, let's dive in!

Chapter 3

CHOOSE CURIOSITY

Essential question: How can you awaken your curiosity to make new discoveries and unexpected connections?

AS THE GREAT PSYCHOLOGIST AND MEDITATION TEACHER TARA Brach has said, "The world is divided into those who think they're right. And that's the whole saying."[1]

I once saw this truth play out on a tropical island where my colleagues and I were consulting for the tourism industry, which was the bread and butter of this small nation. This country's particular "sun and sand" brand of tourism was facing increasingly stiff competition from other equally sunny and sandy countries that offered guests much lower prices. Over the prior ten years, a steady decline in tourist arrivals had created strain throughout the sector.

My particular assignment was to facilitate better collaboration between the island's hotel managers, largely senior executives from multinational corporations, and their nemesis, the industry's labor union. The managers wanted more-flexible labor contracts so as to enhance guests' experiences, while the union saw the changes as yet another attempt to pile on more work without more pay. The stakes were high: if we failed to break a logjam, the likely outcome was a paralyzing strike, with ripple effects that could crush the nation's economy.

The history of the island shaped and aggravated the conflict: The corporate managers were mostly white, with higher educations from abroad, and the union workers were mostly Black, descendants of enslaved people brought to the island by white Europeans during colonization. This painful history, combined with modern dynamics of inequality and cultural division on the island, added layers of complexity and distrust to the relationship between the two groups.

Both sides had an incentive to find a constructive path forward—everyone's livelihoods depended on reaching a solution that would allow the industry to continue operating—yet their skepticism and frustration with one another ran deep. But the hotel managers and union leaders had this in common: total certainty that their story was the right one. And because of this, they could only see each other as opponents and threats.

You don't need to have visited this tropical island to recognize the pattern at play: two sides, each so convinced of their position that they're totally unwilling to hear their opponents. If you've been there yourself, you know how the thinking goes: "*They* are the problem." "Here we go again." You think you already know everything they're going to say and why they're wrong.

In the days leading up to our meeting, understood by all as a last-ditch effort to bring the two sides back to the negotiation table, I had received increasingly angry and impatient phone calls from both exasperated hotel managers and the union heads. At one point, I'd even been hung up on midsentence. This entire initiative, it seemed, was hanging on by the thinnest of threads. Yet this measly thread was all that stood between this tense reality and a paralyzing, industry-wide strike.

When the day of the meeting arrived, it was far from clear we could succeed. Nevertheless, my team and I took deep breaths, and we all got to work. What both sides of the dispute needed in order to co-create a new, shared reality—one in which the tourism industry could rebound and workers could thrive—was a swift dose of curiosity.

CURIOSITY THAT CONNECTS

Curiosity powers your brain's learning engine. Psychology and neuroscience tell us that curiosity is a powerful drive state for information, a sense of "deprivation that arises from the perception of a gap in knowledge and understanding."[2] Similar to other drive states, such as hunger and thirst, curiosity creates a powerful, dopamine-fueled motivation to seek out information to fill that gap. Research has also shown that curiosity primes us for learning, by activating the memory centers in our brains.[3]

The kind of curiosity we're most interested in, when it comes to the *Ask* Approach, is the kind that opens up a channel to what's in someone else's mind and heart. I call it *connective curiosity*.[4] Distinct from *diversive* curiosity (the drive for new information) or *epistemic* curiosity (a more focused form of curiosity having to do with understanding a particular subject area), *connective* curiosity is a desire to understand more about the thoughts, experiences, and feelings of other people.[5] This type of curiosity is most critical for deepening our ability to learn from those around us.

What makes connective curiosity so powerful is that it can also benefit the person we're curious about. In this sense, connective curiosity can be understood as an act of care—and indeed, "care" is *curiosity*'s Latin root!

When you show someone you want to learn from them, they become aware that what they know and experience is deeply important to you—and therefore worth sharing. When you signal *your* desire to understand what another person knows, thinks, and feels, that person's desire to *tell you* actually grows. In contrast, when someone senses judgment, or even just a lack of deep interest on your part, they shut down.[6]

This flavor of curiosity is *especially* important when a power difference is present in the dynamic. Leading with curiosity puts you in a position of humbly seeking to understand the other person. They know or think something you need to understand. You can't force them to share anything; you can only express your genuine desire to connect with them and hear whatever they have to say. This gives them a sense of empowerment that can help counterbalance other factors on the power scale that might otherwise lead them to stay quiet.

YES, YOU CAN *CHOOSE* CURIOSITY

Psychologists have traditionally approached curiosity either as a *trait* that an individual may have more or less of, or as a *state of mind* they may occupy depending on the situation.[7]

I prefer a third way of looking at curiosity—as a *choice*, one we can learn to make in any circumstance.[8] A choice to take a stance that opens us to learning, expanding what we know, and deepening our connection to others.

The fact that we can choose to do it doesn't mean it's easy. Choosing curiosity goes against many pressures, both in our own psychological wiring and in the culture around us. Even when we don't initially feel curious, choosing to open our minds can transform everything else that follows. And it's not a onetime decision—often, we have to choose curiosity, again and again, in each moment of a conversation.

Although it's hard, it is still possible. Victor Frankl, who was a psychologist, author, and Holocaust survivor, reminds us of this possibility even in the most dire of circumstances: "Everything can be taken from a man but one thing: the last of the human freedoms—to choose one's attitude in any given set of circumstances."[9]

I define "choosing curiosity" as:

> **Intentionally looking for new information and different ways of understanding people, situations, and the world around you.**

While everyone has the ability to choose curiosity, sometimes we get so distracted by other stuff going on in our heads—such as anxiety, judgment, or fear—that we begin to feel like there's no space for it. But choosing curiosity isn't like adding another piece of clutter into a messy room. It's a lot more like throwing open a window, allowing light and fresh air to flood in. In fact, the more emotional stuff going on in your head, the more refreshing it is to choose curiosity. It's just good mental housekeeping.

Choosing curiosity doesn't mean abandoning our hunches or beliefs; rather, it's about loosening their grip. Early in my career, I learned a succinct but powerful mantra that I hold close: *strong ideas, loosely held.*[10] Throughout this chapter, I'll introduce what I call **curiosity questions** (CQs). Engaging with these questions can help us keep our strong ideas but hold them more loosely, so we can make room to take in new information and connect to others' perspectives.

To get better at choosing curiosity, and specifically *connective* curiosity, we'll need to look a little differently at two things than we might have in the past: our relationship with reality and our relationship with those around us. To help us think about both, let me introduce you to the most useful tool for choosing curiosity I've ever come across.

TO CHOOSE CURIOSITY, LEVERAGE THE LADDER

Have you ever questioned your relationship with reality? I realize that may sound a bit, well, big, but it's an amazing practice to strengthen your curiosity muscles. We will be aided in this endeavor by a tool adapted (and renamed) from one originally developed by Chris Argyris: the **ladder of understanding.**[11] This tool gives us insight into exactly how curiosity falls apart: our preexisting knowledge, assumptions, and biases lead us to tell ourselves highly certain "stories" about reality, but often our stories have more gaps or errors than we realize. Using the ladder of understanding, we can inject curiosity back into our thinking process, by recognizing when we've jumped to conclusions and inserting more question marks at each rung of the ladder.

You can use the ladder by yourself, as a reflective process to help you choose curiosity when you're in a conflict—or really in any situation or relationship where you feel stuck. Or you can use it as a shared tool to work through an issue together with another person or group. As you'll see, this is exactly what we did with the hotel managers and unions—we threw the ladder diagram up on a whiteboard and worked through the process together, with powerful results.

So let's dive in . . .

Picture a ladder, which emanates upward out of a swimming pool. A strange picture, perhaps, but easy to conjure up and remember. It will make more sense soon, I promise:

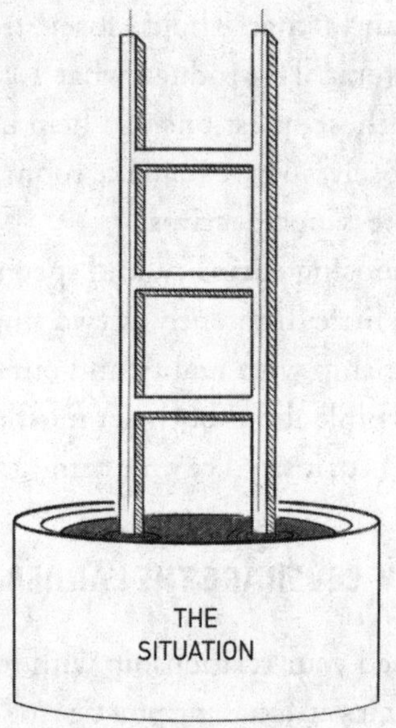

The Situation: A Pool of Zillions of Data Points

The water in the pool, also called "the Situation," represents all the many pieces of information that exist about the situation we're in. As I sit here writing this book, there are literally infinite data points all around me: the temperature of the room, the way the light is coming through the window, the silhouettes of the trees outside, the shape of the chair I'm sitting on, the scents coming from the kitchen, the sound of my wife's voice on the phone in another room, the sound of a plane overhead, the flower arrangement on the table, the clicking of the keys as I type, the blue curtains attached to the black curtain rod, the faint achiness in my back, the feel of my watch on my wrist showing me how many steps I've taken. The list could go on and on. Try it sometime: attempt to take in every single data point around you in the present moment. You'll quickly realize why your brain needs to filter out most of it.

When we try to pay attention to everything, we get paralyzed. We're too busy attending to all the aspects of our experiences to be able to actually do anything. Imagine if, in prehistoric times, a cave person stopped and paid attention to all the points around them. They'd quickly get eaten by the tiger, or if they didn't get eaten, they'd be too entranced by everything around them to go hunt or gather any food. We see it with toddlers too. Have you ever tried to get somewhere quickly when walking with a toddler, for whom everything is fascinating? If you're the toddler, it's amazing! But if you're the adult running late for day-care drop-off and work, less amazing.

We Select a Tiny Slice of Information... Then Ignore and Forget the Rest

As kids, we're relentlessly curious. But as our brains develop into adulthood, we learn to do something simultaneously essential and problematic: we pay *selective* attention to a tiny fraction of the myriad aspects of any given situation. Everything else, we ignore. This is an essential feature of how we must operate to stay sane as we move through life.

But herein lies the bug: that tiny fraction of situational information that we select becomes our total reality. To keep ourselves moving forward, we *forget* that there were so many other parts of the situation that we didn't select (or weren't even aware of).

Let's take a look at how this had played out between the union and the hotel managers in the months leading up to our session. Caroline, one of the longest-standing corporate executives, was the person designated to represent the island's hotel managers. Her counterpart on the union side was Marcus, the leader of the hotel workers' union. While rising up the ranks, Marcus had worked for more than forty years as a porter in one of Caroline's hotels. The two of them had butted heads for decades.

In one conversation, the two sides had talked about modifying the labor contract to consider greater flexibility. When Caroline participated in that conversation, her "reality" was defined by the data point she **selected**, of Marcus forcefully declaring, "We will *not* talk about flexibility!" Little did she remember, at that same meeting, Marcus and other union leaders had also said things like "We want to find a solution here," "We know times are hard for everyone, even the hotel owners," and "We are open to getting creative." But those bits of information swimming around in Caroline's pool didn't come up the ladder with her.

Caroline's Selection

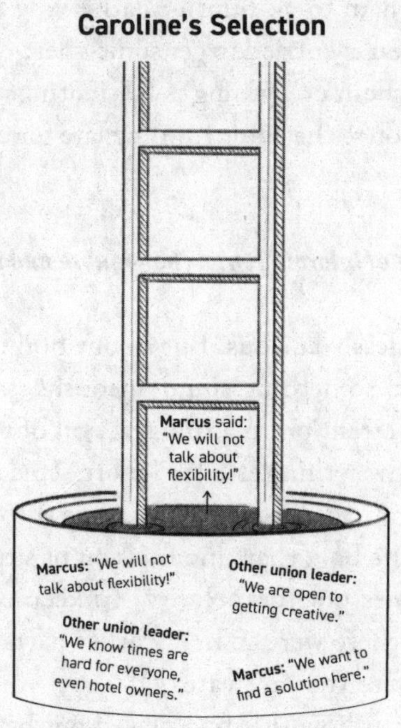

Similarly, Marcus's reality was defined when he **selected** just one of Caroline's statements: "Expanding flexibility in the labor contract is our only way forward." Caroline and other hotel managers had shared far more than this one point. For example, they also said, "We know that the hotel employees are working really hard, and we want to do right by them," "We realize this might have to come with other forms of compensation for employees," and "We are under more pressure than ever before from our hotel owners who are looking at selling the properties." None of those other statements became a part of Marcus's reality.

Marcus's Selection

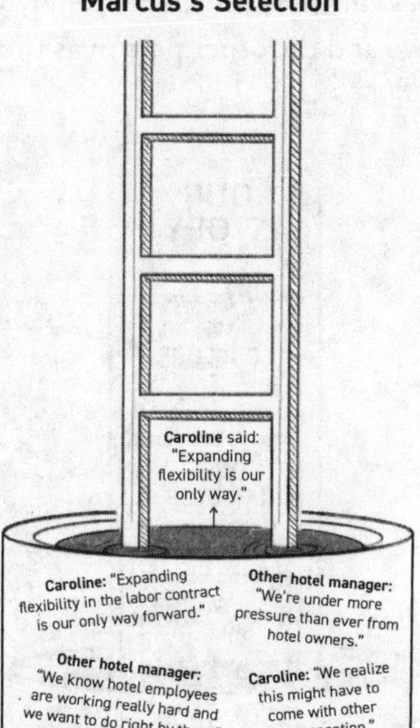

We Process at Lightning Speed... and Reach Highly Certain Conclusions

Once we've selected our fraction of information from the situational pool, just as Caroline and Marcus did, we immediately **process** what that data must mean. We start racing up the ladder, rung by rung, interpreting the data we selected. Sometimes, our interpretations are logical, using inferences. Other times, the processing is more intuitive, or emotion-driven. Either way, it happens really fast, far too quickly to be perceived by our conscious awareness. Psychologists Daniel Kahneman and Amos Tversky have persuasively argued that this kind of "fast thinking" is essential to making critical decisions in a world overflowing with information.[12]

Then, we **draw conclusions**. These conclusions might be about someone else's character, or (what we perceive as) the truth of the matter, or what action we and others should take. Together, the pieces of information we select, the way we process them, and the conclusions we draw create the "**story**" we tell ourselves about any given situation. Especially when we're emotionally triggered, the stories we construct as we race up our ladders can have as much drama as a Hollywood movie, with us as the misunderstood hero and the other person as the malicious villain.

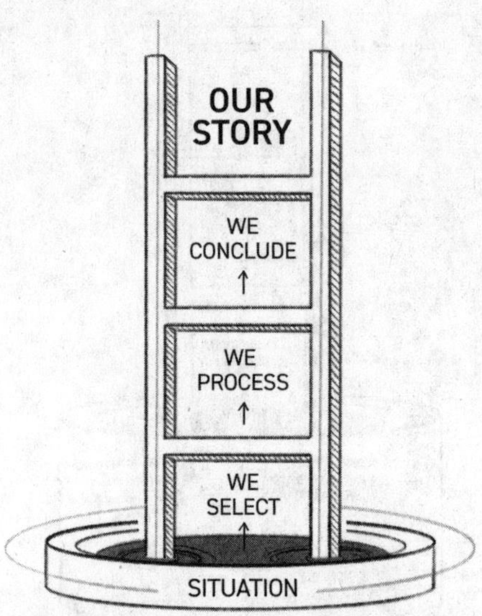

It's important to point out that nothing in life is quite this linear or clean. In reality, the way we construct our stories is full of emotional twists and intuitive turns and messy connections, looking something more like this:

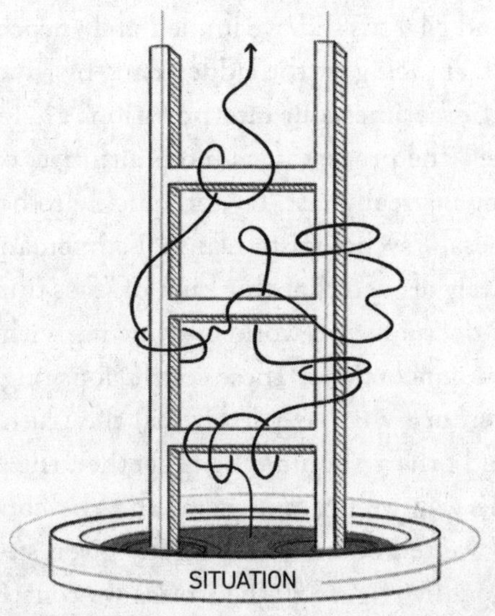

Our Story Shapes Our Steps

However we get to our conclusions, the stories we tell ourselves about reality are powerful. So powerful, in fact, that they determine the next **steps** we take—how we act and react, and how we make decisions, all based on that tiny slice of data we originally selected from the vast amount of information in our situation and how we then processed it.

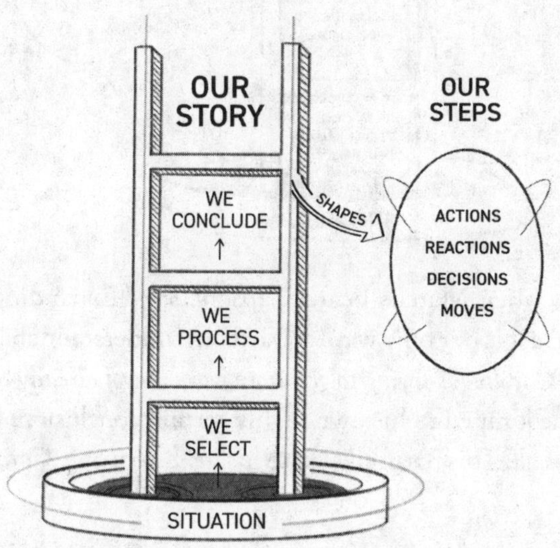

Let's see how this played out with Caroline and Marcus.

When Caroline heard Marcus forcefully proclaim, "We will *not* talk about flexibility," her understandable interpretation was that *Marcus is refusing to discuss* what he sees as the most important way for the entire industry to become more competitive. The way she **processed** that as she moved up the ladder led her to **conclude** with great certainty that *Marcus is stubborn and oppositional*. From here, her natural next **step** was, *I've got to override Marcus's resistance*.

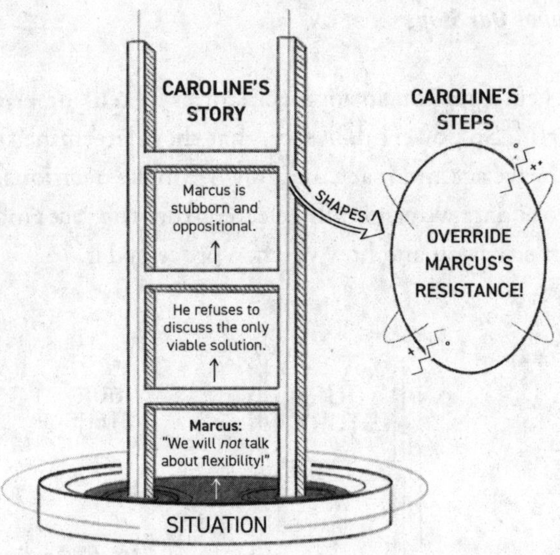

Similarly, when Marcus heard Caroline say, "Expanding flexibility in the labor contract is our only way forward," his understandable thought process was that *Caroline is trying to get more work out of already tired employees.* From there, he jumped to his own highly certain conclusion: *Caroline is trying to exploit us all.* This naturally led to his next step: *Stop Caroline at all costs!*

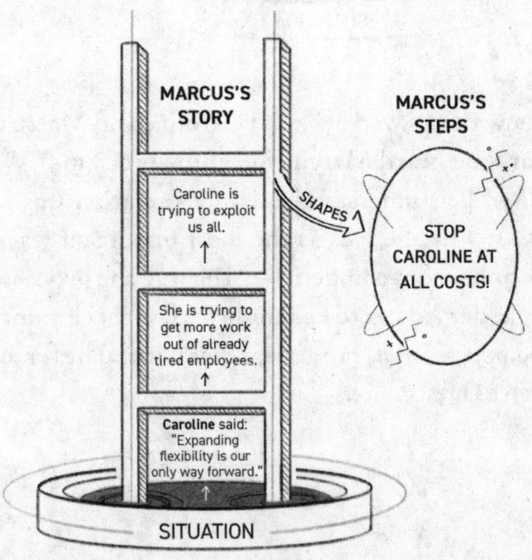

Each time Caroline and Marcus jumped to the next rung of their ladders, it inwardly made sense, based on the tiny subset of information they had each selected and on how they processed them. And yet they could have each selected different fragments from the situation. Or they could have processed each fragment in so many alternative ways. If they'd done so, they might have reached totally different conclusions. So, why did they each climb up their respective ladders in the ways they did?

Our Stuff Shapes Our Stories . . . and We Fall into the Certainty Loop

Part of the reason is a well-documented psychological phenomenon called *confirmation bias*,[13] which refers to the ubiquitous human tendency to select experiences that confirm our preexisting beliefs, biases, prejudices, lived experience, and assumptions about a person or situation, all of which I call our **stuff**.[14] Our stuff is beautifully human at its essence: it's messy, it's got lots of soft spots (some covered over and others still quite raw), it's often filled with contradictions, and hopefully it's ever evolving. We bring our stuff into every situation, and our stuff influences what information we select and how we process that information to reach conclusions.

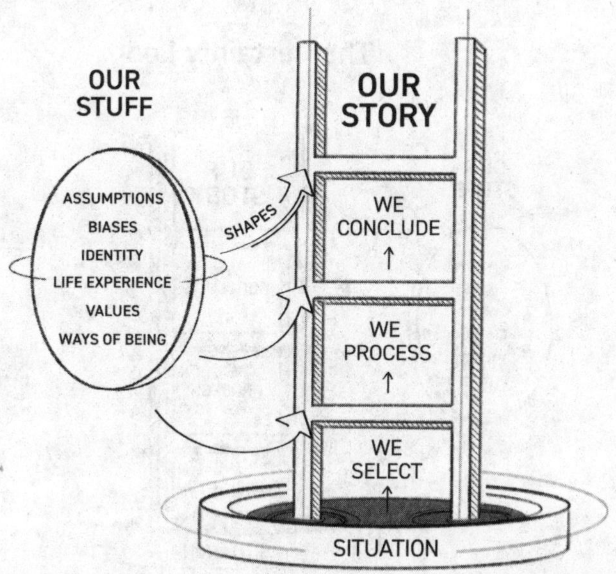

Because our stuff is often quite deeply held—and has been accumulated over our lifetimes—it often leads us to select, process, and conclude in ways that create stories which confirm (and reconfirm) what we already believed. That's why we so often feel that "Here we go again" sentiment when engaged in a familiar dynamic—because here we are, heaving our stuff up our ladders, yet again. Marcus and Caroline were already deeply skeptical of each other, so it didn't take much for them to create stories that confirmed what they'd thought and felt about each other for years prior to this moment.

The act of racing up the ladder to tell ourselves a story isn't, in itself, a problem. It's human, and as we've seen, quite useful in avoiding decision paralysis. The problem comes when we fall into what I call the *certainty loop*. We become caught in this loop when we forget that the story we arrive at is deeply shaped by our own stuff and is only one of many stories that could be crafted about the situation. Our story—and how it then plays out through our steps—stops being a story and becomes, to us, the objective truth, which only serves to reconfirm our stuff's preexisting expectations. This is not limited to situations of conflict; most of us spend large swaths of our day-to-day lives walking through the world stuck inside our own self-sealing certainty loops. If we think our story about any given situation is reality, what is there to be curious about? Not much.

The Certainty Loop

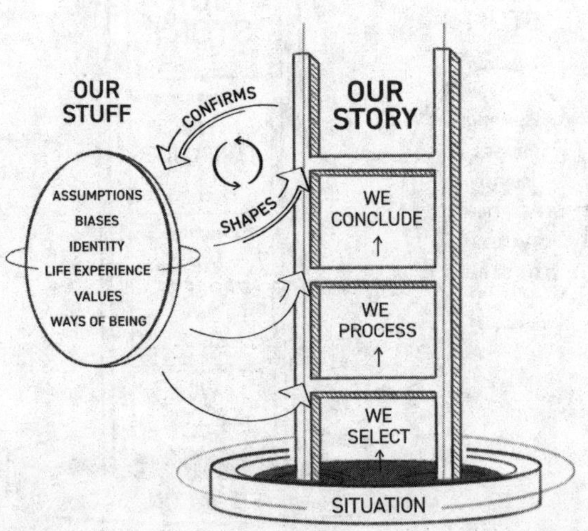

Use the Ladder to Choose Curiosity

How can we interrupt this certainty loop and instead *choose curiosity*? In Kahneman and Tversky's language, we have to *slow down* our thinking. We can start by consciously noting that this process is even happening. When we begin to catch ourselves in the act and realize that our mind has constructed a skewed and incomplete story, we have the chance to identify the gaps in our knowledge, triggering the hound chase of curiosity.

We can then use the ladder of understanding as a tool to unpack our own thinking and find places to inject question marks. After we introduced this tool to them, even Caroline and Marcus—mired for so long in their certainty loops—learned to "walk down their ladders." When things got tense in the room, they jokingly called themselves and each other out by saying, "I think we're all a little high on the ladder right now!" That shared language became a sign to pause and reflect on what they might have been missing or misinterpreting. Little by little, the union leaders became more curious—in fact, they requested a primer on the economics of the industry so they and their members could better appreciate the pressures the managers were facing. And the hotel managers got more curious about what employees valued—as a sign of her interest, Caroline went on national TV together with the union president to affirm her commitment to finding a solution that worked for hotel staff. Eventually, the much-feared strike was avoided, and while never easy, they continued to work toward labor agreements that put the industry on a better path for all.

Despite our mental programming, we *can* choose curiosity. Using the ladder of understanding as a reflective tool helps us inject question marks at each rung, so we can remind ourselves what there is to be curious about.

Curiosity questions to inject question marks into your story:

- What if my story is not the only valid story about this **situation**? What information and experiences might I have overlooked when I **selected** the data points that formed the basis of my story? How could information about this situation be interpreted, or **processed**, differently to reach different **conclusions**?

- In what way is my **story** about this situation serving me and my relationships well, and in what way is it limiting?
- What might be someone else's **story** about this situation? What information might they **select** and **process** to reach *their* **conclusions**? What accumulated life experiences of theirs might have shaped their **stuff**?

All of a sudden, a situation that seems pretty clear-cut is filled with things to be curious about. What a fascinating opportunity to learn!

How Artificial Intelligence Can Help You Inject Question Marks

For help seeing beyond the story you've constructed about a situation, simply type (or dictate) that story into your favorite AI chatbot and then add, "What might I be missing?"

Here are a few stories I entered (all of which might sound familiar from examples in this chapter):

- *I think the union is just trying to get more pay for its workers but ignoring my business's needs. What might I be missing?*
- *I think management is just trying to squeeze more work out of workers and exploit them. What might I be missing?*
- *My colleague Bailey is refusing to take on a project I asked him to do. I am furious. What might I be missing?*

In every case, the response I got back included important and new considerations, which were not part of the original story and which introduced new things to be curious about.

GET CURIOUS ABOUT THE *INVISIBLE* INFORMATION IN YOUR SITUATIONAL POOL

What kinds of information are we most likely to overlook in our pool of data about the situation? According to social psychologists, who have been documenting this challenge for decades, using such concepts as *actor-observer bias*[15] and the *fundamental attribution error,*[16] we humans over-attribute others' behavior to their character and overlook how the situation the other person is in might be influencing them (yet interestingly, when explaining our *own* behavior, we attribute it much more to circumstances we find ourselves in, rather than to our own character). This means that when we interact with others, we are most likely to miss (or misread) data points related to **the circumstances shaping their behavior—in other words, what they're up against.**

In a particularly poignant illustration of this, the Cleveland Clinic developed a video to train its staff to increase their empathy for both patients and colleagues. In the video, people of all walks of life—from patients to visitors to doctors to custodial staff—are depicted going about their business in the hospital. However, each time the camera pans over someone, a caption appears, describing what life challenges they're privately facing. One person has just discovered that his tumor is benign; another, that his tumor is malignant. One person just had a baby, while another is worried how he will care for his wife who has just had a stroke. The video is a poignant reminder that everyone is up against something—and because we don't get captions in real life, we can't know someone else's circumstances unless they tell us. (You can check out the video for yourself at the link listed in this endnote.[17])

Also invisible to us: **others' true intentions and motivations.** As we race up our ladders to construct our stories, we often assume we know *why* someone is doing something, but since others' intentions live inside their heads, *we literally cannot access this information without asking them.* That doesn't stop us from making up stories about their motives—and we now know how those can lead us astray.

Eboo Patel, the founder and president of Interfaith America, knows a thing or two about helping people stay open-minded to learning from others. Patel works with religious leaders of all faiths to create bridges and strengthen the fabric of society. The challenge is that religious beliefs and traditions often directly conflict. "For example, in Catholicism, wine is sacred. In Islam, it's profane," he told me, adding that "Muslims have a single God. And there's Hindus, who have colorful celebrations of many Gods." So, how do you build bridges and stay open-minded to learning when interacting with people who have such fundamental disagreements?

As a trained social scientist, Patel knows that "people tend to do things that work for them, that they think work for them. . . . So, you begin from a place of curiosity." According to Patel, you don't need to change your beliefs or even sympathize to get curious. All you have to do is remember that you also believe and do things that make sense to you. Chances are they do too. So you can ask yourself questions like: *How does what they're doing make sense to them? What's the sense in this from their point of view? How is their view serving them?* This isn't limited to religious differences. When you see anyone doing something that strikes you as off, wrong, or even abhorrent, ask yourself: *How do their steps and their story make sense from* ***their*** *point of view?*

Remember, too, the effect of connective curiosity—or the lack of it—on its recipient. If you wear your judgment on your sleeve, a person is unlikely to share their true experiences and motivations. But if you demonstrate curiosity about their situation and their story—and maybe even their deeper stuff and where it came from—you'll engage in ways that open them to sharing.

The other half of any relationship is how we, ourselves, play into the dynamic—and here we are also likely to overlook some of the information in the situational pool: **how our actions are perceived and their impact on others.**

We're all mostly blind to how our actions come across to others and the impacts they make. Body language can offer clues, but as we've discussed, can also be easily misread or misleading. All we can know for sure is what we said and did, not how it landed. Have you ever listened to audio recordings of yourself and thought your voice sounded strange? That's but a small example of our limited view into how others perceive us.

Tessa West is a psychologist at NYU and director of the West Interpersonal Perception Lab, which studies how people make sense of one another and how they, more often than not, get it wrong. In an episode of the NPR podcast *Hidden Brain,* West recalls how this kind of blind spot resulted in a years-long misunderstanding between her and a student. After a long day of work, she got in an elevator. When one of her students got in on the next floor, West glanced up at her and then looked away. She thought nothing of the interaction and went about her day, but she noticed over time that this particular student seemed nervous around her. It wasn't until several years later that she found out the student read the expression on West's face as animosity and concluded from the glance that her professor hated her! Because she couldn't know in the moment how the interaction was perceived by her student, West had no idea that her small action had such a negative impact on someone over whom she held significant power.[18]

Both of these blind spots—how we come across to others, and our impacts on them—are details that others are unlikely to volunteer, so these data points in the situational pool are completely invisible to us.[19] Connective curiosity is a good start to tease out what could be crucial information.

As a young consultant, I walked into the office of my manager, David Levy. I took a chair across the desk from him. It was our weekly check-in to talk about our client Judy, the head of our client's international division. In the story I'd raced up my ladder to construct, I was hitting a wall and could not get Judy to stop resisting and do what (I believed) she needed to do to succeed. I was getting increasingly frustrated. David leaned back in his chair and said to me, "Have you considered how *you* might be contributing to Judy's resistance?"

With this question, David injected some question marks into my own certainty loop. I temporarily set aside my righteousness, and we began to speculate about the various possible ways in which my well-intentioned efforts—for example, repeated follow-ups, lists of suggestions (each with its own lengthy rationale)—might have been landing with Judy. The more I got curious about the unintended impacts I might have been having on Judy, the more motivated I was to approach her with authentic inquiry. This allowed me to ask her questions about how she was experiencing our partnership, and these uncovered a hidden backstory I was completely unaware of. It turned out that she wasn't resistant to our plan at all—she was delaying because of some sensitive personnel changes that needed to play out before she could move forward. Meanwhile, my relentless pushing was needlessly turning us into adversaries instead of allies. Once I understood this, I adjusted my approach and our collaboration was back on track.

If David hadn't helped me to choose curiosity, I would likely have stayed stuck in my own certainty loop. My attitude and behavior in the face of Judy's supposed "stubbornness" might have endangered the relationship, and with it our work together.

How many times have we all been in the position I was in but didn't have the tools, or the friendly nudge, to choose curiosity about our story? Knowing where our interpersonal blind spots are shows us where to shine a light on information in our situation that would otherwise be invisible to us.

Curiosity questions to expand your awareness:

- What might the other person be up against that I'm not aware of?
- What might be their understandable motivations?
- How might they experience the world, such that their story and their steps make perfect sense?
- How might I be coming across to the other person? What might be my unintended impact on them?
- How might I unwittingly be contributing to the problem I'm concerned about?

DEFENSE AGAINST CURIOSITY KILLERS

While curiosity is almost always the *right* choice, it's often not the *easy* one. The curiosity questions throughout this chapter are a helpful support, and for me, these are often enough to break a certainty loop. I find the questions most effective when I work through them with another person. However, I've noticed some situations when staying curious is particularly hard. I call these *curiosity killers*—here are three perpetrators, along with strategies for overcoming them.

Curiosity Killer #1: Emotional Hijacking

In the experience of Jamie Higgins, an executive coach to top leaders throughout corporate America, this is by far the most challenging of all the curiosity killers. When we get emotionally activated (quite common when people are telling us things we need but might not want to hear), we face a choice: we can reactively race to the top of our ladders, or we can notice our reaction and use it as a cue to slow down and choose curiosity. With practice, negative and uncomfortable emotions can become gateways into strengthening our curiosity and deepening our learning from others.

I faced this choice when I heard, secondhand, that one of my junior teammates, Bailey, had declined to take on a project that I felt I really needed him to do. Blood rushed to my head so fast that I'm lucky a vein didn't burst. Here I was, tired from working so hard and making painful personal trade-offs for the good of the organization, and Bailey comes back with what sounded like a, *Thanks, but I'll pass.*

How dare he be so selfish when we're all making sacrifices, I fumed inside my head. And if not Bailey, who? Who was going to get this done? I was ready to scream. While venting to my co-founder, Aylon, he nodded and commiserated—but then calmly suggested that my, ahem, *strong* reaction might be worth getting curious about. What was going on *inside me* that had made Bailey's response so triggering?

Strong emotional reactions result when we perceive danger—for example, a threat to our status, our beliefs, our identities, or our resources, including time, money, and energy. This process is known as an "amygdala hijack"[20] because the part of our limbic system responsible for processing our emotions takes over our thinking mind (our prefrontal cortex). We might fight (get defensive), flee (avoid the conversation, change the topic), freeze (clench up and shut down), or fawn (people-please, sugarcoat, smooth over). This response narrows our attention to the immediate threat at hand, whether perceived or real, and makes it near impossible for us to broaden our awareness to things like the other person's experience or the possibility that we are missing important information.

In other words, when we feel threatened, our curiosity engine shuts down. What's worse, this can quickly spiral into a vicious cycle, since when we are less curious, we are more likely to become emotionally rigid, more attached to a particular outcome, and more fearful of something not going right, all things pretty much guaranteed to shut down learning.[21]

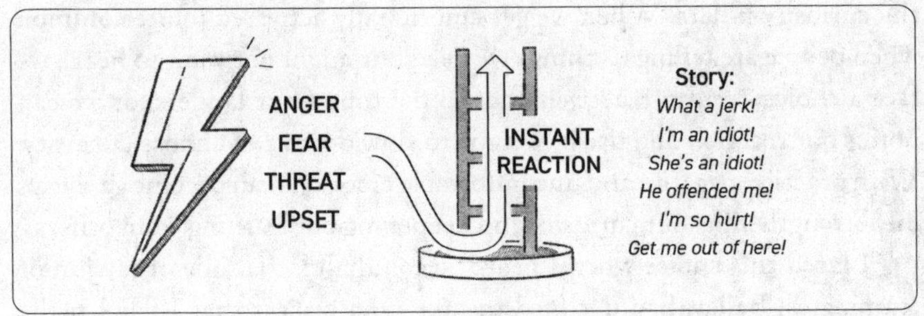

But what if we *could* flip this on its head? What if the emotions, instead of shutting us down, could become curiosity cues? Beyond the knee-jerk reactions of fight, flight, freeze, or fawn lies the possibility of a fifth *f*: entering the *find out* mode, in which we get curious about our own reactions.

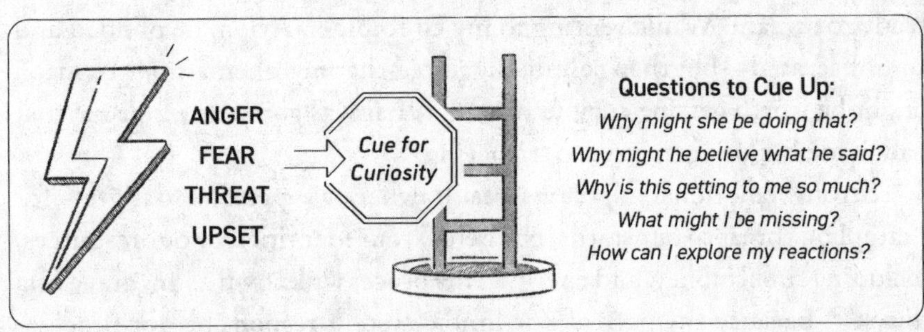

It's not easy, and it takes time to learn, but it's absolutely possible if we're intentional about it. Jim Cutler (remember him from Chapter 2?) told me that he learned to notice and respond to the physical cues of powerful emotions—for example, when he can sense anger or frustration building up in his body. Now, before his hand pounds the table, he takes a deep breath, notices the emotions, and reminds himself to be curious.

Practices like mindfulness or breath work, which I will discuss in more depth in the following section, can also help us get the distance we need from our reactions so that we can notice them arising and then get curious about them rather than being consumed by them. And in the meantime, for the rest of us mortals who haven't yet reached a sufficient level of self-awareness, that's what friends and mentors are for (see also: therapists). We can ask them to help us talk it out—not just to empathize and tell us all the ways we're right but also to help us get curious, just as Aylon did for me when he noticed me getting so worked up about Bailey.

After Aylon's nudge, and a few beats, I was able to say to myself, "That pissed me off, maybe more than was called for. What nerve did he hit?" Perhaps my own exhaustion and the personal sacrifices I'd made for work had taken such a toll that I could not be sympathetic to anyone who would draw different boundaries. Perhaps I was more power hungry than I would like to admit and was therefore incensed when someone I employed would say no to my requests. Perhaps I was just too rushed and stressed to be willing to consider that Bailey might have a justifiable reason to say no.

Now that I wasn't stuck in fight, flight, freeze, or fawn mode, I could *find out: What am I missing here?* As I pursued that question, I discovered that Bailey had said no for an excellent reason. He wasn't prioritizing himself over the team. He wasn't rejecting my authority. He wasn't any of the worst things my emotionally hijacked brain had jumped to. When asked, he explained that he had already committed to other important projects during the time I needed his help, and he didn't want to undermine that equally important work. When he walked me through his other commitments, I saw he was right. If I hadn't chosen curiosity, I might have wrongly undervalued a teammate for making a decision in the best interest of the organization. As *Radical Candor* author Kim Scott shared with me, **"When you're furious, get curious."**

Curiosity questions when experiencing strong emotions:

- What am I feeling? (In my heart? In my body?)
- What are these strong feelings telling me?

- What parts of my stuff (e.g., my life experiences, my identity, my deeper assumptions) might be making me susceptible to having such a strong reaction here?
- What is there to learn from my reaction? How can I explore it?
- What might this strong reaction stop me from seeing or hearing or thinking about?

Curiosity Killer #2: Relentless Pressure for Speed and Efficiency

When our cognitive and emotional resources are drained, when our brains are cluttered with our never-ending to-do lists, when we are rushing from meeting to meeting and barely have time to breathe, curiosity can feel like a luxury we simply cannot afford. Tricia Hersey, the founder of the Nap Ministry and author of *Rest Is Resistance*, argues persuasively that we are suffering from a crisis of sleep deprivation and exhaustion, symptoms of a "grind culture" that cares more about our productivity than our humanity.[22] Hersey's body of work, which frames this crisis as a racial and social justice issue, places emphasis on the ways in which marginalized groups of people disproportionately experience this oppressive pressure for constant performance and productivity. As such, she views the decision to slow down, to rest, and to reflect not only as an act of self-care but as a powerful antidote to a culture in which we are all overworked, exhausted, and disconnected from ourselves and one another. By slowing down, we allow ourselves the spaciousness to imagine different possibilities, which includes curiosity about other people's feelings and experiences that differ from our own.

The practice of slowing down, perhaps more than any other offered in this book, has been the most challenging for me to adopt in my own life. After several decades in the pressure cooker of management consulting and then as a manager, executive, and co-founder in hard-charging organizations, I struggle to slow down and create the spaciousness needed for curiosity to flourish. I have to be intentional and conscious to make it happen, every single day. In theory, as the co-CEO of an organization, I'm more in control of my time than I ever have been—and yet the weight of responsibility I carry, both within the organization and in the broader field, often makes me feel like I have less *right* to slow down and shrink the to-do list than at any other time in my career. I also understand that, in reality, my position grants me the autonomy and financial security to have way more control over my time than most people. And still, when I do take a moment of pause, I struggle to shake the feeling that I should be doing more, moving faster, that I'm falling behind. There's no denying the pace of life has picked up in very real ways, but it's worth considering which time pressures in your life are truly nonnegotiable and which stem from a set of socialized beliefs about how you are *supposed* to be spending your time.

In addition to examining your deeper relationship to time, here are two concrete practices that can help create the spaciousness needed for curiosity.

Calendar surgery... Shortly after joining our staff, my executive assistant, Shanika Verette, clearly but lovingly told me that in all her years of working with CEOs, she had never seen a schedule as jam-packed as mine: no lunch, no breaks. Just back-to-back or even overlapping meetings with colleagues, investors, board members, other CEOs, superintendents, and so on. "How do you have any time to think?" she asked me. Little by little, Shanika pushed me hard to cancel some meetings and delegate others. She turned hour-long meetings into thirty minutes, some weekly meetings became biweekly, and so forth. She added just one new appointment, a monthly meeting with her to review what truly was a priority and what could be dropped. Eventually, all her nips and tucks freed up two to three hours per day (that's ten to fifteen hours per week!) of completely unscheduled time that I previously assumed was impossible. She opened space during which I could actually think. Write down some new ideas. Read. Get curious. Spontaneously call someone to bounce an idea off them or just ask how they were doing. Having this open time has been nothing short of transformational—for my curiosity, my relationships, and honestly, my general health and happiness.

The physiological sigh... This simple breathing exercise is the number one practice that Dr. Andrew Huberman, a professor of neurobiology at Stanford University, suggests for calming the nervous system so as to access parts of the brain shut down by stress.[23] It goes like this: two short inhales in through the nose, one long exhale through the mouth. That's it.

Even a few rounds of this breathing technique can calm the mind enough to access higher thinking states like curiosity. One friend of mine keeps his stress levels under control by making this a twice-daily practice. His "Breathe" alarm goes off at 9:30 a.m. and 4:30 p.m., reminding him to slow down and take a few conscious breaths.

Meditation, yoga, walking outdoors, and journaling are a few other effective ways to renew curiosity. While slowing down our schedules is important to cultivating curiosity, slowing down our bodies and minds is absolutely essential. Committing to making just one of these a regular habit is a powerful act of resistance to cultural forces that prioritize work over wonder.

Curiosity questions to resist speed and urgency:

- Where are the pressures of speed and urgency showing up for me? Where do I feel a sense of stress or needing to rush?
- Where can I find space in my day—even just a few moments—to pause and make room for curiosity?
- What format for doing this works most naturally for me? Taking a few deep breaths? Taking a short walk outside? Meditating?

Curiosity Killer #3: Group Pressures

When we operate in homogenous bubbles, whether in our physical communities or online, everyone around us reinforces the worldviews and biases that contribute to our "stuff." No wonder it's so easy to feel certain. The increasingly polarized and siloed political culture in the United States can be read as the direct result of a nationwide curiosity crisis. Blame technology, blame TV news, blame whomever you want, but the end of the story is still the same: people have stopped thinking they have anything to learn from others who think differently than they do. We each have the power to take action to expand the set of experiences and information we expose ourselves to. In other words, we can swim in a larger situational pool by seeking out new points of view and recognizing the limitations of our own perspective. Journalist Amanda Ripley, author of *High Conflict*, described this to me as "widening the lens"—whether historically or geographically or by including voices often overlooked—as a way of complicating our understanding of situations and thereby stoking more curiosity.

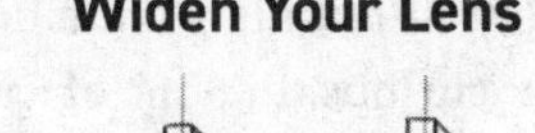

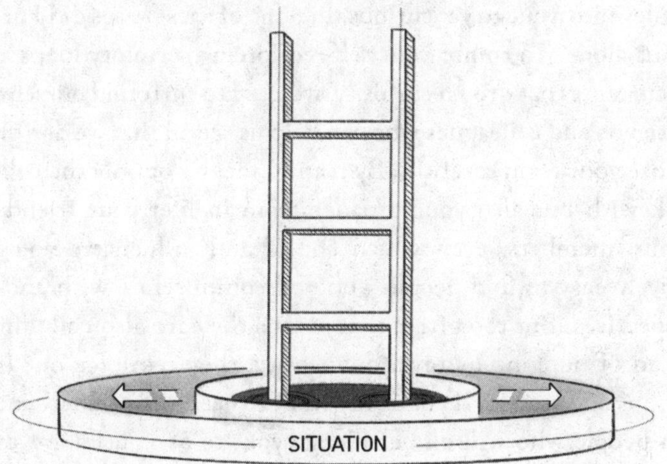

Curiosity questions to counter social pressures that reinforce certainty:

- What voices or perspectives might be missing from what I'm hearing?
- What niggling wonderings, doubts, or questions do I, myself, have?
- What counterarguments might exist that challenge the dominant view? And what aspects of those counterarguments have merit?
- How might the people or culture around me be pressuring me to act more certain than I feel?

CURIOSITY IS A TEAM SPORT

There's a common pattern across the stories in this chapter: it's hard to get curious when we're trapped inside the bubbles of our own history, emotions, and cultures. The union and hotel leaders required engaging with one another (and in their case, an outside facilitator) to break their certainty loops. I required a trusted manager to help me see my blind spots about my client. Similarly, my co-founder Aylon helped me turn my anger about Bailey into a cue to get curious. In none of these cases did I or others get curious alone. To combat our self-reinforcing certainty loops and the cultural currents that drown curiosity, we need to surround ourselves with diverse friends and colleagues who can help us see all that we don't know.

Choose your team carefully. By team, I mean not only the colleagues you work with but also your broader team in life: your friends, your community members, even which shows and influencers you follow. It's relatively easy to find people who will commiserate with and affirm our perspectives. But too often, that means they are also colluding with us. Instead of nudging us toward curiosity, they reinforce our existing assumptions and stories. If you really want to get curious, surround yourself with people who will *also* challenge you: to ask questions, to shine light on your blind spots, to see things from a different angle. If your friends and colleagues aren't doing that today, ask them to step it up!

Are you getting curious yet? If so, now it's time to make it safe, easy, and appealing for others to respond to your curiosity. We'll take up that step in Chapter 4.

SUMMARY OF KEY POINTS

Essential question: How can you awaken your curiosity to make new discoveries and unexpected connections?

1. You can *choose* to deepen your **connective curiosity**—a desire to understand more about the thoughts, experiences, and feelings of other people.

2. Leverage the **ladder of understanding** to get more curious about the following:
    - What information are you selecting from the whole pool available to you?
    - What additional information about the situation might you be missing or omitting from what you selected? Consider what information is *invisible* to you—including other people's situations that they're up against, their motives and desires, as well as your impact on them.
    - How are you interpreting the information you've selected? What conclusions are you drawing? What story are you telling yourself based on that interpretation?
    - How is the story you're telling yourself affecting your relationship to the situation and to the other person?
    - What other alternative interpretations and stories might be possible, and how can you learn about them?
3. Defend yourself against **curiosity killers**:
    - Emotional hijacking—solution: use your emotions (e.g., fear, anger, anxiety) as cues to pause and get more curious.
    - Pressures for speed and efficiency—solution: slow down, breathe, and get all the stuff off your calendar that doesn't *really* need to be there!
    - Groupthink—solution: widen the lens by seeking out new or differing points of view.

EXERCISES

3A. Think of an interaction or relationship where you're feeling less curious than you'd like. Maybe your curiosity is being blocked by your hurt, anger, or defensiveness. Maybe you've got some judgments or blame going on. Maybe you even feel offended or self-righteous. If you can't think of an interaction where this fits, consider identifying someone in the news or social media with whom you strongly disagree. Now, use the ladder of understanding to diagram how you reached the story you hold. Specifically:

- What information did you select from the situational pool?
- How did you process (interpret or make meaning of) that information?
- What conclusions did you reach?
- What action steps did your conclusion make you want to take?
- How might your stuff (your prior knowledge, experiences, biases, etc.) have shaped the story you constructed and spiraled you into a certainty loop?

3B. Notice what effect, if any, it had to slow down your thinking and diagram your story. Did it lead you to get more curious about it? If not, deliberately try injecting some question marks. For example,

- What information might you have overlooked?
- What might have been alternative ways to process or interpret the information you did select?
- What alternative stories might there be about the situation?
- Which of your feelings and reactions might you be able to share or test with a trusted friend?

3C. Consider what curiosity killers might be at play for you:

- Emotional hijacking?
- Relentless pressures for speed and efficiency?
- Group pressures?

For any one that's at play, try out the aforementioned curiosity questions that go along with it.

Bonus points if you do try these exercises together with a friend who can help you step out of your own perspective.

Can you begin to feel more curious?

Chapter 4

MAKE IT SAFE

Essential question: How do you make it easier for people to tell you hard things?

As CO-CEO OF A FAST-GROWING SOCIAL ENTERPRISE, I HAVE relationships with many investors. They are all generous, supportive people who are committed to our success, and many have become friends. Still, there is an elephant in the room when it comes to these relationships: I perceive that they hold some power over me since at any time, they could decide to pull their investment, or expand it. At the same time, they also know that this power dynamic can get in the way of honest two-way communication.

In many of my interactions with investors, I feel this unspoken tension acutely. We have over a hundred employees whose livelihoods depend, in part, on my ability to secure new and renewal investments, and I don't want to let them down. Just as important, we have big goals and solid plans for how to change the world, and we need capital from investors to pursue them.

And so, when I meet with new investors, I feel pressure to put our best foot forward. I come prepared with a list of positive developments. My goal is to be candid, and so I also come with a list of our challenges. However, I will admit that I often fear whether showing our dirty laundry might undermine their confidence. This fear doesn't stop me from sharing our warts, but I often feel self-conscious and wonder about how what I say may be judged.

You almost certainly have experienced power differentials in your life and career, and you've seen how they exaggerate the already formidable barriers to people sharing openly without fear or hesitation. You've perhaps even sat on *both* sides of the experience, as the person with less power or the person with more power. Either way, the fearful dynamic—and its chilling effect on communication—often feels inescapable.

But here's the thing: I personally know that it's not. And one of the ways I know is that I have many investors who have made me feel safe to spill the beans without overthinking. They've not only set me at ease, they've given me reasons to believe that when I open up, it's better for both of us. And they've done it using the same approaches I'm offering in this chapter.

Before I explain how they've done this so well, let's talk briefly about why being able to create safety is absolutely essential if we want to learn what others truly think, feel, and know.

PROTECTING ONE ANOTHER WITH PSYCHOLOGICAL SAFETY

Sometimes being asked to share, particularly in a professional context, feels less like an invitation and more like a social threat. And according to research by Dr. Heidi Grant, the brain registers the pain of social threats no differently than the pain of physical blows.[1] What that means is that being asked to share on a sensitive topic can feel *literally painful*. Small surprise so many people shut down.

To get people to open up, we have to reduce the threat—or otherwise put, we need to create *psychological safety*. Harvard Business School professor and author Amy Edmonson is the world's foremost expert on why organizations need to make it safe for people to speak up. In her seminal study of hospital intensive care units, Edmondson determined that the single most important factor in whether a hospital employee reported errors on the job—a factor that is critical to keeping patients safe—was the employee's perceptions about the consequences of admitting mistakes.[2] Members of teams led by managers who encouraged an open discussion of mistakes and promoted a sense of safety and belonging among team members were much more likely to report mistakes as soon as they happened. Thanks in large part to Edmonson's work, it is now widely understood that cultivating relationships in which sharing feels as safe and beneficial as possible can often be the axis upon which success or failure turns in many industries and situations.

If we want others to answer our questions with any degree of candor, it's up to each of us to *make it safe* for them to do so. Asking someone to let us inside their true thoughts, feelings, and experience is asking them to be vulnerable. It is our job to show them that we are trustworthy and respectful guests *before* we ask them to open the door.

I define "making it safe" as:

Ensuring that it's as comfortable, easy, and appealing as possible for others to share openly with you.

In many relationships, you can take steps to *make it safe* within a single interaction, but in other cases, it may take days, weeks, or longer—you have to use your judgment to determine how long is needed. However, as Amy Edmondson pointed out to me, it's never possible to make speaking up, particularly in a work environment, 100 percent safe or comfortable. There's always risk involved. The risk is higher whenever there's a power dynamic, and some people—for example, people of color whose viewpoints are often distorted by listeners' biases and for whom the stakes of being judged negatively are inherently higher—bear more risk than others. But there's so much we can do to let people know that when they're with *us*, the risks are lower than the rewards.

JUMP ON THE SAFETY CYCLE

The **safety cycle** creates the conditions so that asking another person to share is less like proposing a cliff dive into icy waters and more like proposing a swim in a heated pool—lower risk, worthwhile, and maybe even enjoyable. Working through the cycle is especially important when asking about those thorny but important topics that tend to hide out in people's left-hand columns (i.e., their unspoken thoughts and feelings).

The Safety Cycle

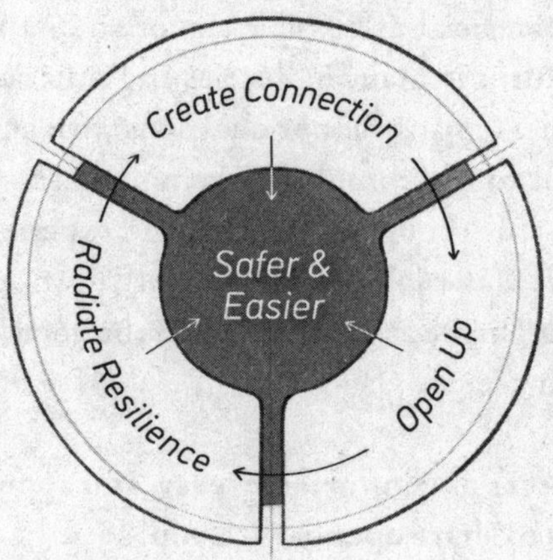

First, Create Connection

When people feel connected to you, and you to them, you both feel safer. You can relax in one another's company. True, personal connection lubricates the emotional gears needed to tackle even uncomfortable topics. There are multiple ways to approach creating authentic connection, and I suggest you practice them all.

Enrich and Deepen Your Stories About One Another

There's a good chance you've already been given this advice in the past, usually along with the recommendation to ask "get to know you" questions about people's lives beyond the office: about their families, their hobbies, or where they grew up. But while these questions can help you get to know someone better, they can also backfire. People who prefer to keep their home life and work life separate might find them invasive or prying. Others might feel too exposed sharing personal details, fearing judgment or manipulation.

The good news is that "Where are you from?" is not the only way to move beyond the superficial to deeper, more caring connections in the workplace. For some people, their relationship with work itself is incredibly personal! There's so much we can get to know about a person by learning more about how they relate to their work: why they were drawn to it, what keeps them up at night, or what their aspirations are and how we can help, to name some low-hanging fruit.

Once a baseline level of trust is present, one of my favorite things to ask someone I'm trying to get to know more deeply is "What's the story behind how you landed where you are today?" Depending on the individual and situation, people take their answers in many directions—some talk about their career trajectory, while others talk about how being raised by their grandparents shaped them. It's important to ask a question that allows people to start wherever feels most comfortable to them. Regardless of how they answer, I always learn something new about them, and even better, I've noticed that people appreciate being asked.

Connection is a two-way street, which means we can't just ask questions—we also have to let others in on who we are. When employees in my organization meet me, the Jeff they see first might be the person who is a decade or two older than them, founded and runs an organization, speaks in bullet points, and holds formal authority over the people he hires and manages. I've come to realize that that Jeff can feel intimidating, maybe even scary, to others. This never ceases to surprise me, since my own insecurities lead me to think, *Who would ever be intimidated by me?*—but when I put myself in others' shoes, I'm not sure even *I'd* feel comfortable opening up to that Jeff.

So I try to introduce teammates to all the different Jeffs that make up *me*. I'm that Jeff who can be intimidated by making big presentations. I'm introvert Jeff, who worries a lot about what to say and how to say it. I'm husband and father Jeff. I'm Jewish Jeff, who observes Shabbat. I'm also Jeff, the middle-aged aspiring guitar player and amateur tennis junkie. And oh, don't forget the Jeff who is such a creature of habit that he still travels an hour away to see his old dentist in his old neighborhood rather than try someone new!

Connection—and the sense of mutual care it fosters—arrives when we get to know one another in such nuanced complexity that we each discover we're not so dissimilar or separate as we might have assumed. When we approach this level of connection, our shared humanity starts to become at least as salient as our differences are. The differences don't disappear entirely, but cracks emerge through which communication can flow.

Model Vulnerability[3]

My friend Adam is one of those investors who understands that making things safe is a prerequisite to the type of honest connection he wants to foster. He summarizes the leader's path to connection this way: "model vulnerability and transparency in yourself, every day. Not just when you are sitting down and asking for someone's feedback, but all of the time, every day, week, and month, in and out." Adam shares his own performance reviews with his direct reports, so they can know what things he's working to improve upon. His entire team knows he goes to therapy every week; it's right there on his calendar. "Because of that, I've experienced them being more open about their own mental health journeys, and we are able to discuss how to create an environment where people are able to talk more authentically about how they are navigating their world." Adam has seen all this openness have tangible, positive effects on the dynamics of his team as well as on their performance. As he shared with me, "When we really know each other, we rely on each other in more specific and nuanced ways, and we ask for help with fewer concerns for how we might be judged."

Modeling vulnerability is a 24/7 way of being, not a tactic nor a single interaction, Adam emphasizes. Indeed, building relationships takes time, and willingness, on both sides. But when it happens, it is much more than a means to learn more from others. It is a source of incredible joy and satisfaction.

Most of us know this—and yet our commitment sometimes breaks down amid the myriad demands on our time and attention. Fortunately that's not the only connective tool you have to help make people feel safe and interested to share. The where, when, and how matter too. To increase the chances of creating connection in real time, **you must find the space, time, and mode of engaging that makes the other person most comfortable.**

Find the Right Space

I'm sorry to say I once was in such a rush to get information that I stopped one of my colleagues on his way to the bathroom to grill him about his take on a troubled project we were both working on. This clumsy approach pretty much guaranteed that I wasn't getting his best ideas, limited our exchange to a couple of minutes, and almost certainly irritated him in the process.

These days, I think very carefully about where I meet with someone if I want to ask them important questions. There's a lot of individual nuance to it, but the bottom line is: Where will *they* feel most comfortable? What is convenient for *them*? Would that place be private or open? Inside or outside? Seated or in motion? I try to think about *their* needs first.

Consider that the *space* you choose will either amplify or soften existing power dynamics. Whenever possible, your goal should be to **flatten the hierarchy**—if not erasing power differentials, at least quieting their presence so that you can connect with them on a more human-to-human level. Irene Rosenfeld, former CEO of Kraft and Mondelēz, shared with me that if she wanted to learn from her employees, she needed to step outside of her larger-than-life CEO persona. And so Rosenfeld connected with employees on *their* turf—on the factory floor, in cars during sales calls, and at small group lunches without the employees' managers present. She made it a point to take her meals in the company cafeteria so that employees experienced her outside her formal role as CEO. Similarly, Bill George, the leadership expert and former CEO of Medtronic, told me he always had a couch and chair for meetings in his office. He recognized the executive desk as the ultimate symbol of hierarchy in the organizational setting—and therefore a total connection killer. On the flip side, if you're the more junior person in a power relationship, getting the "CEO" off their turf is also likely to lead to more candid sharing. It may not be as easy, but you won't know if a VIP in your life will join you for a meal or a walk until you try inviting them.

Make the Time

No one feels delighted to connect when they're in a hurry. Depressurize these interactions by setting aside enough dedicated time. We already know that two minutes on the way to the bathroom won't cut it for most conversations. You need ample time dedicated to the conversation at hand. Think of it like a project manager: decide how much time you need, and then add another 25 percent (or often in my case, as a chronic underestimator, another 75 percent).

My colleague Victoria and I used to have tense disagreements during our very tightly packed thirty-minute weekly meetings covering highly urgent, tactical topics. The meetings didn't leave time for curiosity or follow-up questions that would help us understand where each other was coming from. Finally we agreed to take a one-hour virtual walk each month with no agenda, connection time that was not in competition with other demands and pressures. On these walks, we felt comfortable talking about what was going on behind the scenes for each of us. Very quickly, our weekly calls felt much less tense, despite being as urgent as ever.

The more high-stakes the situation, the more critical creating protected time becomes. When deadlines are fast approaching or the stakes of a project's success feel particularly high, people are likely to be weary of throwing a wrench in the works by raising a concern. Without speed bumps in place, this kind of environment can quickly lead to a communication shutdown.

Corporate ethnographer Leslie Perlow reported this very trap in her study of a growing dot.com company.[4] The company, previously run by its founders and a scrappy team of entrepreneurs, had just hired a team of professional managers. It soon became clear that the founders and management teams disagreed about many aspects of the company's direction.

With the future of the organization hanging in the balance, they knew they needed to reach a consensus, *and fast*. Perlow would watch as the company's leaders outwardly expressed agreement and glossed over important differences, only to admit to her in private that they felt no progress was being made. Yet no one wanted to speak up about how they really felt for fear of opening a time-consuming can of worms that would result in a costly slowdown. But the can of worms didn't go away just because no one dared open it. The company went bankrupt nine months later.

We can all relate to this tendency to bite our tongue when we fear what we have to say could jeopardize a time-pressured situation. Speaking up under these circumstances becomes even more challenging when there is no space for communication outside of project-specific meetings. Looking back, the meetings I had with the TFA team were anything but depressurized. My schedule was jam-packed, and they knew it. We had thirty-minute check-ins with highly structured agendas covering important logistical items. Even if they had felt safe sharing their uncertainty or communicating concerns, there was no time or space for them to do so.

Get the Timing Right

The right time to ask questions is not necessarily the time when *you* want answers. It's the time that works for the person doing the answering—again, not on their way to the bathroom.

I have a teenage daughter, Eden, and I always want to know what's going on in her life and how she's doing. However, I've found that if I ask about her day when she gets home from school, or even over dinner, the best I get is "It was fine, Dad." If I *really* want to get the details, I need to stay up late—way later than my preferred bedtime—and hang out with her in her room before she goes to sleep. At that time, she is not only willing to share with me, but she actually *wants* to do so. I'm always a little tired the next morning from staying up too late, but it's worth it for the chance to connect with her. I love hearing about her experiences at school, what's going on with her friends, and everything else on her mind.

I've been on the receiving end of thoughtful timing as well. My investor Jamie McKee lets me and my team determine the interval between our standing check-ins, saying that she trusts our assessment of what is needed. She doesn't expect me to drop everything to accommodate last-minute requests—she knows that if she asked me to do that, I would feel compelled to do it, and that would weaken our connection. She's also willing to take calls with other teammates of mine in situations when I'm confident they can convey the same (or even better) information as I could. This is also another example of someone flattening the hierarchy. There's no ego or power play when it comes to how we interact; she makes it clear that we're partners in pursuit of a common purpose.

Meet Them at Their Style

Finally, you can facilitate connection by considering the **medium of communication** that works best. While many of us favor face-to-face interactions for their immediacy, for some they are a worst-case scenario—for example, for some people with autism who find eye contact and other neurotypical social expectations stressful. Some people might feel more comfortable starting sensitive conversations in text-based mediums, such as email, because it gives them time to process their reactions, or because they feel they don't express themselves well verbally. Others open up best in a conversation that happens while taking a walk outside. Whatever the case, if you want to make it comfortable for the other person to share with you, figure out what medium works best for *them*.

A more nuanced aspect of fine-tuning communication for our audience is to expand **the *types* of knowledge we are willing to receive**. In many professional cultures, hard facts and figures are the only accepted language. People think they're not allowed to speak up unless they have thorough data, airtight arguments, and polished solutions. The myriad other forms of human knowledge—including subjective observations, personal stories, gut feelings, or hard-to-express intuitions—feel out-of-bounds. But these more nuanced forms of insight are a rich source of information, and the failure to tap into them causes many plans to fail, no matter how good the data looked.

I remember once when I was a junior consultant, watching a frustrating exchange between a senior consultant, whose background was academic research, and a client named Mary who had worked her way up over the years from a call center operator to running the customer service division. Mary was trying to explain why her manager was creating problems for the team. The consultant kept demanding "data and evidence" to "independently evaluate" her "claim." Rather than opening her up further, this barrage led her to yell in frustration, "I know it because I live it!" and storm out of the room. Because he was only open to a narrow range of types of information, he shut Mary down completely. We never learned the full depth of what Mary had to share—which might have informed our work in significant ways.

By contrast, when we invite others to bring anything they want to the table *in whatever form feels right to them*—whether stories, gut feelings, visual sketches, or more conventional data points—we create pathways connecting to realms of their experience that were previously invisible to us. We also signal acceptance and belonging, which are the building blocks of psychological safety.

Next, Open Up

People are far more likely to share what matters to them if we open up about our intentions to learn—*and* if they perceive us as truly open to learning from them. That starts with explaining why we're asking. That way, they don't have to guess at our agenda. They know up front that they're not being tricked or misled into sharing something that we could use against them. Sharing our reasons for asking helps demonstrate that we're sincere in wanting or needing to learn from them.

Doing so provides a great opportunity to **display humility**, which means letting the other person know that you are aware of the limitations in your viewpoint and that you are truly interested in learning from them.[5] Communicating your desire—in fact, your *need*—to learn from the other person can open with statements of intent, such as the following:

- "I'd like to hear your thoughts on what I might be missing or overlooking... This will help us get to a better decision together..."

- "I think you may come at this from a different angle than I do, which is vital for me to understand, since my perspective on this is quite limited..."
- "I am certain we'll find a better solution to this challenge if it's informed by your unique point of view, as I'm likely not considering all the factors that matter here..."

I asked journalist Amanda Ripley how she helps the people she interviews feel comfortable opening up to her, especially at a time when so many people distrust the media. She said, "The first thing people want to know is: What's your agenda?" Amanda relayed to me that early in her career as a journalist, she used to put on a facade of neutrality to disguise the fact that she might have a different political view than those she interviewed. Over time, however, she realized that this actually made the people she interviewed even *more* suspicious of her agenda. So now, when she interviews someone who sees the world differently, she starts by saying something like, "Look. I live in DC. Mostly everyone I know is a Democrat. I am vastly ignorant about almost all of what your life is like in rural Wyoming, but I'm going to try really hard to listen. I apologize if I ask stupid questions." When Amanda opens up in this way, she disarms the people she is interviewing; they can tell she is sharing authentically, and they feel more comfortable sharing honestly with her.

Likewise, the investors with whom I'm most comfortable have done this by showing me "their cards" when it comes to our relationship. As I've learned more about their worlds, I've begun to understand that every investment they make affects their success—their goals, their reputation, their ability to get the next investment done. In other words, my success—which is not in their control—has a material impact on *their* success. Within their various institutions, they have targets they need to hit and people they're accountable to. What's more, they usually feel a deep sense of connection to the mission of the organizations they invest in and want to see real impact happen. Also, like me, they have deeply felt ambitions about doing good in the world. The more I've gotten to understand their worlds "behind the scenes," the more I've seen that I have more power in these relationships than I thought. They aren't so much my Great and Powerful

Oz; rather, they are my partners on the yellow brick road, and our destinies are bound up together.

If it's so powerful to open up, why do so many of us hesitate to do it? I've noticed three common reasons.

You're too focused on efficiency. You need answers, now! Perhaps you're even worried about respecting the *other* person's time. So you cut right to the questions. The better way to respect their time is to first show them why the conversation matters, and why it won't hurt them to engage honestly—and that requires explaining your why. The thirty seconds you take to explain why you're asking and why you need their input will be worth it, for both of you.

You don't want to make yourself vulnerable. It might not feel good to expose a gap in your knowledge, or to admit that they have information you can't get anywhere else. This is an understandable but unfortunate trap to fall into, because sharing that vulnerability would set them at ease.

I asked Amanda Ripley how it feels to lay her cards on the table and tell the people she interviews how little she knows about their lives. "It's uncomfortable. You want to be in control. It feels a little like a teacher telling a student that they don't know the answer. It's like releasing your grip." It was striking to me that if a journalist, who is supposed to be the one asking questions, feels uncomfortable admitting her ignorance, imagine how hard it is for the rest of us. Opening up about what we don't know and why we *need* the other person can be seen as a form of power shifting (or at least power sharing), which can feel high-stakes for any of us who like to stay in control.

Yet doing so quells the social threat with signals of belonging and interdependence: *I need you,* you're saying; *you have something important to share and I value it*. Everyone feels safer to speak when the value of their sharing has been affirmed. One study created teams—of senior executives, of military cadets, and of members of a virtual chat room—for a problem-solving exercise. Just before the exercise, some of the teams were prompted with reminders of their social worth. Whether composed of executives, cadets, or online chatters, the "affirmed" teams were more likely to volunteer information and report feelings of psychological safety. To boot, they solved the task about 50 percent more frequently than other teams.[6]

You don't want to bias them. Many people, especially those in positions of power, are afraid that opening up about their own viewpoint will bias the conversation. But providing the context behind a question offers important information that allows the person to give a more useful answer. You can counter the bias problem by making it crystal clear that you're looking for honest input, not cheerleading, when it comes to your position.

For example, Ryan is CEO of a fast-growing company that operates in a highly dynamic industry. Like many leaders in his situation, he struggles to get his relatively new senior team aligned to his strategic direction. Recently, he asked for my advice about an upcoming meeting, where he wanted to engage his senior team in considering a big decision about a major strategic pivot. His original plan was to lay out all the strategic options, including ones he had already rejected, then ask each person to state their opinion and hope it aligned with his plan to pivot. But as I pointed out, in addition to not being genuine, that approach was unlikely to elicit what Ryan most needed: helpful feedback about his intended path and his rationale for choosing it.

After considering my advice, Ryan revised his approach and headed into the meeting. He briefly shared with his team the strategic options that he had rejected, then explained his preferred option and his reasoning behind it. Instead of asking them to pick an option, he asked them to help him scrutinize his thinking. He explained, "Here's why I think this pivot is the right direction, and here's why I think each of the alternative options isn't right. . . . Now, what I most need from you is to help me see what I'm missing and if there might be a better way forward."

The team listened thoughtfully to Ryan's reasoning, then pressed him on some faulty assumptions he didn't even realize he was making. They pointed out how some upsides of the options that Ryan wanted to discard could be woven into his new direction. Together, they came up with a modified version of Ryan's initial proposal for the pivot, which addressed their points but still accounted for his basic strategic intent. Ryan learned far more from his team than if he'd held back on sharing his own opinion.

Finally, consider this generous form of opening up: letting the other person know that you're open to what *they* want to discuss—not just your own agenda. Executive coach Jamie Higgins calls this setting a **mutual**

agenda. Jamie suggests asking some version of "What matters to *you* that we might discuss?" when starting a conversation. This lets them know you care about their priorities too, and it opens the door to further sharing that may prove important for you both. In a recent meeting with an investor, I said, "I have three topics I'd like to discuss, but I'm also curious: Is there anything you were hoping to cover?" He said, "Actually, I was hoping to ask for your advice on an internal management challenge I'm facing." Had I not opened up space for this in our agenda, I'm not sure he would have let me in on his dilemma nor shared what turned out to be the most important thing we could have discussed that day.

Finally, Radiate Resilience

When it comes to investors who make me feel safe, Jamie McKee, whom I mentioned earlier in the chapter, is a star. The first time we met for a check-in after the investment began, I came to our meeting prepared with a list of progress updates and a few questions to share with her. But just as I was about to launch in, Jamie interrupted me with something I'd never before heard from an investor:

"Before you tell me how things are going, I want to share with you my philosophy of investing," she began. "I know you probably think I want to hear that things are going well with your project. But the truth is, I start with the assumption that things are *not* progressing as you intended them when you pitched me."

I let out an internal sigh of relief. Knowing that Jamie really was comfortable joining me in the trenches made it so much easier to work with her.

She continued, "If you had the power to predict the future perfectly, you would not be in this business; you'd be picking lottery numbers or making bets on horse races. I know things can't possibly be going as you predicted. You may be making faster progress than anticipated, and I also expect that you're facing all kinds of unanticipated twists and turns. I want to hear about *those*. If you tell me things are going as you predicted, I will be suspicious."

Jamie invited honesty into the conversation and made a pledge that she could handle whatever truth I confronted her with. This simple move dissolved any assumptions I had about what she wanted to hear and allowed me to feel safe sharing less-than-shiny information with her, information that was critical for her ability to get a full picture of the state of the project. The result? We both left the conversation with a more realistic sense of the status of the project as well as deeper trust in our relationship.

Jamie communicated her resilience. She wasn't going to run away at the first sign of challenges—on the contrary, she expected them as part of the path to success. This is what people need to speak freely: your pledge that you can handle it, followed by the behavior to match.

Make Things Discussable

Like Jamie, we can let people know that we already recognize they may have thoughts or feelings to express that they might think we don't want to hear, or that are taboo. By showing them that we know this—and importantly, that we're not freaking out at the thought that they may be thinking or feeling these things—we **make things discussable**. This helps demonstrate to them that we can handle their truths. It could sound like:

- "If I were in your shoes, I might be feeling frustrated or even resentful. If that's how you're feeling, I would understand completely. Please don't hold back."
- "I realize you might be thinking that I've got it all wrong. If that's the case, I'm ready to hear it and open to rethinking my assumptions."
- "I recognize we come down on different sides of this very charged issue. Whether or not we change each other's minds, I want you to know that I am sincerely interested in understanding where you're coming from, and what I'm missing."

Remember Dr. Heidi Grant's research showing that painful social threats, such as giving critical feedback, are registered in people's brains no differently than physical pain? Well, Grant's team further found that there was a simple way to reduce their cognitive stress: *Explicitly ask them for the feedback.*[7] Asking for candid feedback is another way to make things discussable, and it communicates that we're resilient enough to handle even uncomfortable truths.

If you've been defensive or reactive when people have shared in the past, you may need a reset. Professor Adam Grant learned to preface requests for feedback on his writing by acknowledging that although he might not have always taken critical feedback well, he really wanted and needed it now. He noticed that having these conversations *before* asking for feedback led to significant improvements in the quality of the feedback he received. According to Grant, now his reviewers give more critical feedback because they understand they are "not going to hurt my feelings by criticizing me, they are going to hurt my feelings by *not* criticizing me."[8]

Own Your Reactions

If you're truly ready for people to take the gloves off, consider using "Crocker's Rules." The computer programmer Lee Daniel Crocker, most well known as an early contributor to Wikipedia, wanted to clear away the clutter and confusion that come when people communicate their arguments while also trying to protect the other person's feelings. So he set forth Crocker's Rules: committing to them means that you're asking others to give input to you without sugarcoating it and promising that you will not hold them responsible for your own reactions to whatever they say. This is a way of promising others that they can speak without concern for how it might make you feel. It's not for the faint of heart, but it releases people to speak freely. (Sidenote: Committing to Crocker's Rules does *not* mean you speak to others this way, unless they similarly request it.)

For a softer approach to assuring people it's safe to speak, you might say something like:

- "I know it's not easy to share anything critical. I promise to listen and embrace whatever you say as a gift, even if it's hard to hear."
- "Sometimes candor isn't easy, but I want you to know that I really value your honesty here."

Doing this proactively addresses their fears of how you might react. Of course, this only works if you can keep your promise—we'll come back to that in Chapters 6 and 7.

If we don't actively make it safe, others are far less likely to feel motivated to share openly with us. It is *our* job to make it feel as comfortable, easy, and appealing as possible, no matter what they need to express. We can do so by applying the strategies presented in this chapter.

Now that we know how to make it safe, we're ready to pose quality questions, the subject of Chapter 5.

SUMMARY OF KEY POINTS

Essential question: How do you make it easier for people to tell you hard things?

To make it safe for others to share openly, follow the *safety cycle*:

1. **First, create connection** with anyone you want to learn from:
   - Enrich and deepen your understanding of one another. Invite them to share about parts of their life or experience, and share yours in turn. Learn to look at them (and help them see you) as a whole person with all the complexities you each have.
   - Find the right space. If there are power differences, avoid spaces that emphasize them. Take a walk. Go to a coffee shop. Meet them on *their* turf.
   - Make the time. Slow things down as much as you can. Carve out more space than you need. Choose a time when you can both give your full attention to the conversation.
   - Meet them at their starting point. Allow for the mode of engaging that makes the other person most comfortable, including the medium (text, phone, in person) and the format of sharing (e.g., data, stories, feelings).

2. **Next, open up:**
    - Let them in on your perspective and your agenda for why you are asking them questions.
    - Be willing to get vulnerable and admit where you're stuck, what you don't know, and why you need to learn from them.
    - Display humility by acknowledging that your perspective may be limited.
    - Make space for their interests by creating a "mutual agenda."
3. **Finally, radiate resilience:**
    - Communicate that you can handle whatever they have to say—especially for topics that may be difficult, awkward, or taboo.
    - Explicitly name your desire for critical feedback and views that differ from your own.
    - Take responsibility for your own reaction to whatever they share.

EXERCISES

4A. Look backward: Think of a relationship or interaction where you feel pretty sure that someone didn't fully tell you what they felt, believed, or knew. Use the safety cycle as a diagnostic to help you understand why it might not have felt comfortable, easy, or appealing for them to share openly with you:

- Create connection:
    - How connected did they feel to you, truly, and vice versa?
    - How comfortable were they with the space, time, format, and mode of engaging?

- Open up:
    - Were you transparent about your motives for the conversation and your agenda for learning from them? Did they understand what you were hoping for and why?

  - How vulnerable and authentic were you about your need for their input?

- Radiate resilience:
  - Did you make it clear that you could handle whatever they had to say?
  - Did you communicate that you wouldn't hold them responsible for your emotional reactions?

4B. Look forward: Think of an important, upcoming interaction where you are unsure whether the other person will feel comfortable sharing openly with you. Use the safety cycle as a planning tool to help you make it more safe, easy, and appealing for them to share with you:

- Create connection:
  - How can you build true connection with each other?
  - How can you ensure the space, time, format, and mode of engaging work *for them*?

- Open up:
  - How can you be transparent about your motives in the conversation and *why* you want to learn from or with them?
  - How can you allow yourself to be vulnerable and authentic about your need for their input?

- Radiate resilience:
  - How can you convey that you can handle whatever they have to say?
  - How can you convey that their relationship with you is safe no matter what they say?

Chapter 5

POSE QUALITY QUESTIONS

Essential question: What questions will best tap into the wisdom of anyone you ask?

MY FIRST DAY ON THE JOB AT TEACH FOR AMERICA, I MET WITH our CEO, Wendy Kopp, and I asked her one single question: "Wendy, you've seen a lot of people come through this organization. Some have succeeded at making a big difference, while others have struggled. What's your advice for how I can be most impactful in my role here?"

I will never forget Wendy's answer. She said, "In a lot of organizations, people feel pressure to appear like they have it all figured out. That wouldn't be my advice to you here. You're going to encounter challenges that you have no idea how to handle, and things are going to feel really hard, even painful, at times. My advice to you is, in those moments, don't try to make it appear like you have it all figured out. Instead, ask the people around you. Ask them to tell you what you're missing. Ask them how they'd approach your challenge. Ask them for help. If you want to make a difference here, don't be afraid to ask."

If you're like most people, you've arrived at this chapter with a history of either not always asking enough questions, or not asking enough of the *right* questions.

And yet, questions are the world's most powerful and underutilized all-purpose, everyday learning tool. Many of our most intractable problems become solvable when we get out of our own heads and invite others to provide their input and perspective. But for most of us, asking questions is not our first stop when we're in a sticky spot.

Take Isaac, the CEO of a health-care start-up that is seeking to make the market for health insurance more accessible through streamlined, user-friendly technology. Isaac has a painful problem you may have experienced in the past: people he relies upon aren't following through on their mission-critical promises to him. Isaac needs to raise his next round of funding to expand his company's impact over the next three years, and a subcommittee of his board of directors has agreed to help him do just that. But in the months since the committee formed, its members have done...nothing. They haven't made larger investments themselves, nor have they rallied their networks of investor friends. Isaac has nudged them, urged them, cajoled them, and done everything he can to motivate them to do what he needs before his current round of funding runs dry.

After a couple of months of angst and anxiety, Isaac finally chooses curiosity. He realizes that he doesn't know *why* they aren't behaving the way he needs them to, and he starts to wonder: *What aren't they telling me?*

Finally, Isaac musters the courage to sit one of them down and ask. He chooses a time and place that works for Anna, a board member he thinks of as the straightest shooter of the bunch, opting for the neutral ground of a local restaurant instead of one of their offices. As we'll see throughout this chapter, in just one hour Isaac learns critical information from Anna about what the board members are really thinking—information that would have remained frustratingly invisible had he not taken the initiative to ask. He leaves not only relieved but with a clear, realistic sense of how to move forward.

And there's something else that's surprising to Isaac: how much closer he and Anna become during the meeting. Isaac discovers that questions have a second amazing power: they are relationship builders. The right question, asked in the right way, is nothing short of a sacred invitation. The question is the knock on the door, an intimate request to be let into another's interior world. It opens up a channel of learning between two people that wasn't present before the question was posed. And that learning can create worlds of new possibilities, for mutual understanding, personal connection, and fruitful collaboration.

WHY IS OUR QUESTION REPERTOIRE SO LIMITED?

You probably have a few go-to questions you rely on; "Help me understand" is one I see getting a lot of use. But for most of us, our go-to repertoire is pretty narrow compared to the range of situations we're in, the challenges we face, and the breadth of things we might learn. My biggest hope in this chapter is to help you expand your repertoire of quality questions.

We're all born with the instinct to ask. As we'll discuss in Chapter 10, kids are natural-born question askers. But by the time we become adults, many of us have stopped asking real questions, other than "Where is the bathroom?" and "Has he lost his mind?" and maybe one or two of our personal go-to questions. One poll found that, among the two hundred executives surveyed, only 15 to 25 percent of interactions included real questions.[1]

Some of this is our neurological wiring. We develop mental maps of the world around us, consisting of millions of neural shortcuts that let us rush up our ladders of understanding in microseconds and save us time and precious cognitive resources that can be used instead to plan, make decisions, and monitor our news feed.

But mainstream culture is conspiring against us as well. The advice offered in an 1877 etiquette guide isn't so far from today's attitudes: "Never ask impertinent questions; and under this head may be included nearly all questions. Some authorities in etiquette go so far as to say that *all* questions are strictly tabooed."[2] And so we worry that asking questions will make us come off as prying or rude. At the same time, we are taught to "perform" confidence and certainty at all times, especially in competitive academic and corporate settings where we face constant pressure to prove our worth. In these environments, asking questions can feel like an admission of imperfection, vulnerability, or ignorance that runs counter to deeply held beliefs about what competence is supposed to look like.

Many of us have been shamed for asking questions as adults. When I was a brand-new consultant at Monitor, a partner named Sam gave all the newbies a speech. He said, "I have a six-month rule. In your first six months here, you can ask me any question you want. It can be a naive question, a dumb question, anything. Just ask. But after six months, only ask me questions that you can't find the answers to yourself, by looking them up or asking one of your colleagues." Only four months into my tenure, I was in a conference room with Sam and decided to take him up on his six-month rule. I was confused about a business term related to financial accounting in the insurance industry that he kept using. So I asked him if he could explain the term to me. He looked at me, his face turned red, and he barked, "You shouldn't be asking me that question. Go figure it out yourself!" *But I'm still in the grace period!* I thought. But all I said was "Okay, I'm sorry."

When people are reprimanded or ridiculed for asking questions in school, in their families, or in their workplaces, the dangers of asking come to outweigh the risks. For those in more vulnerable positions, whether due to age, race, gender, or position in the organizational hierarchy, the risk of asking questions can feel even greater and more chronic. We'll talk more about how this functions in teams, families, and schooling in Section III.

CRUMMY QUESTIONS AREN'T REALLY QUESTIONS

If you were to scour the transcripts of people's toughest dialogues, as I did for hundreds of hours earlier in my career, you'd find plenty of question marks. Yes, people ask lots of questions—but most of them fall into these three categories: *clumsy questions*, *sneaky questions*, and *attack questions*. These are what I call "crummy questions."

Clumsy questions may be well intentioned, but their wording immediately closes down the inquiry, preventing learning. These include closed-ended questions, rhetorical questions, and questions that get lost because they're buried inside statements. Here's one example:

Fred: "We've got to raise our prices, right? All our costs are going up, and we've got to hold our margin steady."

Renata: "True."

Fred's got two clumsy things going on here. First, his use of the question "right?" sounds rhetorical at best. The way he phrases the question makes it hard for Renata to do anything other than agree with him. In addition, by following his question with two other statements, he does not give her any room to answer his question before he moves on, signifying that he's not actually interested in her answer—it's more like he's "telling" in the form of a question. In the end, he has no idea whether Renata really agrees with him. In fact, when she says "True," it's unclear what she's actually agreeing with. This happens all the time.

Sneaky questions, on the other hand, are not designed to learn anything. Instead, they're designed to influence, convince, or maneuver the other person. We see trial lawyers do this all the time, with questions that lead the witness (such as, "Wouldn't you agree that . . . ?"). Other times, people are reluctant to assert their views as direct statements, so they phrase them as questions ("Don't you think it would be better if you stayed home tonight? The roads are so icy."). Finally, sometimes people layer question upon question in a strategy called "easing in," as in the following example:

Dante: Do you think the timeline you're asking for is feasible?

Yuki: I think so.

Dante: Have you considered the time it will take to set up the project in phase 1?

Yuki: Well . . .

Dante: Are you sure we can even get the talent lined up?

In this scenario, Dante clearly has a view that the timeline being requested by Yuki won't work. The problem is, instead of coming right out and saying it, he's asking question after question to try to lead Yuki to this conclusion. Will it work? Maybe in some situations, but it's far less likely that this line of questioning is going to elicit meaningful information about what Yuki really thinks, feels, or knows. And if Dante holds greater power than Yuki, forget it.

While sneaky questions sometimes generate their intended outcome, they are manipulations, and the recipients usually know it. It never feels good to be manipulated.

Lastly, *attack questions* are weapons we use to pounce on others. Examples of these questions include:

- "Why would you ever think that's a good idea?"
- "How could you possibly believe that?"
- "Why can't you be more considerate?"

Attack questions hurt, offend, or put others on the defensive. None of that fosters learning, let alone positive relationships.

Sometimes, we ask questions with positive intent but they come out sounding like attack questions. As question expert and author of *A More Beautiful Question*, Warren Berger pointed out to me, questions that start with "why" are particularly prone to sound like attack questions even when they are coming from a place of genuine curiosity. Consider Jolene, a boss looking over the shoulder of her employee, Ross, and asking, "Why are you doing it that way?" Depending on the tone of Jolene's voice (combined with the extent of the power differential and their respective identities), it would be understandable for Ross to feel criticized by Jolene's question, as if she were accusing him of doing it wrong.

QUALITY QUESTIONS INVITE LEARNING

So, if crummy (clumsy, sneaky, and attack) questions shut down learning instead of inviting it, what's the alternative? The alternative is to ask what I call **quality questions.**

> **Quality questions help us learn something important from the person we ask.**

Quality questions have the following attributes:

- They **signal true curiosity,** reflecting a genuine intent to learn from and understand the other person—not to prove a point or influence or fix them.
- They **are clear and direct,** with no hidden, layered, or confusing meanings, so it's self-evident what the asker wants to know.
- They **invite honesty** by making it as easy as possible for the other person to share openly, regardless of how the asker feels about their answer.
- They **tap into the other person's full story**—to surface the underlying meanings, reasons, emotions, and experiences.
- They **create mutual benefit** by contributing to a meaningful, two-way dialogue in which everyone learns from each other and leaves the conversation with a better understanding of themselves and the other person.

As you consider the quality questions I propose to you in this chapter, your cultural training may trigger mental alarm bells: *Won't they put people on the spot?* The answer, at times, may be *yes*—but all the work you've done to make it safe will create the space in which discomfort is manageable.

Also consider that your fears may be largely imagined. Cognitive scientists Einav Hart, Eric VanEpps, and Maurice Schweitzer have spent years studying what they call "sensitive" questions—about topics that may feel uncomfortable or inappropriate to discuss. They found one of the reasons that people don't ask sensitive questions is that they consistently *overestimate* how uncomfortable they will make the other person. In reality, Hart says, "People are generally less offended and care less about being asked a sensitive question than we think they would be." In fact, people are usually *appreciative* to be asked these deeper kinds of questions![3]

Walking Up and Down the Ladder of Understanding

Remember the framework we discussed in Chapter 3, the ladder of understanding? Just as we each have a ladder that we race up as we process our thoughts and feelings, so do others. They select a small bit of the situation, they process what they select by interpreting it, and they reach conclusions. So if we want to really understand their perspective (i.e., their story), we essentially need to get a full view of *their* ladder.

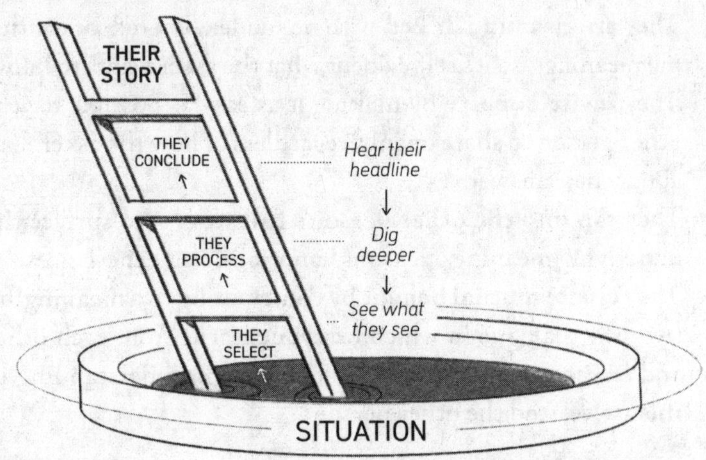

Hear Their Headline

How do you feel about this proposal to ____?

What do you think we should do about ____?

Where do you come down on the question of ____?

What matters most to you in this situation?

It's striking how often people around us don't actually tell us their headline. This is the information at the very top of their ladder—their main, or top-line, views and feelings on something. When they don't, it can feel like they're hiding something, even if they don't mean to be. Why don't they just tell us their headline? Maybe they think it should be obvious. Maybe it feels uncomfortable—or culturally too forward—to tell us what they've concluded. Whatever the reason, asking them their headline takes the guesswork out of it and often makes it easier for them to come right out and say it.

Determined to discover what's paralyzing his board, Isaac meets Anna at a local diner that they both like. After some small talk, he moves them to the topic at hand. "I appreciate you making time to talk, and I'm hoping we can have a really candid conversation about the challenges we've been facing in the fund-raising committee," he says. "I hope you'll feel free to tell me all your views, unfiltered, and don't worry about sparing my feelings. The more we can get to the bottom of this, the better it will be for our shared success."

His first question to Anna is to simply *hear the headline* of what she thinks and feels. "Anna, you know I've been asking you and others on the committee for help raising this next round of funding. So far, we haven't seen much traction in terms of leads. I could make a lot of guesses, but just want to ask you directly: What do you think is going on?"

Anna responds, "Yeah, I've been thinking about this too and discussing with a few other board members. Our sense is that the strategy may need some adjustment."

When Isaac hears Anna's response, he feels simultaneously relieved, frustrated, and confused. He's relieved that he's not crazy; there *is* something going on that is getting in the way of his board doing what he needs them to do. But he's also frustrated and confused because they spent endless meetings discussing and aligning on the strategy for raising the next round.

He takes a deep breath and chooses to remain curious: "Can you say more about what you mean by the strategy needing adjustment?"

Anna goes on, "We really believe in your leadership and the company's mission. But we're worried about the strategy. As we've discussed, the market is getting more and more crowded, and so it's going to get harder for us to make our offering stand out among the rest."

Ah-ha, Isaac thinks. When he first heard her, he thought she wasn't invested in the fund-raising strategy, but now that she has clarified what she means by "strategy," he realizes that her concern is actually deeper. It lies with the company's product itself. Isaac now sees that if they're not invested in the technology's direction, it could make sense why they aren't excited to help raise the next round. This, for Isaac, is the first light-bulb moment.

Dig Deeper

What makes you feel that way?

Can you walk me through your thought process?

What prevented you from [doing ___]?

What concerns were you trying to address?

Once we've heard someone's headline, we're getting somewhere. But it's not enough to know their top-line thoughts and feelings; we need to know what's underneath. We need to **dig deeper**. In the language of the ladder, digging deeper means walking down their ladder with them to understand how they're processing in ways that got them to their conclusion.

Asking *why* is an obvious starting place—except that "why" questions may sometimes sound attacking, and they don't help provide any frame to assist in directing the person's thinking. Many times, people don't yet know quite why they think what they think, and more specific questions can allow *them* to dig deeper into their own reasoning. As writer and leadership expert Margaret Wheatley says, "Conversation is the way that humans have always thought together."[4]

The mutual value that can be unlocked by **digging deeper** is succinctly captured in this parable from *Getting to Yes*, the pioneering book on mutually beneficial negotiations: A son and daughter are fighting over the last orange in their house. The mom resolves their conflict by force—she cuts the orange in half. The daughter takes her half, eats its flesh and throws away the peel. Meanwhile, the son zests the rind of his half to use for a cake and throws away its flesh. Because no one bothered to ask *why*, everyone got less, and half the orange was wasted.[5]

As the story illustrates, there is an important distinction between people's conclusions (*I want that orange!*) and the underlying reasons, interests, and concerns that drive their position.[6] I find that this is a great starting point for creativity because, once I find out what's underneath someone's conclusion, idea, or point, I can then partner with them to think about a range of potential ways to address what they care about, while also accounting for my own interests and concerns.

Back at the coffee shop, Isaac realizes he needs to dig deeper to understand why Anna thinks their product can't compete. He says calmly, "I totally agree that the market is crowded. But our strategy already suggests some ways we can make ourselves unique, even amid the growing competition. I'm curious to understand the reasons you see it differently?"

Isaac's reply lets Anna know that he's not just trying to convince her. He really wants to learn what she is thinking. So she takes him up on it and shares what she and the other board members have been thinking for a while but had never shared with him:

"Isaac, honestly, none of our product's features are going to make it stand out enough. We cost more than competitors. We're harder to use. And we all believe we're better than the competition, but will customers really feel the difference?"

Isaac is a bit taken aback by Anna's bluntness. As direct as she's been in the past, he's never before heard this level of candor from her or from any board member. *Now we're* really *getting somewhere,* he thinks. It's disconcerting to hear and a bit worrisome, but he's glad to know her real perspective.

He still disagrees with her but wants to first check if he's heard her right. (We'll talk more about this in the next chapter, on listening.)

"Wait, Anna, are you saying you doubt whether our product is going to succeed?"

Anna: "Kind of, yes. Not because it's a bad product. In fact, it's great. But it's a crowded market, and there's not enough that will make it stand out. I've seen this happen before in other industries, and products like ours just get disregarded and never get enough market penetration to be significant."

Anna looks like she's going to say more but is quiet for a moment. Isaac wants to jump in, but he decides to wait and see if Anna is going to continue. And she does: "Our product just has too many competitors to be viable."

Anna's words really sting. Part of the sting is finding out that his board members have such doubts about his product. And part of it is finding out that they've never told him this before. Nonetheless, Isaac is grateful to know the real barriers they see.

See What They See

Can you share some examples?
What's a story that would illustrate what you mean?
What's the data that informs your thinking?
What was happening in your world at that time?

Once we've dug into their reasoning, interests, and underlying feelings, the last step in walking down their ladder is to understand their "situation"—specifically what information and experiences inform their view.

Invariably, they have access to experiences and data that we don't have. I call this strategy **see what they see**, and it's a powerful way to find out what we need to know. Some people orient in what Jerome Bruner calls an *analytic way* and respond well to requests for "data points," but others orient in a more narrative way and think of what they see in terms of stories or life experiences.[7] It's important that your questions make space for a range of ways that others may orient. Depending upon the person and situation, you can ask if they would be willing to share a story, give a few examples, or offer some of the data points that are shaping their thinking.

Now on their second cup of coffee, Isaac realizes that if he's ever going to change Anna's mind—or perhaps improve his company's chances—he needs to see what she sees. At some point, he and his board shared the same story about the business. Now, clearly, their stories have diverged. Isaac asks, "Anna, what are some examples of the competitors that you are thinking of?"

Anna names three other organizations that are also putting competitive products out into the field. Isaac then shares his thoughts on those products, and on why his is not only superior in technology but also better aligned to what customers are saying they'll want in the future. "Do you think I'm off on that?" he adds.

Anna says, "Well, do we really have the evidence to back that up?"

Another light bulb goes on. Isaac has a hunch now about the answer to his initial wondering, *What aren't they telling me?* He decides to put it out there—couching the language a bit in case he's off base.

"Anna, I can imagine that if I'm in your shoes, it could feel like a big risk to help me raise funds when you're not sure we have the evidence to prove our competitive edge. Is that why you and others on the board have been hesitant?"

Anna takes a deep breath and says, "You nailed it. There are some deeper concerns as well..."

From there, Isaac and Anna have a candid conversation about exactly what needs to happen with the market testing, the competitor research, and the product itself for the board to feel confident to help raise the next round. Isaac takes detailed notes. Finally, he has some constructive direction to consider—to either make a more persuasive case to the board that they're ready, or go back to the lab for further product development. It's a lot to process, but overall Isaac feels more grounded and sure of his next steps than he has in months.

Clear Up Confusion

Can you explain what you mean by "___"?
How are you defining "___"?
When you said, "__," did you mean [A] or [B] or something else entirely?

George Bernard Shaw famously quipped, "The single biggest problem in communication is the illusion that it has taken place." Said differently, even though the other person has told us their headline views or their reasons or even their data points, that's no guarantee that we understand what they *mean* by the words they're using.

In my experience, it is extremely common that we misinterpret what the other person means and then react based on our erroneous interpretation. It's amazing how often people miss each other in conversations simply by not realizing that they're each using the same term but meaning different things. Sometimes the miss is slight, and other times it's drastic, but both cases need to be cleared up.

This is where a strategy that I call **clear up confusion** comes in. No matter where we are in walking down their ladder, we can pause and ask others a question that clears up any confusion or misinterpretation. This can sound a number of ways, including requests to define terms or simply asking what is meant by a particular phrase.

Clearing up confusion is also a great way to slow down a conversation, which helps everyone involved process more thoughtfully rather than reacting quickly. It also demonstrates to the other person how important it is to you that you really understand what they are intending to communicate.

Quite often, the act of asking questions that creates clarity for yourself also helps the other person to clarify their own thinking as well. For example, when a leader in my organization, Sara, told her team it was "urgent" to finish the proposal, they initially thought she meant they should drop everything else on their plate to get it done. However, they decided to ask her what she meant by "urgent," which forced her to stop and think. Sara realized that as long as it was submitted by the end of the week, all would be fine. Knowing this allowed Sara's team to still move other important work forward while also hitting the deadline on Friday.

WHEN YOU NEED THEIR INPUT

Invite Thoughtful Feedback

Now that you understand how to use questions to walk down their ladder, let's talk about a specific application of the strategy: to elicit high-quality

> *Is there anything I did (or didn't do) that made things challenging for you or others?*
>
> *What, if anything, would you suggest I do differently next time?*

feedback so you can learn how to improve. Often, we don't get feedback unless we ask for it; yet how else will we see past our own perspective, to learn things like how we are perceived, how our behavior is influencing others, and whether blind spots are affecting our interactions?

Walking down someone's ladder to elicit feedback might look like this:

- Hear their headline:
  "Do you have observations or feedback on how I showed up in that meeting?"
- Dig deeper:
  "That's interesting...Can you tell me more about the impact you saw me have when I showed up that way?"
- See what they see:
  "If you can recall any specific examples of what I said, that would be so helpful. Do any come to mind?"

There's one kind of feedback question in particular that we should all be posing when we're involved in a challenging situation, but too few of us do:

"How might I have contributed to the challenge we're facing?"

When we notice a problem, few of us stop to ask this question, of ourselves or others, before we assign blame and take someone to task. It's often easier for us to see *others'* contributions to that outcome than it is to see our own. But as humans, our actions (or inactions) interact as a "system"—a reality sometimes expressed as "it takes two to tango." So one of our first stops when confronting a problem or conflict should be to ask others how we're contributing.

Allan is a school superintendent in his second year of leading a mid-size, urban school district.

Like many school systems in the wake of the pandemic, Allan's district saw students struggling academically. His school board pressured him hard to raise test scores, and fast. Allan, an action-oriented leader with a military background, shared their concerns and felt a high personal level of urgency to get academic performance back on track.

But nearly a year later, Allan's best-laid plans have not borne fruit. Allan's board is furious and frustrated with him personally. He has one year left on his contract, and the board president has made it clear that if things don't turn around dramatically, he's out.

Allan's first instinct is to keep driving harder: more supervision, more consequences for poor performance, longer classes, less recess. He knows from his past experience in the military that sometimes you hit resistance and need to keep pushing through before you see results. But after a tough conversation with his closest friend, he realizes that maybe this way of thinking is blocking him from getting curious about other ways of handling the situation. He realizes he's pushed, driven, and criticized everyone but himself. He decides it's time to take a hard look in the mirror and get some input and ideas from people around him.

On Friday afternoon before everyone heads out for the weekend, Allan decides to send an email to his cabinet-level direct reports—his chief academic officer, chief schools officer, chief financial officer, and chief HR officer. He opens up more vulnerably than he has in the past:

"We are all here for the kids, and clearly my plan hasn't worked. I need to do something different, and I don't know what. I'd like each of you to give me the most candid feedback you can about my leadership. What should I keep doing, stop doing, and start doing? Put some thought into this, and when we each meet this week, it will be our #1 agenda topic."

All weekend, Nora, Allan's chief schools officer, sits with his request. She makes notes and gets ready for her meeting with Allan. When they sit down, Allan looks over and says, "Nora, I'm ready to hear what you have to say. Don't hold back."

Nora goes through her list of "start, stop, and continue." Among the things she shares is "Allan, your plans always look polished and thought through when you present them on PowerPoint slides. But inevitably, they fall short in action. That's because they rely heavily on control mechanisms. Controlling teachers through rules and consequences."

Allan's hackles are immediately raised. Control mechanisms is all he's ever seen be successful in big, bureaucratic organizations. How else are you supposed to manage the chaos and complexity? *What's the problem?* he wonders. And he decides to pose that very question back to Nora, asking, "Nora, could you tell me more about the impact of doing it this way?"

Nora is more than happy to answer a question she never thought she'd be asked. "Allan, forcing people to do things uniformly in the way *you* think is right is no recipe for motivating teachers. And if you make them fearful of being caught out of compliance with your dictates, they're just going to turn around and be dictators to the students. That's why morale is plummeting up and down the system!"

Nora's words cut to Allan's core. He got into this work because he believed in the power of education to lift people up. Now, he's learning that his actions are holding everyone down. He goes home that night and can't sleep. As he tosses and turns, he concludes that Nora has a point. When he gets up the next morning and looks himself in the mirror, he commits to trying a new way, one that benefits from the wisdom of people like Nora, who clearly have important opinions.

Find the Holes in Your Own Reasoning

What might I be missing?

What do you and/or others see as the downsides of my proposal?

What risks am I perhaps overlooking?

If we want quality feedback about our own viewpoints, ideas, and plans, we need to do more than ask these three questions. We need to explain not just what we believe, but why we believe it, and what informs our belief. In other words, we need to first expose them to *our* ladder—and then invite the other person to react to it.

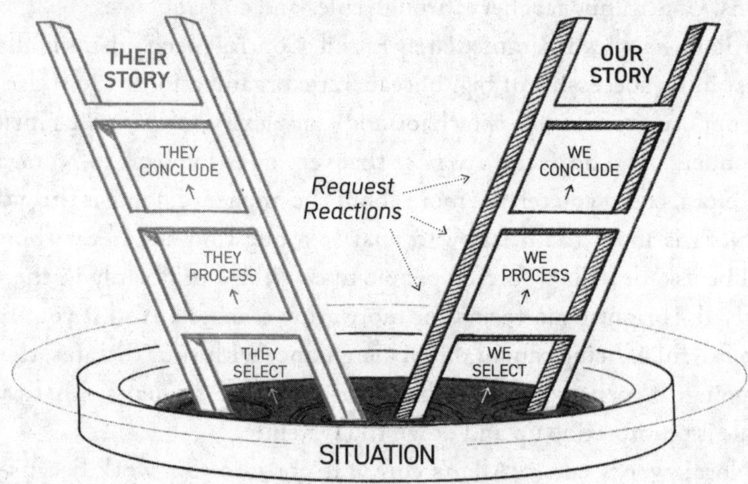

Doing this means we need to express our story clearly and directly, including our conclusions (top of our ladder), our thought process (walking down our ladder), and the data or experiences that informed us (what we selected from the situational pool). Then ask some version of

"What are your reactions?"

If you sense that the other person might hesitate to say anything critical, let the other person know it's perfectly okay to disagree or speak critically. In this way, you are inviting reactions that *disconfirm* your original thinking or approach.

Sometimes *before* asking for their reactions, it can help to first check if you've clearly communicated what you intended to say. This can sound like:

- "I want to check if I'm communicating clearly. What came through most in what I shared?"

- "I'm not sure if my intent is coming through, so I want to check: What were your main takeaways from what I said?"
- "In case I'm not expressing myself well, I want to ask: How are you hearing and understanding what I'm saying?"

If it turns out that they haven't heard what you intended to communicate, rather than blame them for mishearing, you can take the opportunity to clarify what you intended to say, then ask for their reactions.

Using Artificial Intelligence to Generate Quality Questions

There's no guarantee that an AI chatbot will provide you with exactly the right questions to ask someone. What it can reliably do, however, is generate an initial brainstorm that you can filter and build upon. I recently entered this hypothetical scenario into a chatbot:

"I disagree with my teammate about our strategy. He thinks we should focus more on our current products, and I think we should explore new markets. What questions can I ask him?"

Within five seconds, I got back the following list of questions to ask my teammate:

- *What makes you confident in the continued success of our current products?*
- *Have we done any market research that suggests our existing products can grow significantly in our current markets?*
- *What challenges do you foresee if we were to explore new markets?*
- *Can you envision a scenario where diversifying our offerings or entering new markets could strengthen our overall position?*

- *How do you think our current strategy will keep us competitive in the long term?*
- *Is there a way we could test the waters in new markets, while still focusing primarily on our current products?*

After each one came a brief explanation of why this may be a valuable question to ask. While this may not be a comprehensive list of all quality questions one should pose in this scenario, it's a helpful start!

Request Their Help and Ideas

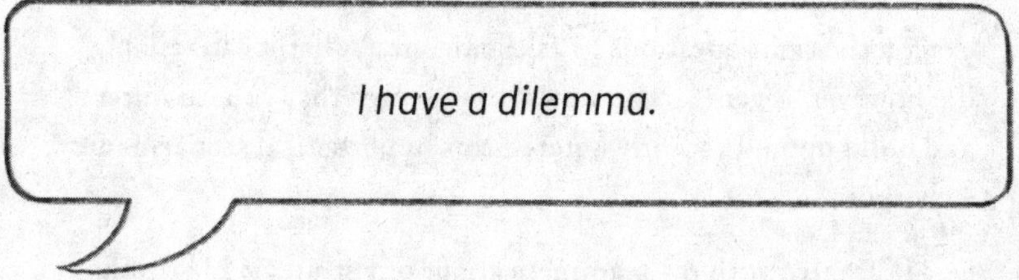

I have a dilemma. These four words immediately capture a listener's attention, and possibly their empathy too. Most people love to be helpful, especially if they're asked to weigh in on something challenging and important. The trouble is, the more challenging our dilemma actually is, the more vulnerable we feel. And the more vulnerable we feel, the more likely we are to keep the dilemma private. That's a real problem, because these are the moments when we could most benefit from having others to help us.

Questions to request help might sound like:

- "Do you have any advice for me in tackling this challenge?"
- "Is there a better or different approach I should consider taking? What might be an example of what that could look like?"
- "What ideas do you have for how we can solve this . . . ?"
- "Can you help me think this through . . . ?"

The people around us—up and down the organizational chart, and across every category of people we meet and interact with in the world—are full of ideas and suggestions. But unless we ask, too many of those ideas will stay hidden. The right prompting can lead people to generate ideas they didn't even realize they had.

Let's return to Allan. His first round of feedback helped him see that his command-and-control approach wasn't working. But all his efforts to develop a new plan had hit a wall because he's still trying to develop all the ideas himself; as the boss, he thinks strategy is his job alone. Meanwhile, his board is demanding a decisive plan from him, and fast. Finally, Allan decides to take a leap of faith and invite help from his team in a way he never had before in any leadership role he's occupied.

He pulls the team together and says, "Look, we have one year to turn things around. There's so much pressure from the board. If I waver, people won't take me seriously. So yes, I need to come out strong. But clearly something's not working. I'm stuck. What would you do?"

Allan's team has never seen this side of Allan. They've been sensing he's felt stuck. They've seen the long hours and the stress he carries in his shoulders. But for him to say it out loud and admit he's stuck? Now, that's new. And liberating. He's treating them as though he trusts them and values their insights.

A rich and open discussion ensues, the likes of which they never had before. Allan leaves the discussion feeling a huge weight lifted from his shoulders. In the past, he's kept his dilemmas to himself, always making private calculations about how to navigate them. By sharing them publicly and asking for help, he not only feels less alone as a leader, for the first time ever, but also gets real insight from his team.

He leaves motivated to gather even more ideas from more people throughout his district. He and his team set up sessions with small groups of teachers as well as parents and students. During these conversations, he not only asks for more feedback but also asks everyone for their best ideas on how to improve the district.

Allan is gratified by the energy that gets unleashed, which astounds him, and the ideas pour out like water from a hose at full speed. Ideas like: responding to student trauma to address mental health, helping students set goals to boost motivation, paying parents and community members to tutor students and reduce burdens on teachers, teaching through projects so students see the relevance of what they're learning. Not all the ideas would work, but some were ones that Allan had never thought of. More important, he was no longer alone—by tapping into the wisdom all around him, Allan began to build a coalition that could, together, tackle the community's toughest challenges.

CAN YOU KILL THEM WITH QUESTIONS?

We now know that a question mark doesn't guarantee a quality question. Well, the inverse is also true. The defining feature of a quality question is *not* necessarily a question mark. You can say to a friend, "Tell me what you really think," or "Help me understand why you feel that way." It has no question mark, but it has all the curiosity it needs to convey a true desire to understand the other. The biggest determinant of a question's quality is the *genuine intent* behind the question: Are you truly interested in and open to real learning?

At the same time, if we are *only* asking questions of the other person, we can come across as—in the words of my friend and colleague Susan "killing them with questions." Unless we are conducting an interrogation or cross-examining a witness, the best questions come interspersed with expressing our own views and feelings and thoughts. After all, learning is a two-way process. This is what my friends and teachers at Action Design call "combining advocacy *and* inquiry," which is a fancy way of saying we need to both share and ask.

One version of this is what Warren Berger calls the "question sandwich." It starts by naming your intent for asking a question, then posing the question, then saying why you're curious. Remember Jolene, the boss who looked over the shoulder of her direct report, Ross, and said, "Why are you doing it that way?" Imagine if she'd said, "Hey, I notice you're doing it differently than others do, and I'm intrigued. Can you tell me why you're approaching it that way? I ask because maybe you can help us all come up with a better way." Consider how different the impact of that question would be. What's helpful about Berger's idea, as with all the approaches above, is the combination of asking a good question with sharing our own views and intentions.

There's another way to save yourself from killing them with questions: Get really good at what comes *after* the question. This is what we'll take up in the next chapter, "Listen to Learn."

SUMMARY OF KEY POINTS

Essential question: What questions will best tap into the wisdom of anyone you ask?

1. Beware of **crummy questions**, including:
   - **Clumsy questions** that are worded in a way that closes down inquiry and prevents learning
   - **Sneaky questions** that influence, convince, or maneuver the other person in a self-serving way
   - **Attack questions** that hurt, offend, or put others on the defensive

2. To invite honest sharing, ask **quality questions**—designed to help you learn something from the other person. Quality questions can be used to:
   - *Explore their ladder of understanding* to gain insight into their internal thought process
   - *Hear their headline* to find out their conclusion, or position, on a topic
   - *Dig deeper* to access what's underneath their headline
   - *See what they see* that you can't—the information and experiences they're drawing from
   - *Invite thoughtful feedback and ideas*
   - *Find the holes in your own thinking*

EXERCISES

5A. Look backward: Think back to an interaction that didn't go as you'd hoped. Capture some essential snippets of the dialogue on paper (or if you happen to have a recording of it, get key parts of it transcribed). Count the number of assertions you made and the number of quality questions you asked. What was the ratio of assertions to quality questions?

Now, consider if any of the question strategies in this chapter might have made a difference to improve the results of your interaction. Which ones? Why?

5B. Look ahead: From the question strategies presented in this chapter, choose one that you don't currently have in your repertoire. Try inserting it into an upcoming interaction. See what you learn and how it affects your connection with the other person.

Chapter 6

LISTEN TO LEARN

Essential question: How can you hear what someone is really *trying to tell you?*

IMAGINE THIS SCENARIO: YOU'RE A DOCTOR AT A HOSPITAL. TWO police officers arrive with a belligerent prisoner who needs sutures. He has slashed his own wrist, multiple times, with the corner of a tube of toothpaste. You don't know what his crime was, but his behavior now suggests he's cruel and violent. He hurls racist, threatening remarks at a nurse, and when he sits so that you can work on his wounds, he curses and berates you nonstop. It's affecting your ability to sew him up. The police just stand there, doing nothing. You can't throw him out, but you can't take more of this verbal violence. What do you do?

The esteemed surgeon and author Atul Gawande was the actual doctor in this predicament. As he explained in a 2018 *New Yorker* essay,[1] he was so put off by the man's ugly behavior that he questioned, briefly, whether all people are truly worthy of care, a bedrock principle of medicine. But then he remembered something he had once been taught about brain function. When people speak, they are expressing more than their thoughts. They are expressing something they want heard even more: their emotions.

Instead of trying to stop listening, he decided to listen *closer.* Gawande sought to listen to the man's emotions, rather than his words. And what he heard led him to say this to his patient:

"You seem really angry and like you feel disrespected."

At that point, the man stopped cursing. His tone changed. He started telling the surgeon about what it was like "inside." How he had spent the last two years in solitary confinement. "All it took to see his humanity—to be able to treat him—was to supply that tiny bit of openness and curiosity," Gawande reflected.[2] Both men relaxed, and Gawande was able to care for him.

Gawande's story poignantly illustrates the fundamental lesson of this chapter: how we listen matters. The quality of listening we bring to an interaction profoundly shapes what gets shared—and how the other person feels about themselves and their contribution. If we want to be worthy of responses to the questions we ask, we have to become skilled at what I call **listening to learn.**

"Listening to learn" means:

> **Intentionally opening ourselves to all that another person shares, in order to understand what's essential about their message and experience.**

The challenging reality is that most of us were never taught how to listen. One survey found that 96 percent of people think of themselves as good listeners,[3] yet research has also shown that we retain less than half of what people tell us and that the average person listens with only 25 percent efficacy.[4] Research shows that we are actually *worse* at listening to the people closest to us than to total strangers.[5]

We are taught how to read, to write, to speak and defend our opinions, but not to listen. Worse, we are taught to associate speaking with intelligence and ambition but staying quiet with being dumb or disengaged. And yet, as Susan Cain argues persuasively in *Quiet: The Power of Introverts in a World That Can't Stop Talking,* it is often the quietest among us that have the most astute observations to share.[6]

Perhaps we have failed to teach listening skills because we, as a society, have equated *listening* with *hearing* and therefore assume that it is an instinctive activity, like seeing or tasting. But as any art critic or sommelier will tell you, there is an ocean of difference between passive sensory perception (hearing, seeing, tasting) and active, skilled perception (listening, observing, distinguishing French tannins from Italian ones).

Growing up, I was fortunate enough to have my ears tuned by a small subset of American society who are true sommeliers of listening: practicing Quakers. Fundamental to the Quaker faith are the twin beliefs that each person has equal access to the divine and that God may speak through a person at any time. Quakers see everyone around them as potential sources of God's wisdom. This makes listening not only an essential act, but a sacred one. Quakers aim to "listen as if God is speaking."[7] Because listening to and learning from one another is so central to their communitarian approach to life and leadership, Quakers have developed a set of practices and conventions that can turn anyone into an expert listener.

I experienced this myself every summer for nearly a decade at a Quaker camp called Shohola.[8] A ritual called "Weekly Thought" gave three hundred of us boys—not a demographic group well known for patience or the ability to hold space for others—the structure to sit quietly and listen respectfully for forty-five minutes to whatever our fellow campers and counselors felt the need to share.

In a clearing in the woods, we all gathered in a rough circle on still-damp ground on Sunday mornings at 10:00 a.m. After a few minutes of settling, someone eventually stood up, walked toward the center of the circle, and spoke his mind. The rest of us just... listened. I can remember my friend Juan talking about growing up in poverty so severe that his family would duct-tape his jacket at wintertime to keep out the wind. And how that same family's love and faith allowed him to persevere, earn a college degree, and put himself on a path of success. Juan's brave candor moved many others to stand up after him, sharing their own personal stories about experiences and moments that were imprinted within them.

For the vast majority of us, the idea of being listened to in such a way is completely foreign. It may even sound a little daunting. But what made it possible and actually enjoyable for the person standing in the center of the circle was the safe space created by the listening of everyone else.

Think of this chapter as your own "listen to learn" summer camp, complete with a starter set of strategies that will allow you to learn more than ever before from your conversations. Your improved skills will lead more people to tell you more things, more honestly, than they have in the past. Like Atul Gawande, you will learn to hear the messages beneath the words when people speak. And like the Quakers, you will perfect the art of holding space for people's most vulnerable admissions.

THE THREE CHANNELS OF LISTENING WITH INTENTION

Listening to learn starts with setting a particular intention. It is distinct from listening to prove or persuade, to fix or advise, or to come off as a good listener. Carl Rogers, a founder of human-centered psychology and one of the all-time greatest listeners, argued that real listening requires us to think "*with* people instead of *for* or *about* them," putting aside our ego so that we can be of service to the other in expressing what they really think, believe, or feel.[9] The value of giving your complete attention to another person is often overlooked in modern life where, as Kate Murphy, author of *You're Not Listening,* points out, "we are encouraged to listen to our hearts, listen to our inner voices, and listen to our guts, but rarely are we encouraged to listen carefully and with intent to other people."[10]

When we consciously remind ourselves of our intention to listen, we are more likely to think and behave in ways that align with that intention. This piece is easy to forget, but taking even five seconds to remind yourself of your listening intention can be incredibly powerful. It creates a foundation for effective listening that the strategies below build upon.

Foundation set, it's time to *triple* the range of communication you've been listening for in the past. While at Monitor, I had the chance to work closely with David Kantor, a leader in the field of family dynamics and interpersonal communication. David could watch people interact—whether a couple whose marriage was in distress, or a dysfunctional leadership team—and almost instantly detect what was going on beneath the surface. How did he do this? Among his secrets: you have to listen simultaneously through three channels—content, emotion, and action.[11] Let's consider each in turn.

Three Channels of Listening

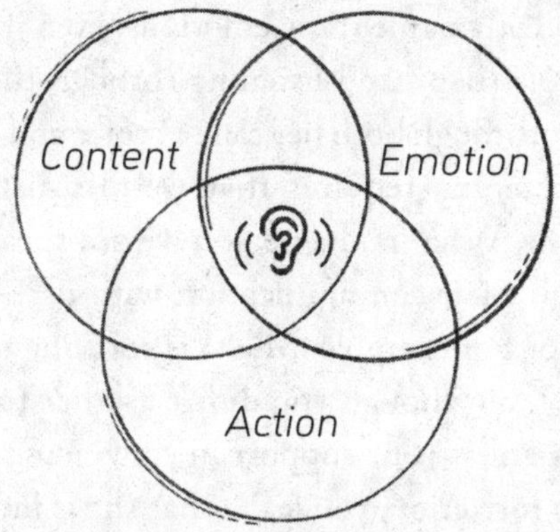

Perhaps the type of listening we are most familiar with is listening for the *content* of what someone is telling us. These are the facts of the matter and the claims they are making. This includes concrete information, as well as their beliefs, reasoning, and conclusions. Imagine that your employee, Mieka, has come to you to discuss a problem she's having with a client who seems unsatisfied with every solution she has presented. Listening for content entails hearing the details of what happened, what solutions Mieka had presented to her client, how many phone calls had taken place between them, and what aspects of the solution the client was unhappy with.

A second channel for listening is *emotion,* as Gawande did with his patient. Through this channel, we listen to understand what feelings are being communicated, including what needs and desires are behind those feelings. For those of us—myself included—who have been trained and socialized to prioritize highly rationalistic forms of thinking and knowing, learning how to pick up on these emotional messages can take some work. Sometimes, I get so caught up in listening for the facts that I forget to tune into the emotional information as well, but experience has taught me that this channel is not only incredibly rich but often the most essential thing that's going on.

For example, when we tune into the emotional channel when listening to Mieka, we might notice the tone of frustration in her voice, or her hunched shoulders and furrowed brow indicating her disappointment with herself that she was unable to help a client she cares deeply about. Mieka may or may not explicitly name these emotions; even if she doesn't *express* them, she is *displaying* them, and listening through the emotion channel lets us perceive them through both her tone of voice and her body language.

Finally, good listening requires that we also listen for the *actions* inherent in their talk. What is the person we are speaking with actually trying to *do* through their communication with us? And what are they trying to get *us* to do? For example, Mieka is stacking up evidence against her client's opinion, even though you didn't ask her to. This could mean that she is trying to enlist your support in convincing her client that she is right. In listening for action, you learn that she is intending to hold her position with her client (rather than compromise or pivot) and also that she is trying to get you to back her up.

Learning how to listen through all three of these channels simultaneously can be a challenge at first, but it's critical if we want to truly understand what someone is telling us. Imagine listening to a piece of music for the first time. To the unskilled ear listening at surface level, all the sounds combine together. But if you try to isolate each aspect of the song—maybe first the lyrics, then the drums, then the guitar, and so on—you can begin to train your ear to hear in more nuanced ways. Over time, you train and practice until your ear develops so that you can hear all the different pieces at once. All of a sudden, the richness of the song opens up. Anyone who has learned to listen this way will tell you that it's like unlocking a door into the musician's mind.

When it comes to listening to people, it can take practice to listen to all three channels at once. Award-winning journalist Jenny Anderson shared with me how important it can be to listen again and again. When a person she is interviewing says something that sounds important, Jenny will sometimes pause the conversation and ask if they can repeat what they said, just so she can listen even more closely to all facets of what they are telling her. Whenever possible, she even records the interview. Afterward, she listens to it over and over again, and she is shocked by how each time she listens, she hears something new and important. This matches my own experience of recording meetings and reading the transcripts, where each time I reread it, I see something I had missed previously. If Jenny, a professional question asker and listener, has to listen over and over again to hear everything being communicated, imagine how much we all miss in hearing most things just once! (Sidenote: One unexpected opportunity with more meetings happening over video these days is that it's easier than ever to record those conversations—with others' permission, of course—and listen again to the most important moments.)

Now that we know *what* to listen for, let's talk about the *how* of listening to learn.

How AI Can Help You Listen Through All Three Channels

These days, you can easily record any call or video meeting and use an AI transcription app to get a decent transcript of your dialogue. (Ask permission to record, of course!) Once you have the transcript, ask your favorite AI chatbot to review it and answer three questions:

1. For the *content* channel: What were the key points or messages that [Person X] was conveying during our meeting?
2. For the *emotion* channel: What emotions might [Person X] have been feeling during our conversation?
3. For the *action* channel: What actions was [Person X] taking throughout the dialogue?

When I've tried this, it's been fascinating to see the richness I get back, and the quality will only improve as AI's abilities to listen directly and evaluate tone of voice become even more sophisticated. The idea, however, is not to let AI do the listening for you. Rather, it's a chance for you to have the perceptions of another set of "ears"—in this case, an AI chatbot with no stakes in the game—to compare to your own takeaways. AI's answers may not be perfect, but they give you another perspective against which to triangulate what you are hearing.

SEVEN PRACTICES FOR LISTENING TO LEARN

What follows are seven practices that you can try out right away—maybe not all at once but over the course of a week or two. None of them requires intricate skills, and you'll be amazed at how much better you listen—and how much more you learn—when you practice them.

1. Ditch the Distractions

I once had an in-person meeting with a potential investor. I walked into the library of his well-appointed offices, with thick woven carpets, ornate lamps, and books adorning the shelves. We sat down in plush leather chairs across from each other. As he sat down, he took out his phone and began looking at it and typing. I figured he was dealing with something urgent, so I waited. After about a minute went by, he said, "Go ahead. I can listen to you while I'm doing this." I started to share some new developments that I hoped would interest him, but he spent the entire conversation looking down at his phone and typing, never once glancing up. I stammered a bit, shared much less than I typically would have, and left to pursue investment elsewhere.

While this may seem like an extreme example, I would be lying if I didn't admit that I can get distracted easily myself, especially on video calls where I flip between the video screen, incoming emails and text messages, and yes, maybe even social media. These things feel innocuous, even productive, in the moment, but they chip away at our attention and retention. Just think of how many conversations you've had when you feel your phone vibrate in your pocket, and for the next five minutes, all you can think about is who texted you. Research shows that simply having our phone nearby reduces our cognitive capacity to listen and process.[12] Further, when we engage with these distractions, other people feel our diminished presence. Think of a child telling a parent about their day at school, and the conclusion that child must reach when the parent keeps glancing down at the message that just popped up on their phone.

The trickier task, but no less important, is to learn to minimize *internal* distractions. Oscar Trimboli, in *How to Listen*, writes that people speak at an average speed of 125 words per minute, but listen at a speed of 400 words per minute.[13] When I discovered this, a light bulb went on for me—if I have an extra 275 (400 minus 125) words per minute of listening capacity that is not being filled by the person talking, no wonder I get distracted and look to fill that void! This finding describes numerically what we all know experientially: it's hard to slow our brains down, so they race forward, always thinking, thinking, thinking, reacting internally to what we've heard.

But trying to understand what someone is telling you when you are not fully present is like trying to skim Tolstoy—you barely get anything out of it! So put the damn phone away, shut the laptop (or if on a video call, close out all other windows and mute your email), and stop looking at your watch. My current hack, when I'm on video calls and tempted to start checking email, is to literally sit on my hands. That way, every time I'm tempted to start multitasking, I'm reminded to stay focused on the people I'm speaking with and give them my full listening.

Finally, the more you train yourself to listen for content, emotion, and action, the less room you'll have to take in external distractions. This makes it easier to stay present.

Psychologist and Buddhist teacher Tara Brach identifies fear, along with judgment, as two core reactions that create *internal* distractions that prevent listening. Judgment isn't just about evaluating the other person as good or bad, but about racing up our ladders of understanding to slap a label on everything as we receive it—whether negative (wrong!, scary!, rude!) or positive (smart!, exciting!)—and deciding automatically how we feel about it. Suspending judgment means resisting the (very seductive) trap of evaluating, labeling, or categorizing either the other person or the information they are sharing with you as they share it. We can make all the judgments we want later on, but in the moment of receiving, it is critical that we do our best to stay low on our ladders of understanding by simply listening with open presence.[14]

Legendary music producer Rick Rubin argues that suspending the judgmental part of ourselves is essential to true listening. When he sits down to listen to a piece of music that he really wants to understand, he makes an effort to minimize external distractions (by going into a silent room or his car) and to actually "turn off" the judgmental part of his brain. Only by suspending judgment, Rubin says, can he really "be with the music." Rubin, a lifelong meditator, points out that while we can never truly rid ourselves of our judgmental distractions, we can choose not to engage them when they appear. In his transcendental meditation practice, Rubin does this by bringing his attention back to his mantra whenever he notices a judgmental thought. When engaged in deep listening, he treats the music as the mantra, bringing his attention back to it again and again whenever he notices thoughts appear.[15]

In addition to judgment, we are distracted by fear: fear of rejection, fear of being less than, fear of being judged, fear of not getting the outcome we want. Perhaps the other person shares something that triggers an insecurity in us and suddenly all we can think about is defending ourselves or feeling badly about ourselves. As with judgmental thoughts, the trick is not to stop having these internal experiences, but rather to get into the habit of noticing them and then simply refocusing on the other person.

2. Zip Your Lip

While I'm sitting on my hands, my mentor Diana Smith is using a different hack when taking important meetings. At the top of the pad where she takes notes, she writes the following message to herself in capital letters:

"STHU!!!"

Not only does this acronym (which stands for "Shut the He_ _ Up") remind her to avoid interrupting the other person, but it also cues her to sit quietly in those moments when no one is talking. So many of us, at least in Western cultures, are habituated to fear silence and to avoid it at all costs. It's awkward, it feels unproductive, we feel like we should be saying something…anything! So much good sharing gets thwarted by this inability to just shut up and wait. Because, as the best listeners know, the most interesting sharing often occurs only when we let silence work its magic.

Silence, as awkward as it can feel, is an immensely fertile space in which both parties can pause, reflect, and gather their thoughts. When I interviewed writer and activist Parker Palmer for this book, he underscored how important it is "to respect the silence and make room for the silence, as much as we have to respect and make room for each other." As Parker pointed out, silence itself is an esteemed member of any group or relationship, capable of making an important contribution if given its due time.

Let's see how this plays out in a different kind of relationship: parenting.

Monica is the mother of thirteen-year-old Jared. Jared plays shortstop on his middle school's baseball team and has been MVP for the past three seasons. He has good friends, gets decent grades, and has been a generally happy kid—until recently. Monica has noticed that Jared has become quiet and withdrawn. He stays home instead of hanging out with his friends. Last week, one of his teachers reached out to check in because she felt that Jared was disengaging in school. Monica, trying to keep her worry in check until she knows more, finds a quiet moment with Jared when they are in the car together, riding home from baseball practice.

"Jared, how are you feeling these days?" she asks. "I'm okay," he replies. Monica knows in her heart that her son is not okay, so she persists a bit. "For real, Jared. You don't seem like yourself, and I really care about you. You can tell me anything—the good, the bad, the ugly. I just want to know how you are doing," she says, doing what she can to make it safe for him to speak.

But . . . he doesn't say anything.

After a few seconds, Monica feels the urge to say something—but she fights it. They continue down the highway, and minutes pass. Monica is just about to break the silence and tell Jared how much she loves him, when Jared finally speaks: "Life just feels less fun than it used to." It's not words that any parent wants to hear, but now Monica has an opening to learn what's going on. She is relieved. (We'll return to Monica and Jared in a moment!)

Someone's silence doesn't mean they have nothing to say. Rarely the case! Often, they need a moment to think about how to phrase something or to gather the courage to say what they really think or feel. We've been conditioned to feel silence is uncomfortable, so we jump in fast to fill the void. But when we give in to this urge, we are not only cutting off the sharing that might have emerged from the silence but also signaling that we do not have the patience or curiosity to wait with others as they think.

Educators have long understood the value of silence. In the 1970s, education researcher Mary Budd Rowe coined the phrase *wait time* after observing that when teachers waited just *three seconds* after asking a question before speaking again, students exhibited significantly higher levels of creativity and learning. In the years since, educators and scholars have determined that one of the reasons this period of silence is so important for learning is that it allows both teacher and student to *think*—to process their thoughts, feelings, and reactions—in a way that enriches the sharing and learning that follows the silence.[16] Understanding the benefits of wait time helps teachers to resist asking their students a question and then immediately answering it themselves or calling on the first student who happens to raise their hand.

Try it yourself: Next time you're in a group conversation and after posing a question that doesn't get an immediate response, count to ten in your head before saying anything more. I have made this a habit, and usually by the time seven or eight seconds have passed, someone jumps in with a valuable insight.

3. Watch Your Face

Keep in mind that the other person is listening to you too—and that your reactions, said and unsaid, can have a profound effect on what and how much they decide to share. CEO Chong-Hao Fu is a world-class asker and actually trains his facial expressions to reflect the energy he wishes to bring to important learning interactions: warm, open, and nonjudgmental. Otherwise, he knows that people might decide it's not safe to share with him. He controls his external body language by paying close attention to his internal state, focusing on slowing his breath and relaxing his body.

Child and family psychologist Fred Muench explained to me that one of the top predictors of whether children continue sharing with their parents is how reactive they are. When parents get upset, angry, or otherwise emotionally heightened, it radically decreases the chances of their child sharing honestly again.

When Jared, whom we met earlier, shares he's been feeling down, what if Monica, in response, were to start crying and say, "Oh my God, no, Jared, no! Is it depression? Depression is an epidemic these days!" An outsize emotional reaction, whether in your words or your body language, is a great way to scare someone—especially if that someone is your child—into silence.

But Monica doesn't lose it. Instead, she stays calm and tries to dig deeper: "Life can sure be hard. What's the hardest part for you these days?"

Jared pauses, then says, "Baseball."

Baseball? Monica is taken aback. For years, baseball has been Jared's rock, the center of his life, the bright spot when other things were hard. Baseball would have been the very last thing on Monica's list of guesses as to what's been getting Jared down. She sits quietly for a moment to see if there's more.

Eventually, Jared goes on: "It's just not as fun for me as it used to be. And besides, I don't think I'm as good as I used to be. All my friends are talking about how we're going to play on the high school team next year, but I actually don't think I *want* to play next year in high school. But my coach is expecting me to. So is the high school coach, who has already been talking to me. And so are my friends. I feel like I'm going to let everyone down. Everyone expects me to keep playing, but I'm not sure I want to."

Monica is shocked, but she does her best to remain calm and unreactive so that Jared stays engaged as she asks more follow-up questions. She needs to know more, a lot more, in order to be able to help him the way he most needs. But already, the problem seems less daunting than she initially feared.

4. Paraphrase and Test

If you can get these three practices down, you will already be better at listening than 99 percent of the population. But truly listening to learn requires that you balance these quiet, receptive strategies with more active responses that allow you to test, clarify, and expand the information you are receiving.

Follow-up questions are one of the most powerful yet underutilized listening tools at our disposal. Organizational psychologist Richard Davis points out that the information we get from our initial question often isn't that great, yet most people simply accept what they hear and move on to the next question (or end the conversation). Meanwhile, he argues, "The key to understanding people lies in the follow-up question."[17]

The most powerful follow-up practice is the simplest: it's called **paraphrase and test**. To do this, you share back in your own words what you think you heard the other person say and then check whether you heard them correctly. For example:

- "It sounds like your biggest concern right now is how to balance caring for your aging parents while also being present for your young children. Is that right, or is it something else?"
- "I hear you saying that you feel overwhelmed by the amount of work on your plate right now and that you feel frustrated by the lack of resources at your disposal to get it all done—is that correct?"

Not only do responses like these demonstrate to the other person that you've been paying close attention to them, they give them the opportunity to *verify* or *clarify*, which helps *you* be sure that you are hearing them correctly. When paraphrasing what you hear from others, it's important to try to stay as close as you can to their original meaning and not mix in your own interpretations or evaluations.

There's no way to fake this one—you have to *actually* listen deeply in order to attempt to paraphrase what they've told you. As Harvard Business School's Hanne Collins points out, that is exactly what makes this practice far more valuable than other types of signaling, such as nodding, laughing, or the classic "mm-hmm" and "ah." The quality of the listening increases, and the speaker feels more heard.[18]

Journalist Amanda Ripley told me that she began using this strategy after learning about it in 2018 from Gary Friedman, a divorce mediator she wrote about in *High Conflict*. Gary taught this strategy to his clients and many others—he called it "looping" (as in, looping back to the other person to check if you understood them correctly). After that, Amanda started using this strategy regularly in her journalism. She now finds that "fifty percent of the time, I don't get it right and they tell me more." The very act of sharing back what we tell others and checking if we heard them correctly demonstrates so much interest that it alone often invites more sharing. Amanda told me she now uses this strategy everywhere: "as a parent, spouse, friend, and with strangers."

5. Pull the Thread

Another way to keep asking is a practice I call **pulling the thread**. This simply refers to asking questions that invite the other person to extend their sharing more deeply, such as:

- "Can you say more about that first concern you shared?"
- "That's so interesting—tell me more about that."
- "Could you share more about that idea you mentioned briefly?"

These kinds of follow-up questions have the potential to unspool all kinds of useful information. Why does this work so well? Sometimes, the other person doesn't initially state explicitly what's most important about their thoughts or feelings. Maybe they're hesitant and holding back. Maybe they want to see how much you really care or will persist with them. Maybe they, themselves, aren't totally clear or self-aware, and your questions will help them think things through. Or maybe they've only shared 125 of the 900 words going through their head in any given minute. In any case, **you can't assume that what they've shared so far is the totality of what's really going on—or even the most important part.**

Whatever prompt you use, pulling the thread can inspire someone to *develop* ideas during the conversation that they might not have even considered. That's the magic of great listening: your attentiveness and interest creates safety and belonging that ignites *their* creativity.[19] I experienced this with Samra, a teammate. As I kept asking versions of "What more?" and "Are there any additional ideas you want to share?" her suggestions kept getting better and better, culminating in an inspired idea about how to solve a really difficult and chronic problem with one of our clients. After Samra's brainstorm, I sat back in my chair and marveled at her genius—and the surprising power of asking some version of "What else?" again and again.

Psychotherapists have noticed a phenomenon they call *the doorknob moment*. The doorknob moment comes at the very end of the therapy session. Just as they're about to leave, sometimes even as they walk out the door, their clients let loose their most important insight. Something about the urgency of the session ending leads them to finally spit out the thing that's as important as it is difficult to say.

You can preempt the doorknob moment when your time together is nearing the end but with enough time left for something important to come out. Just ask:

"Before we go, is there anything else you want to share?"

My friend Max Koltuv, who coaches CEOs, does exactly this at the end of every coaching session by asking, "What else is on your mind that I can help with?" just before the session ends. Invariably, his clients share their most juicy and important challenges that hadn't surfaced until then.

For instance, a client might spend the entire session talking with Max about long-term strategy while holding back some very important development, like that their organization is being investigated by the state for an alleged wrongdoing. They must know how important this development is, yet they need this small push of "What else?"—and the urgency of the meeting ending—to share it.

Michael Bungay Stanier, author of *The Coaching Habit*, calls this the AWE Question, an acronym for "And What Else."[20] You'll be in awe of what comes out when you ask it regularly.

6. Back Off to Move Forward

The flip side of asking if there's anything more they want to share is to **respect the limits of their sharing**, even if you didn't find out everything you'd hoped to learn.

Earlier this year, I tried to approach my daughter, Eden, about a pattern of behavior I had noticed and was concerned about. Eden looked down and said, "Dad, I don't want to talk about it." I replied, "I'm just curious and care about you," and I got back a "Daaaaaad. I doooooon't want to talk about it!!!" So I backed off—Eden's content, emotion, and action were all aligned: she wanted me to back off. A boundary was up, and I needed to respect it. I just said, "Okay, no problem. But I'm here if you ever do."

Every person is entitled to their boundaries, and healthy relationships are built on a healthy respect for one another's limits. Sometimes respecting another person's boundaries means *not asking* more questions in the moment and instead letting the conversation rest. It may even mean saying out loud something like "I feel like there's possibly more to talk about here, but I respect your limits. If at any point in the future, you want to share more, I'm here and always interested to listen." Acknowledging and respecting someone's boundaries goes a long way in helping them feel safe being vulnerable with you in the future, since they know that you will not push them further than they are willing to go.

Sure enough, about a week later, I was hanging out in Eden's room one night. She was doing her homework on her laptop, and I was reading a book. At one point, she looked up and said out of the blue, "Okay,

I'm ready to talk about it." From there, we went on to have a meaningful conversation about what she was going through and what help she did or didn't want. It was also clear that Eden only wanted to talk about this for about five minutes, at which point another boundary went up. But by respecting each boundary and letting her know I was there for her, the door stayed open for more sharing and support over time.

7. Check In

Last but not least, to really listen, it's important to know how the other person experienced the interaction you just had. If they felt shut down or stifled or even put off, they're far less likely to trust and share openly with you in the future. Conversely, if the interaction went well for them, it's helpful to understand what they appreciated so you can do more of that in the future. One of the most underused but powerful moves you can make at the end of an interaction is to **check in on the interaction you just had**. This can include questions like:

- "What worked or didn't work for you in how we just talked about this?"
- "What, if anything, would make this kind of conversation feel better or easier for you in the future?"
- "To what extent was this conversation useful or not?"

In many settings, it can feel countercultural to talk frankly about the interaction we just had with someone. In some cultures, it would be more acceptable for people to gossip about it afterward to others who weren't there, but never to each other's face! They'd walk away and say, "Wow, I feel like he totally misunderstood me," or "He seemed really frustrated with me," or "Clearly, she just wanted me to agree with her point of view. There was no room for actual discussion."

When this kind of thing happens, a misunderstanding can go unaddressed, which breeds distance and resentment in any relationship. More important, if we had a negative impact on the other person that we weren't aware of (especially since intent and impact do not always line up), it's likely that the person will decide it's safer and more comfortable to stay quiet in the future. But conversely, if we can find out how the other person experienced us, we can address it before it has the chance to fester. This last step is easy to overlook or rush, but it deserves our care and attention. It's the difference between closing the door gently with a smile and slamming it shut, shaking the whole house and making it unlikely the person will invite us in again.

JOIN US AT A "NO B.S. LISTENING PARTY"

Lastly, a "what not to do." I first learned about the concept of B.S. listening—and a version of this term—from author and racial justice educator Debby Irving.[21] The B.S., in this case, stands for "back-to-self." How often have we had someone share something with us only for us to respond by exclaiming, "That's so interesting because I had a similar experience... Let me tell you all about it!" While it's nice for us to share how we can relate to what they've said, when we do this (whether out loud or in our minds), we've immediately taken the focus off them and put it on us. In other words, we've engaged in B.S. (back-to-self) listening!

B.S. listening not only makes the other person feel slighted, but it can also lead them to stop sharing. Which means we stop learning from them. There are moments, of course, where it's appropriate and helpful to make connections back to ourselves. If all we ever did was ask follow-up questions in perpetuity, it would make for very strange discourse. But I am inviting you to notice how quickly you move the conversation away from the other person and to consider whether you might be engaging in B.S. listening. If so, a good approach is to ensure you've asked at least three follow-up questions—whether *paraphrase and test* or *pull the thread* or any other follow-up questions that naturally strike your curiosity—before moving the conversation off the other person.

So "no B.S. listening" means staying with the other person rather than bringing it back to oneself. Debby shared a provocation that has always stuck with me: What if we threw a "no B.S. party"? The single ground rule at this party is that no one is allowed to practice "B.S. listening." Said differently, whenever someone shares something, guests need to ask at least three questions before shifting the conversation back to themselves or anything else. Imagine how different our world would be if we all lived life as if we were at a "no B.S. party"! How much more would we learn from one another? How much closer would we be? How might our misconceptions start to be replaced by more understanding?

SUMMARY OF KEY POINTS

Essential question: How can you hear what someone is *really* trying to tell you?

1. Set the **intention** to listen without trying to fix, advise, or persuade.
2. Learn to listen through **three channels** at once.
   - **Content:** the facts they share and claims they make
   - **Emotion:** the feelings, needs, and desires beneath the words
   - **Action:** the intentions and goals motivating what they are sharing
3. **Ditch the distractions.** Turn off your phone, close your email, and give the person in front of you your full attention. Put aside your internal judgments, fears, and reactions for the moment (you can come back to them later!).
4. **Zip your lip.** Resist the urge to fill up quiet pauses and let silence work for you.
5. **Watch your face.** Monitor your reactions and try to stay as inviting as possible while the other person is sharing.
6. **Paraphrase and test.** To make sure you have the right takeaways, test your understanding by repeating back to them what you think they are saying.
7. **Ask again.** Keep opening the door by asking versions of *What else?* Often the best and most unexpected insights come out at the end of the conversation.

8. **Back off to move forward.** Respect the boundaries of their sharing while letting them know you are open to hearing more if and when they feel ready to share.
9. **Check in.** This is a chance to gain deeper insight into the other person's experience of your interaction and to allow any remaining misunderstandings to surface.

EXERCISES

6A. Practice listening through the three channels of content, emotion, and action. Listen to a clip of your favorite TV show or a movie. Listen three times: once just for content, once for emotion, once for action. Compare the differences in what you take away.

6B. Tell a friend you are trying to practice your listening skills. Ask them to tell you a story and practice asking follow-up questions. Then tell it back to them and test your understanding of what they said. Keep going until the other person says, "Exactly!" or "You got it."

6C. Practice "no B.S. listening" with a friend or colleague or family member; even better, hold a "no B.S." lunch or party, where everyone has to ask three follow-up questions before taking the attention off the person speaking.

Chapter 7
REFLECT & RECONNECT

Essential question: How do you turn talk into action?

THE HARDEST PART OF LEARNING FROM OTHERS ISN'T ASKING THE questions, or even listening to the answers. It's deciding what to do with what we hear.

The pandemic years turned out to be a catalyst for fast growth in my organization. Lockdowns and interruptions had left schools across the country urgently seeking guidance. Educational redesign is our mission, so we grew rapidly to meet the need, from thirty-five people to more than one hundred, all while operating remotely amid the strain and struggle of the pandemic years.

It's probably impossible for any organization to quickly triple in size without experiencing growing pains, and we were no exception. Minor cracks emerged across the organization, but overall we held it together pretty well. While everyone felt some strain, our largest project team—which was taking on a new set of clients with intense needs that we hadn't before encountered—felt it most acutely.

My co-CEO Aylon and I, and others on our senior team, started to hear a low-level buzz about concerns. Some were classic HR issues, such as a lack of role clarity and performance feedback. Others were more serious, calling into question whether parts of the project were well enough aligned with our mission. And yet others expressed general concern about the way forward, in the form of questions like "Are you sure we're ready for all this growth?"

We'd tried a number of solutions and optimistically thought things were turning for the better, but after months it was clear they weren't; we were at risk of losing some of the amazing people we had hired just a year earlier. Our super-talented and dedicated teammates were pouring their blood, sweat, and tears into their work with school communities. Many of them were making good headway, but it too often felt like two steps forward, one step back, and our internal challenges compounded their sense of frustration.

Eventually, we concluded there was no way around this without getting together in person to talk it all out and hear directly from every teammate. So Aylon invited the project team to Chicago for two days of planning and rebuilding.

The team of nearly twenty gathered together in a circle in a large meeting room. Because of COVID-19-related travel restrictions, some of them had been together in the same physical space only a handful of times. Even so, there was a real sense of love and connection in the room. But there were also furrowed brows and crossed arms, suggesting the months of strain that had come before. People sipped coffee from paper cups and doodled on their notepads, chatting up their neighbors, unsure about what the day was to bring.

Together with Lavada, another senior leader on the team, Aylon offered the group a warm welcome. Something you should know: My co-CEO is a seasoned executive and leader—but also a celebrated jazz guitarist. He can take the stage and, with a few notes, set the emotional tone of a room. He's just as good at doing this in a professional setting, using his words, voice, and presence. "It's been a challenging year, I know," he told the group. "But we're going to find the way forward together." His smile and deep, warm voice immediately communicated safety. He also made clear up front that people's jobs were not in jeopardy.

Then Lavada asked everyone to answer two questions, in round-robin fashion: "In the previous year, what could I have done better, and what could the people around me have done better?" She and Aylon imagined that the questions would function as an emotional icebreaker that would further build connection and energize the planning work that would compose the majority of the two-day meeting.

Instead, the floodgates opened. Rather than rattling off quick lists as we imagined these individuals would, it was like the room collectively took a deep breath and began to cast off a year's emotional weight. People took their time telling sad and regretful stories, at times pausing for tears, about where they had struggled, what they needed but didn't get, and moments when their work felt like it was going sideways.

Aylon and Lavada had scheduled three hours for this initial share. But by the conclusion of day one, *people were still going*. In the end, three-quarters of the two-day meeting were spent answering these two questions. Critical information and themes emerged to inform the next steps we would take as an organization. But it was also a day and a half of listening to many teammates share painful workplace challenges—a situation both directly and indirectly created by, well . . . *us*.

Everyone left the session with a clearer sense of the organizational changes that needed to happen, and with hope for the future. Soon thereafter, the project took a real turn for the better. In the end, we managed to retain over 90 percent of the team and went on to see strong results across many parts of the project. But there was another, more personal question, introduced by all the feedback: Why had we taken so long to act—and how could we get it right next time?

Aylon and I had much to reflect on. We owed it to our employees to get every ounce of learning out of what they'd shared—and to let them know what we'd be doing with it.

When someone has given you the gift of candid, thoughtful answers to your questions, you owe them two next steps: to *reflect* upon what you've heard, to process and decide what you'll do with it. Then, to *reconnect* back to them. This pair of steps is essential to making meaning of the answers you get and creating actionable insights that strengthen your work and your relationships. Just as important, they're how you keep the learning going over time. When we process what we've been told and then offer our reflections back to those who shared it with us, we ensure we've got the right takeaways, grow our collective understanding, and reinforce open communication.

BEFORE YOU REJECT, *REFLECT*

Not *everything* you learn from others is going to be useful. Some of it might even be counterproductive or harmful if you were to rush to action. What makes asking empowering is that **you get to decide what to do with what you hear.** They say that words are like toothpaste; once spoken, they can't be put back in the tube. While that may be true, you don't have to use the toothpaste that came out of the other person's tube. You can even dump it. How do you make that call?

All of us need a way to separate the wheat from the chaff—to process the input we receive and consider what (if anything) to do with it. The powerful sorting mechanism available to all of us is *reflection*. We need to sit with what has been shared, discern what it means to us, and—when appropriate—use the information to help change things for the better.

As a vehicle for figuring out what and how to change, reflection is one of the most high-value uses of your time. It doesn't require you to become a monk who sits cross-legged on a mountaintop for days on end, but it can nevertheless feel like a lost art in our harried modern world. So I've outlined a simple process you can use, called **Sift and Turn**.

First, Sift It

Some of the best learning opportunities often arise during emotionally intense moments—such as feedback conversations, arguments, and heated discussions. In these moments, it's easy for us to race up our ladders of understanding and walk away with overly simplistic takeaways:

they're just being too self-centered, I'm a terrible person, this job sucks, and so on. The world is rarely that simple, so it's valuable to sift through what you heard to discern what's important to think about and what to discard. The process will also help prevent rumination, which is when you turn things over again and again compulsively, leading to spiraling thoughts or spinning your wheels.

Radical Candor author Kim Scott is an ardent believer in being open to, well, . . . *candid* feedback, yet even she urged me to include this caveat. When we spoke, she was in the midst of preparing for a podcast by soliciting stories about times people had received *ridiculous* feedback—off-the-wall, sometimes even offensive stuff derived from the other person's biases, hang-ups, and challenges. The stories were flooding in: "There's a world of pain out there, a world of BS," Scott told me ruefully. She told me her own painfully ridiculous feedback story, about a boss in the tech sector many years back who once told her to wear tighter pants to work. (As if this story couldn't get worse, he actually didn't stop there—he sent someone out to buy her a new pair, then gave them to Kim with the bill!) Scott, who didn't have a lot of confidence in her fashion sense, actually wore the pants—until she realized they were making her stomach hurt, and that her boss's comment was chauvinism masquerading as advice. Ultimately she quit. (Scott tells the full story in her book *Just Work: How to Root Out Bias, Prejudice, and Bullying to Build a Kick-Ass Culture of Inclusivity.)*

Scott's experience was a wildly egregious situation; regardless, we've all likely experienced some form of "ridiculous" feedback. Sifting through the information you receive from others does not mean you're being unreasonable. This is especially true if you're part of an underrepresented group and therefore more vulnerable to receiving input that's tainted by bias. Said Scott, speaking as a woman in tech, "There's been so much written about soliciting feedback that's about being open to it, and not being defensive. But we are defensive for a reason . . . If you take it all in, you can be inundated by crap."

Before you begin sifting, consider documenting what you heard from the other person. It's best to jot it down right away, since memory degrades quickly. Documenting the exchange provides clarity and prevents you from second-guessing or immediately interpreting what you actually heard. One good form of documenting an interaction after the fact is the two-column-case format that we explored in Chapter 1.

Once you've documented it, you can consider what, if anything, is valuable for you to reflect on. The sad fact is, sometimes there's no goodness to squeeze from what someone else has shared. If the information you've received from them feels erroneous, unfair, or in that "ridiculous" category, you may just want to sift it out and move on with your life. But before you do so, share it with a few other people (ideally with different perspectives from your own and from one another's) whom you know will be honest and help you to check your thinking. Even if all they do is confirm that it's crap, your friends might help you identify the best next steps (like, maybe, a stop at HR!).

But what about when there seems to be some value in what you've heard? Then it's time to start squeezing the meaning out of what the other person shared, with three reflective turns.

Now Turn It... and Turn It Again

One of my favorite quotes, from ancient rabbi Ben Bag-Bag, gets right to the heart of reflection's power to make meaning: "Turn it and turn it, for everything is in it."[1] The rabbi was talking about reflecting on sacred religious texts, but the quote equally applies to the "text of life"—that is, the words we hear others say to us. If you can read others as closely and carefully as you read a cherished text, turning and turning the words they share, you can discover whatever value lies in what they've offered you.

The **three turns**[2] is a structured set of questions to help you reflect upon what you heard from someone so you can pull the most important insights out of what they shared with you. I present these turns in a particular sequence here, but they can be taken in whichever order feels most appropriate to your situation:

- Turn 1: Reflect on your **story** about the situation.
- Turn 2: Reflect on the **steps** you should take next.
- Turn 3: Reflect on your **stuff** and whether there are deeper factors to explore.

To make these turns, we'll be using our central framework, the ladder of understanding.

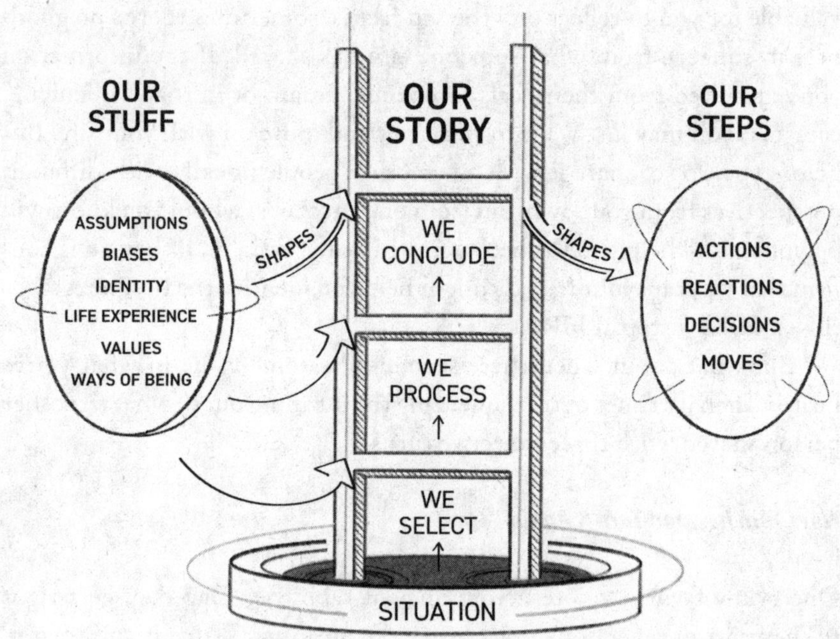

As we discussed in Chapter 3, anytime we enter a situation, we climb up the ladder of understanding to develop our **story**, which naturally leads us to take next **steps**—we act, we react, we decide—all in ways that are consistent with our story. But, of course, the story we tell ourselves in any given situation isn't random. It's a product of our **stuff**—the assumptions, experiences, identity, values, biases, and ways of being that we accumulate over our lifetimes. We carry all that stuff with us, and when we encounter a situation, we draw on that stuff to help us know what aspects of the situation we select to pay attention to, how to process what we select, and what conclusions we draw. Said differently, our preexisting stuff influences the story we tell ourselves in any given situation, which determines what steps we take.

The problem is that, typically, our stuff leads us to form a story that confirms our deepest-held prior beliefs. So we get stuck in the certainty loop, which leads us to act in ways that confirm our old story—unless we interrupt this cycle with tools of reflection. In reflection, therefore, *we have the opportunity to break the certainty loop's self-sealing cycle and learn something new.*

Turn 1—Reflect on Your Story

When you make this turn, you ask yourself a simple question:

How does what I heard from others affect the story I've been holding about this situation?

When you sit with this question, you have the opportunity to nuance, challenge, or revise your story. This can involve rethinking the role that you, yourself, play in the story, the role of others, and the task you set out for yourself. Perhaps you realize there are other aspects of the situation you weren't thinking of, or other conclusions you could draw.

Remember, from Chapter 2, Jim Cutler, whose close friends and colleagues revealed that they thought he lacked the commercial drive to lead the business? When Jim reflected on the feedback he received, he began to reconsider his story about his leadership of the business. His initial story had been that he was crushing it: by building a great team and creating valuable content and selling meaningful projects, he was on the road to success, and that his colleagues were in agreement. As he learned from the 360-degree feedback process, however, his colleagues had a more critical view of his work. As he reflected, Jim realized that they might have a point: maybe more commercial success was possible for the business; maybe he could be driving the business toward better results. Maybe he wasn't "crushing it" after all—but could be, if he made some changes.

To continue our story at Transcend, after that emotional team confab in Chicago, Aylon and I came together to reflect on *our* stories about the situation. In Aylon's case, he realized that he had been operating with a story that the highly capable and seasoned people we hired didn't need a ton of management structures to do their best work. Earlier in his career, he'd established such systems and enforced them at larger companies, but he often felt like they put him in the position of "nannying" junior employees. At Transcend, meanwhile, we'd had the luxury of hiring experienced team members who were highly motivated by the mission of the organization. In such an environment, these systems seemed less important than giving people the space to do the work they were motivated to do. Reflecting on the feedback from the offsite, he realized that his story about performance management systems was off base: even highly motivated, veteran staff needed explicit goals, progress-monitoring systems, and clearer role definitions to guide their work and help them perform at their best.

We also realized that, together, we had constructed a story that since this was a time of such high and urgent need for schools, we had to do everything we could to rise to meet the need, even if that meant growing the organization much faster than we'd planned. We'd assumed that with our strong, mission-driven culture and amazing team, we could hold off on some of the work of building the management structures that keep bigger organizations strong and healthy. Now we could see that our employees had been carrying the burden of our overly confident but ultimately unsustainable story.

Turn 2—Reflect on Your Steps

Once you make Turn 1 and begin to revise your story, it often opens up the possibility of new and different steps you can take, which is the essence of Turn 2.

When you make this kind of reflective turn, you ask yourself this question:

Based on what I heard (and how it affects my story), what steps can I take?

When you ask this question and sit with it, you get powerful insights about what you can start, stop, or continue doing in response to what you heard. Maybe it's an action you can take or change. Maybe it's a new decision or move you can make.

Once Jim revised his story to account for the feedback he heard, it became natural for him to ask what he could do about it. This led him to hire two senior commercial leaders for his division, who brought in significant new revenue. Their presence in the division went a long way to addressing the concerns that people had about how fast revenue would grow. This allowed Jim to do what he did best—set vision, inspire and develop people to work toward it, and engage in the substance of the work—while ensuring the commercial side of the business was booming.

Once Aylon and I revised *our* story (based on what we'd heard from our team) to acknowledge the underinvestment we'd made in foundational systems, the practical steps we needed to take became very evident. We set in motion a series of projects to invest more deeply in onboarding, training, communication structures, planning, talent management, and knowledge management (so people could find others' work products instead of reinventing the wheel). We also put in place goal-setting and performance-monitoring systems and started using them on a regular basis. Finally, we invested in much more detailed strategic planning processes to consider the many new opportunities in front of us and more deliberately decide what our team could feasibly handle and deliver with quality.

Turn 3—Reflect on Your Stuff

When you make this final turn, you look to reexamine some of your deepest-held assumptions, biases, and values at the core of your identity and your life experience. Reflecting on your stuff creates the possibility of traveling up the ladder more effectively next time. Ask yourself this question:

How does what I heard relate to my stuff? What might it reveal about my deeper worldviews, biases, assumptions, and ways of being?

This is the deepest, often most emotional level of reflection—and also where the most important learning occurs, because if you don't evolve, you'll likely keep bringing the same old stuff to every new situation you encounter (hence the phrase, "Wherever you go, there you are."[3]). It can be painful to question your deeply held worldviews and ways of being—after all, they've gotten you here, and it can feel scary to lose them. This is also the place where you may have to confront the not-so-pretty biases and prejudices you (like all of us) have internalized over the course of your life and to begin the hard work of *un*learning them. I sometimes feel embarrassed when I look hard at my stuff because it doesn't live up to the ideals and values I espouse for my life. However, if you are willing to look at your stuff, it's the most powerful reflective turn of all, as it has the greatest power to help you grow and evolve in profound and lasting ways.

When Jim made this turn, he reflected hard on where his superpowers really lay. He realized that being a CEO of a fast-growing commercial business unit might not be his highest and best calling, nor how he most enjoyed spending time. This wasn't easy, as it required him to get over the part of his ego that felt like he "should" be doing this. This deeper insight freed him up to ask what he truly felt were his unique superpowers. Over time, he handed off leadership of the business to others and moved into other functional and advisory leadership roles, both at Monitor and elsewhere, where he thrived, was happier, and continued to have tremendous impact. He now lives a rewarding life where his values, work, and impact are highly aligned.

When Aylon looked more deeply at his stuff, he asked himself why he'd been so swift to brush off earlier warnings that the project was approaching a point of crisis. The question took him back to his upbringing, in an immigrant family that was hyperprotective of their children. Although he grew up in coastal Southern California, he was never allowed to swim in the ocean, because it was "too dangerous." His mother saw improbable danger in every direction and insisted that Aylon heed her warnings. To compensate, Aylon had developed a lifelong habit of assuming that any warning was most likely someone catastrophizing. This optimistic leaning had served Aylon well in life as well as in his past leadership roles, allowing him to inspire others to forge ahead amid uncertainty and challenge. But now he saw that it had its downside.

This insight helped Aylon see why it took so long for him to take action as trouble brewed. But further, it led us to realize that the dynamic had often played out in our relationship as co-CEOs. I was brought up with the implicit mantra that "only the paranoid survive," and instead of resisting that message from my father, I'd internalized it. So I'd come to Aylon with concerns and he'd confidently dismiss them, sometimes—but not always—being right that my anxiety was inappropriately high. After examining our dynamic and where each of our parts in it comes from, Aylon and I now have a more balanced way of bringing each other concerns, examining them together with greater care, and using data and input from others to inform where we land.

Tools for Reflection

For me, reflection comes in the quiet moments, the spaces in between—like when I take a walk or a shower, do the dishes, or take the time to talk things through with my wife or a trusted friend. It's easy and tempting for me to fill in every crack of free time with stimuli (podcasts, news, calls), but that blocks the open space for reflecting. However, when I do make time to deliberately sit with the reflective questions listed in the Three Turns, I'm more likely to take information that others have shared with me and turn it into meaningful insight and action.

If the three turns feel difficult to work through inside your head, consider:

Journaling. Writing helps many people organize their thoughts and make the process of reflection more concrete. Instead of just thinking through the three turns, write your way through them.

Conversation. Just as curiosity is a team sport, it can be very helpful to reflect with someone else, especially since the stories we construct and the certainty loops that trap us in those stories can make it hard to shift our thinking. A critical friend can gently help us see that our story is just one possible way of understanding reality. You can increase the likelihood that your friend will be critical by telling them that's what you really need. (Remember the safety cycle from Chapter 4? Radiate resilience.)

Coaching and/or therapy. Working with a paid professional can add safety, structure, and long-term support to your reflective turns.

However you move through them, it is very helpful to capture your conclusions: write them down, say them out loud, tell them to a friend. This helps us to solidify them, remember them, and hold ourselves accountable for acting on them. You'll find a template for taking these three reflective turns in your own life at www.AskApproach.com.

YOU'VE REFLECTED. NOW RECONNECT.

Once you've reflected, it's time to close the loop by **reconnecting** with the person who generously responded to your ask. Whether and how well you do this may well define your relationship going forward. Asking questions can strengthen your relationship—but only if you both feel rewarded by the exchange. You don't want the kind of conversation you had to be "one and done." **Your response will determine whether the door you've opened stays open, to sustain sharing and learning over time.**

Maybe you asked someone how you could improve as a boss. Maybe you asked for ideas to improve a client challenge or personal relationship. Maybe you just asked for some tips to improve your running form. Whatever the line of questioning, I can guarantee you that the interaction left your friend, family member, or colleague with questions of their own, questions like: *Will what I shared have any impact? Was it well received? What's next?* If they shared anything that made them feel vulnerable, they may have what Brené Brown calls a "vulnerability hangover,"[4] where they feel exposed, perhaps even embarrassed about what they revealed or fearful of how you might use it. So don't leave them hanging!

Start with Gratitude

Gratitude makes a difference even—maybe especially—in those cases in which you reflected on their input and decided not to act on it. (More on that soon.) This can entail something as simple as a heartfelt thank-you, which goes a long way to let someone know their input was valued, especially if they're feeling uncertain about what they shared. Chong-Hao Fu, whom you met in the previous chapter, trains himself to think of feedback as a *gift* and always responds with a thank-you, no matter how challenging it is to hear. Framing it this way internally, as a generous service someone has provided us in our quest to learn and get better, can help us respond positively even in those times when a conversation leads to a mixed bag of emotions.

Saying thank-you is not just good manners. Research has demonstrated the positive effects of expressing gratitude on the person saying the thank-you as well as the one receiving it, including increased levels of emotions like joy, optimism, and enthusiasm, and decreased levels of stress and anxiety. It makes us feel closer and more connected to the other person and actually increases how much each person wants to help and support the other.[5]

Thanking the other person for the advice or information itself makes sense, but your expression of gratitude may have even more impact if you focus it on their gifts. Research by Sara Algoe, a professor of psychology at UNC Chapel Hill, and her colleagues has demonstrated that expressions of thanks that focus on a person's positive qualities—such as their courage, their wisdom, or their creativity—are most impactful.[6] For example, "I am so grateful for your unusual thoughtfulness and care as a person that is reflected in the feedback and advice you shared."

Show Them the Impact of What They Shared

Gratitude is often just a starting place. People want to know what you're doing with the content of what they've shared—and may hope for or even expect some promise of action. In short, **let them know what the impact of their sharing was.**

David Kantor's listening framework from the last chapter—content, emotion, and action—works as well here as a way to express the impact of someone's words on you:

Showing impact in the channel of *content* means summarizing what you've heard, what (if anything) you learned that you didn't know before, and your substantive takeaways. This helps show the other person that you really listened to what they said and how their sharing influenced your thinking or taught you something new.

In the *emotion* channel, you can share the emotional impact they had, while also empathizing with their experience. Careful here, though: you don't want to burden them with or blame them for your emotional reactivity. For example, it's not helpful to share that you are feeling really bad about yourself because of the feedback they gave you, or that you are pissed off and aren't going to be able to focus for the rest of the day. It's fine to share the negative or painful emotions their sharing stirred in you (for example, "It was really painful to hear what you shared, but I'm glad you did..."), as long as you don't hold the other person responsible for your reactions. The point of sharing their emotional impact is to let them know that they have moved you in some way and, in so doing, you return the gift of vulnerability to the other person.

Finally, in the *action* channel, you can let them know what you are contemplating or committing to do based on what you learned. This proactively mitigates a common concern people have: that nothing will come out of their attempts to share, a conclusion which is basically guaranteed to discourage them from bothering to share openly with you in the future. As the saying goes, actions speak louder than words, and this is certainly true when it comes to learning from others.

When I was chief learning officer of TFA, we sometimes partnered with outside organizations to provide additional support and professional development to our teachers. One year, we piloted working with an organization we'd never used before, and early survey data showed that our teachers rated their programs lower than any other forms of support they got. I sent the data to the organization's president, Nick, and scheduled a meeting. In the back of my mind, this was Nick's only chance to convince me that I shouldn't start the process of canceling our contract and getting the teachers better support from a different provider. I was skeptical.

The day of our meeting, I walked into Nick's office nearly convinced it was the end of our relationship—and yet an hour later, I walked out feeling enthusiastic to keep working together.

How did he pull off this turnaround? Nick convinced me—through the channels of content, emotion, and action—that our teachers' survey feedback had made a real impact on him.

When we sat down, he let me know right away that he understood and agreed with the content of the survey data. "It's clear we're underdelivering," he said. "Your teachers aren't feeling supported by our faculty, and our material isn't hitting their most important needs. They want more practical support, and we're giving them too much theory. I can see exactly why they aren't getting what they need."

Then he shared the survey's emotional impact on him: "Hearing this is absolutely crushing. I know how hard it is to be a teacher and how insulting it feels when your time is wasted. It kills me to know that we are the lowest-rated support of all that your teachers are getting. I pride myself on building a different kind of program, and this flies in the face of that."

Finally, he promised strong action: "Here's what I'm going to do. I'm going to sit down with our lead trainer this afternoon and go through this data. We will make a series of personnel changes immediately so that your teachers get our best-rated trainers. I will also personally review the materials with them to ensure it's practical. And I will observe the class sessions every week for the next month and call you to discuss what I'm seeing."

Nick's response left no doubt in my mind that he'd not only learned from and thought hard about what I had shared with him but that it was a good use of my time to sit down with him. It also left me confident that if further issues arose, talking to him again would be worthwhile. Instead of the relationship ending, I left feeling connected and optimistic that our conversation would have real impact. More important, however, Nick actually delivered on the insights he took away from our conversation. Within a very short period of time, things turned around and his program became the highest rated of all our providers'.

When You Don't Plan to Take Action

What happens when you reflect and decide the learning you got wasn't useful after all? Or maybe you agreed with what you heard, but something prevents you from acting on it?

In these cases, sharing your *process* of reflection—along with your honest conclusion—is a great way to reconnect. On the face of it, this can feel awkward, and you may resist following up—but, in fact, it's a great opportunity to deepen your connection with the person and maybe even learn something you didn't see coming. You might say something like, "I thought carefully about your advice, and I want to walk you through why I'm not inclined to do what you suggest—maybe you can help me see if I've missed something, or my sharing will inspire some new thoughts for both of us." Then you walk them through your reflective process, and yes . . . ask for their reactions!

People don't offer input with the expectation that it will always lead to total agreement or direct action. They *do* expect that their input be given serious consideration, and that the *potential* for impact is there. This way their time is not being wasted. That's why you **reconnect**—to follow up with the other person, even if it's to say, "Here's why we won't do that."

Shereen El Mallah is a developmental psychologist and researcher at University of Virginia who specializes in a practice called Youth Participatory Action Research (YPAR), which is a fancy term for helping young people become researchers on issues that matter to them. She saw the profound impact of reconnecting when one school network she worked with, Community Lab School, implemented a system-wide process for following up on what students shared when asked for their input. *Any time* their schools collect feedback and ideas from students, that information goes into one of three buckets: (1) *on the way*—we can and will take immediate action on this; (2) *on the radar*—although immediate action can't be taken to address the issue/concern (e.g., budget constraints, timeline restrictions), here is our long(er)-term plan to fix the problem; or (3) *out of our hands*—we hear the feedback but for X reason we can't act on it. These three buckets help the school follow up with students after they give input, and the effects have been remarkable. Students are more engaged and eager to share feedback with the school, and the information they do share is far richer than in schools without this full-circle feedback process. This practice has been so empowering that the students actually took over responsibility for sharing the bucket presentation with their peers. Shereen now requires all the schools she works with to commit ahead of time to creating accountability channels back to students who give them input. What if every business did this with their customers' suggestions? With their employee feedback? What if every political leader—or faith leader—did this with their constituents?

PUBLICLY MODELING THE REFLECTIVE PROCESS

Reconnecting to share your *process* of reflection is equally important, and rewarding, especially when the other person's words had real impact. Aylon and I decided to do this publicly, in front of the entire organization, about a month after the big Chicago meeting. We had already begun implementing important changes to strengthen our management systems, and it seemed that things were moving in the right direction. But we wanted to show how the feedback we received, though personally challenging, had led us to grow as leaders; we also wanted to model the three turns to encourage this kind of reflection throughout the organization.

This all seemed like a great idea until the day came that we actually had to do it.

The occasion was the return of our annual organizational retreat after a three-year COVID-19 hiatus. We asked Jenee, our chief learning officer, to help us publicly reflect in front of everyone. She sat us down on the stage and asked us to walk through each of the three turns we'd made while reflecting on what we'd learned from the past year's challenges. Out loud. In front of everyone.

Suddenly, there we were, microphones in hand, walking everyone through our story, our steps, and our stuff. Even though we exposed how our leadership choices had caused painful (though thankfully recoverable) consequences felt by many, Aylon told me later that the process was incredibly cathartic for him, and even enjoyable.

As for me? Opening myself up in this way in front of so many people at once was honestly uncomfortable, from start to finish. I was sweating and sometimes stumbling on my words. I didn't look up at the faces of the crowd much, I think because I was afraid of what I might see: judgment, disappointment, maybe even shock. Still, I didn't let those feelings stop me from sharing from my heart, being honest and candid about what I had learned.

After we finished our last turn—Aylon talking about his childhood, and me, my unmitigated drive for more and more impact—Jenee thanked the team for listening. There was a brief moment of silence, during which I stared at my hands, wondering if we'd made a giant mistake. Perhaps we'd lost their confidence altogether.

Then I heard a clap, which rapidly became another and another. Only then did I look up at the team. People were standing to clap, a rousing ovation that lasted nearly a minute. I was relieved, but also overwhelmed with gratitude and a feeling of belonging.

WHAT DOESN'T KILL YOU...

Some of you may find that **reflect and reconnect** may be the most challenging of the five *Ask* Approach steps. This chapter gives you a structure and some tools, but similar to public speaking, it may take practice to become confident in your ability to confront and revise your story. What's more, it requires you to examine your own deeply held beliefs and to overcome powerful conditioning about the risks of vulnerability. And the risks can be real, especially for those in positions of lower organizational or social power who face higher pressures to speak and behave in ways that don't ruffle the feathers of those in power. But more often than not, the rewards of this practice, including deeper insight, powerful action, and closer, more honest relationships, far outweigh the risk.

Aylon's and my public reckoning felt about as uncomfortable as I could imagine, yet we lived to tell the tale. And in fact, it was so impactful that teammates asked us to make it a feature of every annual leadership retreat. I expect the next one will be easier for me because I've now experienced, very viscerally, the deep fulfillment of reflecting and connecting with others about what they've taught me.

After our three turns, teammates came up to us, clearly moved, and said they'd never seen leaders of organizations make themselves so vulnerable so publicly. Others came over and said that their experience watching us in the room that day confirmed that they were working for the right organization; they felt more, not less, confident in leaders who were willing to share so openly and deeply about their own mistakes. I learned from their reactions that what mattered perhaps even more than our mistakes was showing the team that we had not only listened to their feedback but learned from it in ways that would make us, and the organization, stronger. And they learned something equally important: they learned they were powerful and their voices mattered.

SUMMARY OF KEY POINTS

Essential question: How do you turn talk into action?

1. After someone has shared, it's up to you to decide what to do with what you've heard. To **reflect**, you need to *sift* and then *turn* the information.
2. First, **sift it.** Separate the wheat from the chaff. Decide what is worth reflecting on more deeply and what isn't. Share what you heard with a trusted friend to help you gain perspective on the information.
3. Then reflect on what you heard through the three turns:
    - **Reflect on your story.** How does what you heard affect the story you've been holding about this situation?
    - **Reflect on your steps.** Based on what you heard (and how it affects your story), what steps can you take?
    - **Reflect on your stuff.** How does what you heard relate to your stuff? What might it reveal about your deeper worldviews, biases, assumptions, and ways of being?
4. Once you've reflected, it's time to **reconnect**.
    - Start by expressing gratitude for them—and their positive qualities reflected in their input.
    - Let them know how what they shared has affected you . . . and what you plan to do with it
    - If you *don't* plan to act on what they've shared, explain why and invite reactions.
5. Consider incorporating reflective practices like journaling, coaching, therapy, or conversations with trusted thought-partners to support your reflection.

EXERCISES

7A. Walk yourself through the three reflective turns. Think of something meaningful you heard from someone else, then ask yourself:

- Turn 1: Reflect on your **story**: *How does what I heard affect the story I've been telling myself about this situation or person?*
- Turn 2: Reflect on your **steps**: *Based on what I heard (and how it affects my story), what steps can I take?*
- Turn 3: Reflect on your **stuff**: *How does what I heard relate to my stuff? What might it reveal about my deeper worldviews, biases, assumptions, and ways of being?*

Find a thought partner who can listen to you make these reflective turns and gently serve as a critical friend to draw out your reflections and, where helpful, push your thinking.

7B. Now, reconnect. Go back to the person who originally shared with you the input that you reflected on. Let them know how their sharing affected you. What are you grateful for? What did you take away? What will you do with it?

SECTION III

Building *Ask* into Leadership and Life

SECTION III REVEALS HOW THE *ASK* APPROACH CAN BECOME A TRUE superpower—for ourselves, our teams and organizations, our young people, and even for healing our divided society.

It takes practice to incorporate the *Ask* Approach in ways that feel fluid and natural, but Chapter 8 gives you the supportive framework and strategies you need to master this, or any new skill.

In Chapter 9, you'll see how the power of asking can improve the effectiveness of teams and organizations—including what you can do to increase asking throughout your workplace, at any level of your career.

How about the next generation of leaders? Chapter 10 will help you support the young people in your life and community to become great *Ask*ers, and it offers ways to coax their natural sparks of curiosity into a lifelong engine for their creativity.

And finally, in the Epilogue, we'll look at how the world might improve, one conversation at a time, if we all entered interactions with renewed curiosity about what we can learn from every single person, regardless of how different—or difficult—they may initially appear.

Chapter 8

Make It *Your* Superpower

Essential question: What does it take to become a world-class asker?

WHEN I WORKED AT MONITOR AND BEGAN SEEING HOW POWERFUL Chris Argyris's approaches were, I got incredibly motivated by the challenge of how to build my own—and everyone else's—skills at using the methods. It's one thing to read about these practices, but it's another to truly build the muscles to be able to apply them when they're needed most. How do you turn a great set of ideas into a practical arsenal of concrete skills?

So I asked Chris how long he thought it took people to master his approaches. His simple response: "About as long as it takes to learn how to play a half-decent game of tennis."

As luck would have it, I knew something about playing a halfway decent game of tennis. After all, I've been an amateur tennis player ever since junior high school, and *at best*, my game is only half-decent!

It turns out that the process of getting better at tennis—or really any set of skills—is very similar to how we can master the *Ask* Approach. In this chapter, we'll examine what that process is; along the way, we'll call out concrete strategies you can use to get better and better, until you make asking your own superpower.

"YOU ARE ALL INCOMPETENT!" (THAT'S OKAY!)

Building any superpower starts with recognizing our own incompetence and meeting ourselves where we are. When I worked at Monitor, our CEO, Mark Fuller, was infamous for giving a speech each year to the incoming cohort of new consultants. His speech was titled "You Are All Very Smart and Motivated, but You're All Totally Incompetent." When new hires first heard their CEO call them incompetent, they were taken aback. After all, these were people who had graduated from the most elite colleges and business schools in the world, with the very best grades and the most impressive track records of prior success. They had worked their entire lives to be not just good at whatever they did, but to prove their excellence. "Incompetent" was the last thing they had ever been called—and perhaps deep down, the word they most feared ever being used to describe them.

Now, here was their new CEO—the most powerful person in their new work universe—calling them "incompetent." Of course, at a literal level, Mark simply meant that these new hires hadn't learned the tradecraft of being management consultants. As such, it was true: they were incompetent at being management consultants. In making this point, Mark reminded them that, yes, they were highly capable people, but he normalized the idea of their being incompetent at their new jobs. After all, he had just hired and paid good salaries to this group of "incompetent" people, so being incompetent couldn't possibly be that bad. Moreover, why *should* they be competent at something they had never done before? It was perfectly understandable to be incompetent in this situation; it might have even been weird to *not* be incompetent.

When we don't yet know how to do something, we are *incompetent* at it. In our society, there can be a negative connotation with the word "incompetent"—as if it's a harsh judgment on someone or a permanent flaw in our character. But the fact is, we are all incompetent at many things, and there's no shame in admitting it. This shame is learned, which means it can be unlearned. After all, when we were children, no one expected us to automatically know how to do everything we tried. It was understood that not knowing how to do something was exactly where the learning process began. Unfortunately, as we entered adulthood, many of us absorbed the message that we were no longer allowed to be beginners. Few beliefs are more stifling to continued growth and learning than this.

For example, just because I'm an incompetent flutist doesn't mean I'm an incompetent person. It simply means I haven't committed the time and effort to learning how to play the flute. By contrast, I am a competent driver, not because I was born knowing how to drive, but rather because I spent time learning the skill. Similarly, many of us are incompetent when it comes to truly learning from others, not because we are bad or selfish people but because we have not (yet) invested in building the skills of the *Ask* Approach.

The question is: How do we go from being incompetent to competent?

THE MASTERY SPIRAL

We'll take on this question using a simple but powerful framework for capability building, called the **mastery spiral**.[1] (Sidenote: This framework—and more important, the strategies for progressing through it—applies pretty much to *any* complex capability you want to master, so tuck it away for when you want to get good at yodeling, pickleball, knitting, playing the tuba, or [name your own learning goal].)

Throughout the chapter, we'll work our way around the spiral, beginning at the top, where you may find yourself starting with aspects of the *Ask* Approach: feeling stuck. When trying anything new, we often feel stuck and aren't sure why—we may not even realize that the problem is our lack of certain skills. For that reason, we call this stage *unconscious incompetence*. As we start to realize the gaps in our capabilities, we see what we're doing wrong as we become more *conscious* of our incompetence, which is where the learning begins. As we discover and try out new skills, it's often a bit wobbly and takes a lot of concentration, but we start to get it; we call this *conscious competence* because we need to concentrate a lot to do the thing. And finally, with enough practice and feedback, we start

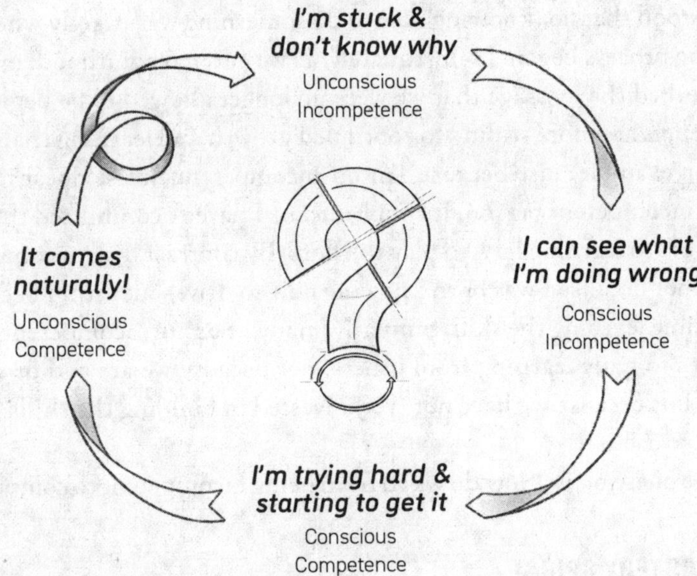

to really internalize the capability to the point where it's so natural that we don't even have to think about it—in other words, we have *unconscious competence*. Then we start applying our skills in more challenging circumstances and may find ourselves stuck again... until we again spiral our way upward. Lo and behold, as we go through these stages over and over again, in ever more challenging circumstances, we develop our superpower!

Learning how to drive is a great example of what the mastery spiral feels like. As kids, we imagine we can just hop behind the wheel and join a high-speed car chase. Then, when we become student drivers, we learn that driving safely and speedily requires a whole set of distinct actions, all performed simultaneously: checking our mirrors, learning which pedal to use, how to signal, how to handle turns, and more. At first, it's impossible to do any of these things well, let alone simultaneously. Then we start to acquire skill, but it still takes conscious effort (and occasionally, a white-knuckled adult yelling, "Check your mirrors!") to perform each of these tasks successfully. But finally, after a lot of repetition, we get to a point where we perform all these tasks without having to think about it at all;

we can drive safely and easily maintain a conversation at the same time. We have reached unconscious competence!

To see how this applies to mastering the *Ask* Approach, I'm going to introduce you to a business consultant named Alexa and the distressing dilemma she brought to a workshop I led for management consultants. To be clear, mastering this material doesn't require you to attend a workshop, but because it's an idealized learning environment, it's a great way to see the stages play out in action. Think of it like we're watching the game tape together after a big game—we'll pause the tape a few times and call out the learning strategies.

"I'm Stuck and I Don't Know Why" (Experiencing Unconscious Incompetence)

Alexa was a management consultant in her early thirties, based in our New York office. This was her second job after graduating from a top-tier business school, and if all would go well for the next few years, she'd be on the partner track. Alexa brought her case into a daylong workshop, which included herself and five other consultants. I was the workshop's facilitator.

Alexa had a client named Bryan, the senior vice president of manufacturing at a struggling company that made and sold industrial products. Alexa's team was brought in by Bryan's CEO and had just completed two months of intensive research on the company and their industry. Now, she was ready to make her formal recommendation about what should happen next: to streamline costs and save the business, two of the six mega-factories under Bryan's management should be shut down.

Alexa's manager had asked her to preview the recommendations with Bryan one-on-one before the team's meeting with the CEO. It was important to get him on board so that he wouldn't oppose them during the final presentation. She was anxious about the meeting, fearful that he would react badly when she informed him that their recommendation entailed a major downsizing of his division.

And she was right: Bryan was immediately defensive and launched in with a series of objections. Alexa, feeling impatient, knocked down each and every objection as if they were pins in a bowling alley. Ultimately,

Bryan said he needed more time to review the team's analysis and ended the meeting abruptly. As she walked out of the room, Alexa had a sinking feeling that Bryan would play politics with the CEO to undermine her recommendations. She felt that any future conversation with Bryan was likely to hit the same wall because he was simply intransigent.

Alexa felt stuck. She was frustrated with Bryan's reaction and didn't know how to move forward. The meeting with their CEO was coming up soon, so time was running out.

This was exactly the kind of scenario we asked participants to identify for our workshop. As prework, Alexa captured her conversation with Bryan in the two-column-case format. Alexa's write-up portrayed, in painful detail, how Bryan dismissed Alexa's recommendations after she'd failed to persuade him. In the right-hand column, Alexa recounted key segments of their dialogue, as if she were writing out the script of a play. In the left-hand column, she captured her unspoken frustration with Bryan's reactions. Now that it was down on paper in this format, she had something to work with.

"I Can See What I'm Doing Wrong" (Moving Toward Conscious Incompetence)

As Alexa presented her case to her colleagues in the workshop, it was clear how exasperated she was. She felt like she kept hitting a wall with Bryan and couldn't get him to see the only obvious conclusion from her analysis. As a result, he never really embraced her recommendations, and further, her relationship with him felt strained in a way that really drained her. She'd gotten into consulting to help her clients, and here she was locking horns with Bryan. He was old enough to be her father, and she didn't like being in a position where she might have to argue with him, or worse, to have to go above his head to tell the CEO that she disagreed with him. None of it felt good, and she was stuck. And yet, she still didn't know why.

As we got into the discussion of her case, I encouraged Alexa and the group to take a look at Alexa's action steps—the behaviors we see in the right-hand column of her case—to see how she might have been contributing to the challenges she was experiencing. The first thing we did was a simple count of the ratio between Alexa's statements to Bryan and her questions to Bryan. Very quickly, Alexa and the group concluded that she had made only statements and asked zero questions. When Alexa—a very data-driven person—saw in black-and-white that she literally asked her client no questions, she was taken aback.

Let's pause our tape: Seeing that she didn't ask any questions was Alexa's first moment of shifting from *unconscious* to *conscious incompetence*. She was still stuck, but now she at least knew what she was doing wrong.

Now that Alexa had more awareness of her missteps, we dug deeper: What had stopped her from asking more questions?

As she reflected on this, Alexa said, "I probably didn't ask him any questions because I felt like I was there to share findings with him, and there wasn't anything I needed to ask him about. Was there?" From there, Alexa's peers earnestly took her up on that question and began to brainstorm some things she might have asked him about.

One person gently suggested that asking Bryan questions was an important step before reaching her conclusions. He might have information that could improve the final plan. Even if he didn't, the group pointed out, understanding where Bryan was coming from would have allowed Alexa to make a more compelling case for her original recommendations, perhaps convincing him. And finally, by not asking Bryan any questions, Alexa likely left him feeling that she didn't care what he thought or didn't value his thirty years of experience at the company—none of which was a good recipe for client investment, let alone cultivating a positive relationship with Bryan.

Alexa sat with this feedback from the group. It was clear this was not the most comfortable moment of her day, or even her week. But we had built a culture that embraced learning, even if it was uncomfortable. So she leaned into the opportunity and said, "You all are right. I missed a lot by not asking Bryan any questions. I wish I could rewind the clock."

Next up was to examine her story, looking for clues as to why she hadn't asked Bryan any questions. Her story at the time went like this: When she walked into the room with Bryan, she believed she had done her analysis and had come to the right answer. Any objections from Bryan were wrong, or even worse, defensive. She didn't consider the possibility that he might be able to show her something she had missed. She believed that her task in the conversation was to deliver the recommendations with enough finality and confidence that Bryan would concede, so that she could move on to deliver her team's conclusions to the CEO without Bryan becoming an obstacle.

As Alexa pieced together what her story was, it became abundantly clear that her action steps were perfectly aligned to that story: if her core task was to get Bryan to agree with her, it was understandable why she would assert her views, quickly push back on his concerns, and not ask him any questions.

But her colleagues in our workshop also showed her the many consequences of not asking questions. She had already experienced the worst one firsthand: Bryan fighting her in his office, and potentially in front of the CEO.

When Alexa looked at her story, her steps, and her results all mapped out—we literally diagrammed them out on a flip chart—she felt a kind of surprise that was simultaneously chagrined and enlightening.

Let's pause our tape again.

That moment of feeling simultaneously embarrassed but also enlightened, as gut churning and painful as it can be, is essential—that is the emotional experience of shifting from being *unconsciously* incompetent to being *consciously* incompetent. This realization can be extremely uncomfortable, even overwhelming, but it is also a moment of real possibility as you see for the first time how you got yourself stuck. You only need to develop new competence. And the first of those competences is to sit through that discomfort and not let it scare you off. It will pass, and you can move on to the excitement of skill building.

Strategies for Building Conscious Incompetence

- **DO: Locate or re-create your game tape.** To see what you need to do better, you need observable data of yourself *in action*. This could mean looking back on emails or texts you sent, or (even better) watching a recording of yourself during an interaction. The best athletes watch themselves in action on game tapes—why shouldn't you? Nowadays, especially with many meetings happening virtually, it's easy and often not a big deal to ask others for consent and press the Record button. It's even easy to have the meeting transcribed in real time. Whether you record it or have it transcribed, you have the chance to do what great athletes never stop doing: review your actions live. (If you can't access a record of yourself in action, use the two-column-case template to re-create the game tape. Even if your memory is not perfect, most of the time it's still good enough to learn from.)

- **DO: Look at your actions . . . *with* a friend or colleague.** Take a look at what action steps you took—or didn't take—and how those contributed to the results of your interaction. Pay special attention to whether and how well you took (or didn't take) each step of the *Ask* Approach. Then ask yourself what internal story you held and how this shaped the action steps you took. There are real limits to how well we can see our own incompetence. That's why pro athletes not only watch their game tapes, but do so with their coaches and teammates. Recruit your friends and colleagues to help you see what you need to do better.
- **DON'T: Let the discomfort stop you.** If you feel embarrassed, upset with yourself, or even ashamed, remember that this is normal. Look at it as a symptom of discovery, a clear sign that you are on a path to growth. Try to release any self-judgment and instead remind yourself that this is part of the learning process.

"I'm Trying Hard and Starting to Get It" (Creating Conscious Competence)

The next, and critical, stage is to start developing the new skills. This is the path from conscious *incompetence* to conscious *competence*. When we build conscious competence, we begin to develop the new skills, but implementing them takes a lot of concentration and effort.

The first thing to do when building conscious competence is to learn about the skills. You can do this through reading, watching videos, attending workshops, or asking an expert to teach you explicitly. The good news for you is that, if you've made it this far in the book, you've already done that research when it comes to the *Ask* Approach.

Once you know in your head what to do, you've got to put it into action. For example, no amount of watching YouTube videos will get you to master riding a bike. You have to actually get on the seat and pedal. The same thing goes for interacting with others. With riding a bike, there are training wheels (or balance bikes) to get you started. When it comes to interactions, the closest equivalent to training wheels is the role-play. A lot of people, when they first contemplate role plays, feel anxious and awkward; don't let that stop you—it will be worth it, I promise.

As she prepared to step into a role-play, with one of her colleagues playing Bryan, Alexa started with step 1 of the *Ask* Approach: she needed to **choose curiosity** when it came to Bryan and the knowledge he might have to contribute. With the group's help, she picked out a couple of curiosity questions to think about:

- What data might I have been unaware of that was informing Bryan's conclusions?
- How might my own behavior be influencing Bryan's reaction?

Feeling more genuinely curious now, Alexa was ready to role-play a conversation with Bryan. To help her prepare, she and her colleagues brainstormed some ways she could **make it safe**. She could let Bryan know that she was genuinely interested in his perspectives, whether or not they aligned with her recommendations. She could also acknowledge that his insights were essential to moving forward.

They then developed some **quality questions** that Alexa could pose to Bryan:

- "Bryan, can you tell me more about the prior times you've considered closing factories? What considerations did you weigh, and what risks were you concerned about?"
- "What do the sales fluctuations look like, and how do these play into your thinking that all the factories need to stay open?"

- "What might we have missed or overlooked in our approach?"
- "I'd love to hear more about the company's commitment to these communities. What is the story behind that?"

Alexa chose one of her colleagues to play Bryan. When the moment to begin approached, Alexa was reluctant to get started. So many people I've worked with hit this wall before their first role-play. *How could something contrived and artificial as a role-play possibly help?* they wonder. But Alexa suspended her reservations enough to give it a go.

As the role-play began, Alexa asked her first couple of new questions to the person playing Bryan. He replied in a warm tone and shared more information back with her than she'd received in a full hour of actually meeting with the real Bryan. *So far, so good,* Alexa thought; *I've got this.*

But then the person playing Bryan threw her a curveball. He didn't answer the question as openly and directly as Alexa expected. In fact, he started pushing back, saying, "I just don't think your recommendations make sense. I can't support them."

Wait, this wasn't what Alexa had been expecting from asking Bryan more questions! She got flustered, and all the original feelings she had about Bryan being an immovable obstacle came rushing back. In fact, she shifted back into a mode of telling him, in a combative tone, why he was wrong.

"Time-out," I called, so we could debrief what just happened.

Let's pause here for a moment. Building conscious competence isn't neat and clean. Sometimes you fall off the bike, just as Alexa did. This is why role-playing in lower-stakes environments (such as in workshops or with trusted friends) can be so helpful—if you get flustered or forget what to do, you can just get back on the bike and try again.

Now, back to the action:

I offered Alexa the chance to take a break and request that someone else take her place in the role-play (as if they were her). She was relieved and asked her colleague Greg to tag in. He simply said to Bryan, "I take your concern really seriously. Tell me more about the problems you see with our recommendations..."

That simple request changed everything. Bryan started to open up.

Alexa jumped in and said, "Okay, okay... let me try that again." She did, and things started to go much better. She even began implementing one of the **listen to learn** strategies—paraphrase and test—by asking Bryan, "Here's what I hear you saying... Did I get that right?"

We again paused the role-play to **reflect**. Alexa named what she saw herself doing differently—asking questions, really listening, asking follow-up questions, adjusting her internal story based on what she'd heard—and the person role-playing Bryan shared how different that felt to him compared to the beginning. He said he felt more heard and valued, and that it really seemed like Alexa cared about understanding where he was coming from. All of that led him to want to share much more.

During this first phase of skill development, you are learning a new process and working through each step deliberately. It can feel clunky, awkward, and cognitively demanding. Don't rush through it. During this early practice, Alexa began to experience conscious competence—the evidence that she now possesses skills that work and that would let her have a very different kind of interaction with Bryan, one where she can learn far more *and* better connect with him. But it didn't yet come naturally—she needed to concentrate, slow her reactions, take some deep breaths, and be very mindful with her words. Although she sometimes fell back on old patterns, she was forging a new set of skills.

Strategies for Building Conscious Competence

- **DO: Break it down.** Work through each step of the *Ask* Approach, one at a time. Take the time to study and try implementing each skill as you go.
- **DO: Prepare in advance.** It's not always easy to think of the right questions to ask in the heat of the moment. Especially when you're building up your competence, it's helpful to have some questions you can start with. Write them down in advance. You can even tell the other person that you've written down some questions you want to make sure you get to during the conversation.

- **DO: Insert speed bumps.** You don't have to always think on your feet with an immediate answer or question to ask. It's totally fine to say, in the middle of a conversation, "Hang on, this is too important to rush through; let me just stop and think about what you said for a moment." During that time, you can remind yourself to check if you've heard the other person correctly, or to ask a follow-up question.
- **DO: Practice in low-stakes situations.** It's important to start in situations that feel easier and more comfortable, and where it's okay if it doesn't always come out right. Role-plays with willing volunteers are among the safest, lowest-stakes situations, but you can also put your skills to work in real situations with friendly colleagues or friends. Let them know you're working on this and invite them to let you know how it's felt for them.
- **DO: Look for role models.** Make a practice of identifying and observing people in your life who are already good at the skills you'd like to master. When possible, ask them to tell you how they do it! But you need not limit your role models to those you know personally—they can be celebrities, historical figures, even fictional characters. (For me, it's the ever-curious TV character Ted Lasso!)
- **DON'T: Be surprised if it feels awkward.** If not, you're probably not pushing yourself enough to build new competence. New behaviors, preceded by new ways of thinking, are naturally awkward. Pay closer attention to the *outcomes* of your new approach; as you develop a track record of gains, it will become easier to embrace the initial awkward feeling. And if you fail, that's normal; congratulate yourself for trying!

"It Comes Naturally!" (Building Unconscious Competence)

This won't happen in a one-day workshop, but when Alexa ultimately reaches unconscious competence, the training wheels will come off and she won't have to think about the steps anymore. Her new skills will be habitual and natural. Difficult conversations won't seem quite as hard, and with time, they will get even easier. As journalist and lifelong learner Adam Gopnik writes in *The Real Work: On the Mystery of Mastery*, with practice, "the separate steps become a sequence, and the sequence then looks like magic."[2]

Alexa, like any of us, won't get there overnight. She'll need to deliberately practice choosing curiosity, making it safe, posing quality questions, listening to learn, and reflecting and reconnecting. She'll need to try it over and over again and gather feedback on her attempts. This might mean recording herself and listening to it after the fact. Or writing more two-column cases and looking back at them with peers. Or working with a coach who can observe her or reflect with her on past and upcoming interactions. But it could also look like asking friends or colleagues to let her know how her attempts are being received.

Here's the key to mastering anything to the point where it feels natural: deliberate cycles of repeated practice and feedback. Practice alone isn't enough—we have to blend practice with feedback from others that allows us to keep course-correcting and refining what we do.

My friend Tom St. Hilaire is a financial adviser to families. His success depends upon whether he's actually learned from clients what their most important goals are, what their current situation is, and what they truly think about his recommendations. He's dedicated himself to improving his asking and listening skills during his entire career, and at this point, he's truly a pro.

How did he get so good at this? For years, Tom would go to client meetings together with his partner, Hailey. This allowed him to use every meeting as an opportunity to both practice his questioning and listening skills and to get objective feedback on what he could do better. After each meeting, Tom and Hailey would debrief, walking through what they each heard. Hailey would point out places where his listening failed him—where he missed something, or misinterpreted a statement through the lens of his assumptions. Sometimes Tom and Hailey would disagree on what they heard, which gave them a chance to push each other's thinking. But every small correction, no matter how minor, gave Tom a chance to get a little bit better and fine-tune a new skill the next time. Perhaps even more important, it reminded him to stay humble and curious, no matter how many hundreds of families he listened to and advised.

Tom continues this practice to this day, whenever he and Hailey are in meetings together. Imagine how much better, how much more *competent,* we all could get if we honed our skills as deliberately as Tom does.

Strategies to Build Unconscious Competence

- **DO: Master one skill at a time.** For example, practice listening for content, emotion, and action one at a time as you are learning. Or asking questions to *clear up confusion,* such as, "Can you say more about what you mean by that…?" Focus only on that skill in your interactions until it's habitual and natural. Once you've got it, take a moment to appreciate the new muscle you've built, then pat yourself on the back and move on to the next skill.
- **DO: Practice, practice, practice.** The more you practice a skill, the more natural it will feel. After you're comfortable using it in one setting, try it in a different situation.
- **DO: Get feedback each time you practice**, whenever possible. For example, say, "Hey, this is something I'm trying to get better at. So, it would be helpful to know, how did it feel when I asked you those follow-up questions?"
- **DON'T: Stop growing.** Just as Tom, who has been doing this for decades, still practices and asks his business partner for feedback every time—and continues to benefit from it—so can we all!

Now, Level Up

Once you've made it to unconscious competence, you feel like a natural. Congrats! So, now what? You're done learning, right?

Well, yes and no. It's a spiral of mastery. As your life changes and you take on greater challenges and responsibilities, you'll need to stretch your *Ask* skills to meet these new demands. I like to think of leveling up as a series of cycles spiraling upward—almost like a strand of DNA; at each new level, you enter a new dimension of unconscious incompetence. You'll know when you reach that point because—suddenly, painfully—you'll feel stuck again. To return to our driving example, that moment might strike when you first leave the calm streets of your neighborhood and jump on the freeway at rush hour.

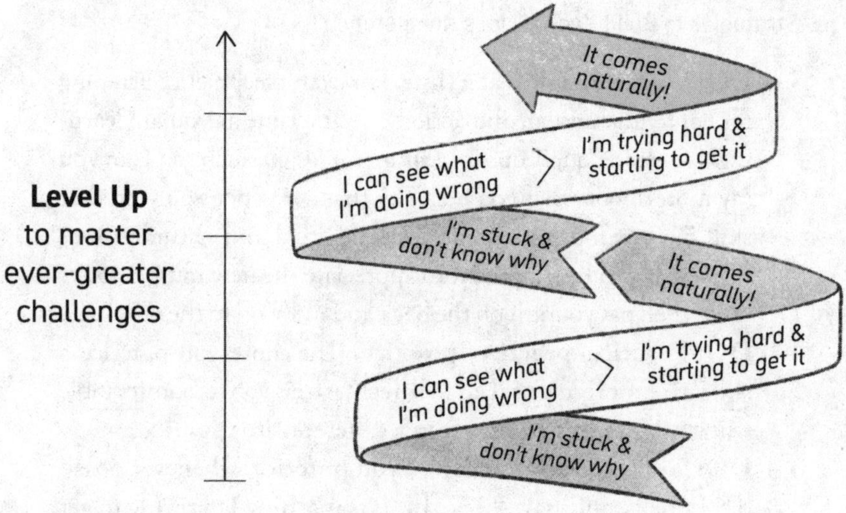

That moment came for Alexa when she got promoted to associate partner and began working with Whitney, the CEO of a new client company. All of a sudden, Alexa's job was no longer just to develop and deliver their team's analysis, but also to grow the firm's relationship with Whitney and sell new consulting projects.

After months in the role, Alexa was getting nowhere. Again and again, Whitney politely declined to consider buying new consulting projects, even though Alexa was genuinely convinced that these projects would help Whitney's business. Again, Alexa felt stuck—at the edge of her competence but unaware of what she was doing wrong.

So she did what she remembered worked for her in the past. She wrote a two-column case and brought it to our follow-up workshop, nearly a year later. In that workshop, her colleagues quickly helped Alexa see what she was doing wrong. She was pushing her ideas onto Whitney without first taking the time to understand Whitney's world: her hopes for the company, her deepest fears, her perspective on the business, her complicated relationship with her corporate board, and even her personal career aspirations. How could Alexa possibly deepen her relationship with Whitney and her company—let alone be helpful to them—if she didn't know any of this?

Alexa's first reaction was defensive: "But how can I possibly learn that kind of stuff when our meetings are fifteen minutes long and we can barely cover the tactical work of the current project?"

But had Alexa ever invited Whitney to a longer meeting?

I encouraged Alexa to try an "experiment" of sorts. What if, at the close of a meeting, she said, "Hey, Whitney, I'd love to have a different kind of conversation with you. I know what I think about your business, but I'd really like to get a better sense of *your* perspective. Would you be game to grab lunch one day?" Often, trying out an experiment at the level of our action steps is enough for us to realize that those new actions are beneficial.

Alexa wasn't quite ready to go there. So we looked at her internal story. Alexa believed that Whitney would never want to talk to her about anything other than a piece of analysis. And because she believed that, she felt that higher-level questions would seem inauthentic, and an invite to lunch could only end in embarrassing rejection.

As a group, we brainstormed alternative stories about Whitney that might make it easier for Alexa to stretch into these new action steps. One group member suggested a possible Whitney story that really caught Alexa's attention: *It's lonely to be a CEO, and it's very hard to find people you can trust with your most honest thoughts. It would be incredibly helpful and relieving to have an outside adviser who is actually interested in listening.* I encouraged Alexa to try on this new story, not because it was true (none of us knew if it was true) but to see if it felt like it might liberate her enough to try the experiment. As Alexa considered this new perspective, she was surprised at how it immediately inspired a greater level of care and empathy for Whitney than she had ever felt before.

Alexa agreed to try it out in a role-play. She took a deep breath and, with her partner, had a very different kind of conversation with "Whitney," one that would be far more likely to open up a deeper relationship and one filled with learning.

At Alexa's next meeting with Whitney, she kept in mind that she was just running an experiment, and no matter what happened, she would learn something. This mindset of trying out a different story to see what would happen kept Alexa's nervousness at bay. When their time together was up, Alexa smiled and asked Whitney to lunch, using a variation of the language Alexa took away from our workshop. Whitney didn't bat an eye. "Sure we can. Talk to my admin and get it on my schedule." A week later, Alexa and Whitney met at a sun-filled café for lunch. As they chatted, Alexa began to understand how much Whitney was juggling. She asked questions that gave her insight into Whitney's real needs and listened deeply. She heard that Whitney was actually far more open to Alexa's support than she had imagined, but that she was also overworked and anxious about her strained relationship with her board. Alexa walked away from the meeting with a deeper understanding of Whitney as a person. She felt hopeful that Whitney saw her in a new light as well, as someone who was willing to listen deeply enough that her recommendations might be worth considering. Only time and further conversation would answer that question, but no matter what, Alexa was happy to notice she was now looking forward to their next interaction.

Strategies for Stretching to the Next Level

- **DO: Remember the spiral.** When you feel newly challenged, stuck, or stymied, remember that you have merely reached the edge of your current competence level, and now you have an opportunity to grow. Instead of thinking, *This person is a jerk,* try a new attitude: *This situation goes beyond my current level of competence. It's an opportunity for me to stretch up and expand my skills.* This attitude is fundamentally more empowering and encourages you to then take the steps to stretch and grow.

- **DO: Experiment with new action steps.** When you grow to the next level of your competence, by definition you may not have the repertoire of stories and steps needed to handle the new situation's challenge and complexity. But you can experiment with one *Ask* skill at a time. See what happens. If you like what you get, try doing more. If you don't, consider a different strategy (or ask someone for help).
- **DO: Experiment with a different story.** If you're not ready to experiment with different action steps, then experiment with a different story. If you think the other person is wrong, experiment with this story: "They may actually have an important point, but I don't yet see what it is." If you think the other person is out to get you, experiment with "They may not intentionally be trying to hurt me. They might be at the edge of *their* competence." You don't have to actually believe the experimental story; you just need to try it out enough to experiment with different steps and see what happens.
- **DON'T: Interpret the results of your experiment alone.** When you're at the edge of your competence, you're liable to interpret your experiment based on assumptions from your old story. Getting someone else's eyes on what happened can help you break free.

Over time, the cycle of learning itself becomes second nature. The awkwardness, the curveball reactions, even the experiments that falter, become tangible signs not of failure but of necessary struggle as you progress along the cycle. If you stick with it, you'll start to see meaningful differences within weeks and months.

But there's one thing you can do right away, in this moment: Imagine life as a series of fascinating experiments, in which the most challenging people and situations are not working against you. They are portals through which to gather information, test hypotheses, and deepen your understanding of the world. Stay in that mindset, and your superpowers will keep on growing.

SUMMARY OF KEY POINTS

Essential question: How can you become a world-class asker?

1. To get good at any new skill, we have to work our way around and up the mastery spiral:
   - To move from **unconscious incompetence** toward **conscious incompetence**: Walk through a recent challenging interaction with a friend or group and look for areas where you could have applied aspects of the *Ask* Approach.
   - To create **conscious competence**: Break down the steps and work through them one at a time. Concentrate as you implement them one by one.
   - To build **unconscious competence**: Take your new skills out into the real world in increasingly challenging situations. Practice and ask for feedback each step of the way.
2. Expect awkwardness, frustration, discomfort, and backslides—these are all part of the learning process!
3. Try one new skill at a time, not all at once.
4. Practice your new skills with trusted learning partners to supercharge and speed up your mastery.
5. Start in low-stakes situations and environments—with friends, family, or close colleagues—and work your way up to more challenging situations.
6. Learning any new skill requires ongoing *practice* and *feedback*.
7. When you reach the next level of challenge, try experimenting with new action steps (and if needed, new stories), even if you aren't yet sure if they'll work. You'll learn a lot by trying them out and reflecting with a trusted peer on what happens!

EXERCISES

8A. Try out the *Ask* Assessment to reflect on your overall level of competence in asking questions and your skills at each part of the *Ask* Approach. You can find it at www.AskApproach.com.

8B. Think about a professional or personal situation where you truly felt stuck. Try looking at that situation through the lens of competence—is there an *Ask* skill you hadn't implemented well? Consider each step:

- Choosing curiosity
- Making it safe
- Posing quality questions
- Listening to learn
- Reflecting and reconnecting

8C. Now, pick out one of these skills and work intentionally to build your competence in it. Try one or more of these strategies:

- Write out how you'd say or implement it before trying it out.
- Find a trusted friend or colleague to role-play it with you.
- Use it in a low-stakes situation, and ask those around you for feedback.
- Practice it in a range of (perhaps more challenging) situations, continuing to ask for feedback.

Chapter 9

Make It Your *Organization's* Superpower

Essential question: How can you unlock the collective genius of your team?

WHO DOESN'T LOVE A GOOD COOKIE? I KNOW I DO. ESPECIALLY when I can dip it in milk.

Well, one day, a gentleman who also loves a good cookie peeled open a fresh pack of Oreos, only to find a crumbled mess of broken cookies. When he bought another package at his local store, he found the exact same issue.

Our story might have ended with him making an ice cream sundae topped with the broken cookies—except that this gentleman was actually a newly minted board member at Mondelēz International, the parent company of Oreo. And so, he went straight to the top. He brought the quality issue to the attention of the entire board and to the CEO of Mondelēz at the time, Irene Rosenfeld.

Irene was stunned. If a quality-control issue had shown up in the cookies of one of her own board members, chances were there were already crumbled Oreos in packages all over the country or even the world. How had this happened? Every Oreo factory had systems in place to catch and fix exactly this type of problem. And why was she just finding out about it now? Irene decided that the best way to find out what had gone wrong in the packaging system was to ask the people at the front lines: the factory workers.

It turned out that the plant that was packaging the cookies had recently installed a fancy new machine that could package up to six times the number of cookies at once compared to the previous machines. But, clearly, something had gone awry with this machine, and the cookies were crumbling.

Most likely, the employees on the line had noticed something was off, and if they did, they weren't sharing their concerns aloud. Or if they were, their supervisors weren't escalating it to the people who needed to know. Who would want to be the bearer of bad news or the one to slow down progress, especially when demand was booming? Upper-level management remained unaware of the problem for far too long. While, thankfully, there were no health or safety concerns, it took months to rectify this problem and cost Mondelēz financially.

If only the company could have tapped into the knowledge of frontline workers *before* it was too late, so much time and money and headache could have been saved. This experience led Irene to wonder, what would need to change for the organization to consistently tap its own collective intelligence? What would it look like to be an organization that centers asking and learning in its strategy and decision-making?

So far in this book, we've primarily explored asking as an act that happens between individual people. But Irene's observations as the Mondelēz CEO are ones that *all of us* should be asking about the organizations in which we work. **Whether you lead an entire company, a team of five—or even if you're simply a member of a team—you are in a position to build asking more deeply into your organization.** You'll see immediate benefits from doing so.

ORGANIZATIONS ASK TOO

In today's world, so many of our most important actions and decisions occur by and through the vehicle of the organization. It is through organizations that we innovate, respond to macro-challenges like market disruptions and climate change, and distribute precious social resources like aid and education. Just as individuals can learn to make better decisions, be more creative, and understand our impact on others more deeply by asking those around them, organizations can also tap into the collective intelligence of those around them: their customers, partners, and employees.

Why the Stakes Have Never Been Higher

The stakes of asking at the organizational level have never been higher. Whatever the industry, we are all operating amid unprecedented uncertainty. A mounting body of research shows that, in this context, many aspects of the *Ask* Approach are strongly predictive of organizational performance. Teams in which members feel safe admitting mistakes, expressing uncertainty, and communicating openly consistently perform better, learn faster, and are more innovative than those with lower levels of psychological safety.[1] Increased curiosity in the organizational setting has been linked to richer information exchange, more creativity, and reduced conflict.[2] Organizations that are better at learning from their members are better at adapting within uncertain environments,[3] a critical skill in a world characterized by rapid technological development, cultural change, and environmental precariousness. My own experience building and leading organizations has shown me over and over again that finding out what our staff and clients really know, feel, and believe creates vastly better outcomes, often in a fraction of the time.

Collections of Individuals vs. Collective Genius

An organization, by definition, is a collection of individuals working together toward a common goal. The goals of organizations can vary widely, from producing smartphones to curing cancer to educating children, but all organizations share the common feature of collectivity. And wherever there is a collective of people, there is the potential for *collective genius*.[4] Collective genius happens when a group of people come together and share their ideas, knowledge, experiences, and brainpower. It unleashes a cognitive power and capacity for creativity that exceeds that of any single individual. By harnessing and amplifying collective genius, 1 + 1 + 1 equals infinite potential. To me, few social phenomena are cooler or more exciting than collective genius (especially since in many conventional organizations, 1 + 1 + 1 equals 2 at best). The old model of individualistic competition within organizations stifles the kind of collective sharing and learning required for breakthroughs and success.

Collective genius isn't just a passive by-product of collections of individuals, or of organizations, for that matter. As Bruce Patton, world expert on interpersonal communication and co-founder of the Harvard Negotiation Project, explained to me, it is the product of *effective interpersonal learning*. In other words, the key that distinguishes organizations that tap into and benefit from collective genius from those that don't is *the degree to which members are able to consistently learn from one another*, which, Bruce points out, often requires having potentially difficult conversations. As I've argued throughout this book, the best way to learn from those around us is to *ask*. This holds true at the organizational level as well as the interpersonal. So, how can organizations tap into their own collective genius? Just like you, they need to make asking their superpower.

Organizations that "ask"—whether public or private, large or small—make decisions that consistently tap into the genius of key stakeholders, the most important of which are end users and employees. Companies that ask build it into the bones of the organization itself, into HR practices like hiring and training. They ritualize practices of asking among employees and teams, and they operationalize asking through annual learning cycles and meaning-making activities. Lastly, their leaders demonstrate curiosity, humility, question-asking, and listening through their own behavior, setting the tone from the top.

Tap into the Genius of End Users

Emily Weiss didn't set out to break the beauty industry. And yet, that is exactly what happened when Glossier, the direct-to-consumer beauty brand she founded burst onto the scene in 2014, building a devoted following amounting to a $1 billion–plus valuation less than a decade later.

Key to the brand's wild success was, from the very beginning, its customers, in whom Weiss recognized an immense and untapped source of valuable information. "I was interviewing hundreds of women from around the world," Weiss reflected, "and I realized that there was a real disconnect between the beauty brands and the customer. They weren't communicating with her—they were talking down to her . . . rather than having a conversation, which was leaving a lot of women at arm's length." Before Glossier even had its first prototype, the company was working directly with would-be customers to co-create the vision, a relationship that would come to define the company's approach to everything from product development to marketing to customer service.[5]

One way in which Glossier centers the collective genius of its end users is by integrating customer service in every wing of the company, rather than sequestering it in some satellite office or outsourcing it to a third party like many organizations do. In this way, the company is constantly asking its customers questions: *What's working? What's not? What else would you be interested in seeing from us? How can we serve you better?* The company has even used a Slack channel—an easy, comfortable digital space for building connection, similar to our "make it safe" recommendations in Chapter 4—for its most loyal customers to provide detailed feedback on its products. While most organizations struggle to get people to fill out even basic surveys (the accuracy of which is variable at best), Glossier has a consistently engaged and enthusiastic customer base more than happy to share information that is invaluable to the brand's continued success.

Glossier is not alone in finding ways to engage end users to produce a constant inflow of quality learning. Major organizations like Google, Intel, and Samsung (to name just a few) are increasingly hiring corporate ethnographers, psychologists and sociologists, and others specifically trained in communications and qualitative research for just this purpose. I spoke with Sheethal Shobowale, a senior user experience (UX) researcher at Google and an expert at asking in ways that unlock the greatest learning from Google's end users. Sheethal and other UX researchers on her team employ many of the practices explored in this book in ways that make it safe for clients to share openly and honestly.

They ask questions designed to unearth the most useful information about end users' needs and experiences, listen deeply, and translate what they learn into actionable insights. This process consistently produces information about aspects of the products that only the user can really see, since, as Sheethal pointed out, "When you've looked at something for so long, you forget how different it is for someone using it for the first time."

Because it puts time and resources into *asking*, Google is able to access a wealth of knowledge that would likely remain unspoken if it relied on users to reach out with feedback. Moreover, customers value being involved in the design process. They are often eager to share their thoughts and experiences. Sheethal emphasized the mutually enriching nature of this process—the information shared by end users is invaluable to project managers, product designers, and engineers who can digest that data into better products and a better user experience. Sheethal often hears these teams referencing user quotes from her interviews in their product development meetings.

Strategies to Ask End Users

- **DO: Make it a priority to know and understand your end users.** Treat them like thoughtful, complex people who have brilliant ideas as well as a wide range of needs, desires, and hopes that would be incredibly valuable for you to know. Watch them in their everyday lives. Build these priorities into people's job responsibilities. Develop and focus on questions to learn about them. Don't stop after you do it once.
- **DO: Create multiple ways for your end users to tell you what they think, feel, and want.** Don't rely on them to proactively make suggestions or comments. Go ask them!
- **DO: Develop ongoing relationships with consistent users.** Invite them into your teams and communities. Make it not just safe but worth it for them to give you critiques and crazy ideas.
- **DON'T: Forget to thank them.** Circle back and let your end users know the impact of their feedback.

Find Wisdom in the Front Line

In my experience, the most valuable, and essential, source of ideas, knowledge, and information in any organization lies in its employees, particularly those closest to the front lines. Teachers, nurses, factory workers, customer service representatives, sales staff, retail employees, cashiers, and truck drivers are all examples of employees whose proximity to real "action" gives them access to information largely invisible to those higher up in the organization.

While "tapping the front line" has become widely acknowledged as an organizational necessity, few companies have successfully moved from theory to effective practice. Efforts to involve the front line are typically too superficial or disconnected for employees to trust that any time and energy they invest will affect decision-making. Many companies do some version of "ask quality questions" but forget all the other steps of the *Ask* Approach.

I found myself guilty of making this mistake when I first arrived at Teach For America and was charged with leading my realm (teacher training and ongoing support) through a massive five-year expansion. One of the reasons I and others in the corporate sector had been recruited was that we had experiences advising and running organizations at the scale TFA wanted to reach. We took on this challenge with gusto and confidently started applying all kinds of corporate, data-driven management techniques to this education organization: we implemented goals, metrics, accountability systems, dashboards, organizational designs with rational spans of control, and so on.

As we went about this, all the growth-related numbers kept ticking upward just as we would expect, except for one. For several quarters, our satisfaction surveys showed that morale among teachers and staff was slowly decreasing. Even as we succeeded in tripling the size of the organization while maintaining consistent technical quality metrics, we were dampening people's spirits. My team and I had been so busy optimizing for scale and performance that we'd overlooked the ways in which these changes were affecting the people on the front lines.

We started to realize that we couldn't simply apply, in a top-down way, whatever ideas we drummed up in our conference room at headquarters.

To make better organization-wide decisions, we needed information that only those on the front lines had access to—for example, the unintended consequences of our performance metrics on how teachers were teaching and students were learning. Meanwhile, the extent of our "asking" among teachers and staff had been limited to surveys, focus groups, and interviews. Teachers doubted these data-collection tools would produce useful change and therefore didn't take them seriously. As a result, we had no deep insight into what they really thought, knew, felt, or even wanted. This realization gave us a swift kick in the pants to **choose curiosity** to a far greater extent than we had before.

We then needed a different and better way to learn from our colleagues in the field. We investigated the fields of design thinking and action research, and developed a new approach to decision-making that involved our front line. Calling the initiative "Collaborative Innovation," we knew the first thing we'd need to do was to **make it safe** for people to share and not be intimidated by what could be perceived as "higher-ups from headquarters." So we started by gathering together many small groups of teachers and their supervisors. We shared the challenges and dilemmas that had led to all the organization-level changes, then asked **quality questions** designed to surface their best ideas to create a management system that balanced the need for organization-wide information with the unique local realities in each region. We let them know that anything was discussable and all ideas were valuable to surface. We used design protocols to surface people's best, wildest ideas, and then we asked staff to prioritize those ideas and even build prototypes of how new management systems could work. We **listened** hard **to learn** their best ideas.

Although I hadn't yet created the *Ask* Approach, you might notice that Collaborative Innovation is remarkably like its five steps, with a twist of organizational design theory. And just as this approach can lead to new revelations and solutions in one-on-one conversations, so it did with our broader organization. Alongside some of our original performance metrics, teachers and their supervisors added their own personal vision statements, which served as their true North Stars to guide their efforts. These gave local control back to the teacher, whose vision statement would include goals that were personally energizing and aligned with the unique needs of their individual classrooms and communities. The passion that had brought them to teaching began to rebound, now that they were working toward aims that supported them in bringing their best to their work. The process of co-creation not only tapped into the organization's collective genius but also unleashed enormous energy and inspiration in our staff.

This experience taught me that the job of leaders isn't to come up with the solutions. It's to get really curious about the experiences and knowledge hidden in the minds of the organization's stakeholders and to build the culture and systems that unlock that collective genius. Teachers and staff who supported them knew, better than we did, how to address the challenges, and we in management needed to create a very different relationship with them in order to access that insight.

Strategies to Ask Employees

- **DO: Reduce the effects of power dynamics** as much as possible by acknowledging that you have a dilemma or puzzle and *need their partnership* to take it on. Name the value you see and place in their perspective.
- **DO: Let them know in advance how final decisions will be made** and what roles they will play in making and/or influencing the decisions. Ideally, let the decisions get made as close to the front lines as you can.
- **DO: Let them in on the challenge by exposing them to all the data points you can**, while asking them to help you revise your understanding of the issues by adding additional information that they uniquely see.
- **DO: Empower them to develop new solutions** by asking "How might we . . ." questions and generating as many creative ideas as possible *before* any ideas are evaluated or discarded. Invite them to prioritize the solutions they see as most relevant and share their reasons why.
- **DO: Consistently report back to employees how their ideas and feedback informed organizational decisions.**

When you can't act on their ideas or feedback or can't respond right away, let them know why and what you plan to do next.

- **DON'T: Feel like you need to have all the answers.** Instead, bring your thorniest questions to the people who are closest to the action: those on your front line.

Build Asking into Your People Practices

Organizations that ask need individual employees that ask too, if they want learning to really take root. Essential places to bake this skill set into your people practices are in hiring, training programs, and feedback rituals.

When I was interviewing to work at Monitor Group, the business consulting firm that was my first professional home after graduating from college, the final step of the process—unbeknownst to me—was receiving critical feedback on the performance task I had been asked to complete. This caught me off guard, as it hadn't happened in any of the other interview processes I'd participated in—typically, they either gave me an offer, or told me I didn't get the job.

I later learned that this critical feedback was a test, one given to every candidate who made it to the final stage. The purpose was to see how the potential hire responded to critique. Would they jump to defend themselves, listing reasons why the feedback was wrong? Would they take it silently, just nodding and moving on? Or would they demonstrate a deeper curiosity about the feedback—and maybe even ask a few questions? While I was a bit bewildered when I received the feedback, I must have demonstrated a sufficient level of curiosity and openness to learning, because the next day they let me know I had gotten the job!

Thanks in part to this practice, the people I met at Monitor are, to this day, some of the most curious, inquisitive, and growth-oriented individuals I have ever known. And the company didn't rely merely on this initial competency. Rather, they further developed it through frequent training. For example, every consultant at Monitor got a full-day training in what was called at the time "giving and receiving feedback." As people grew in seniority, the duration and intensity increased to multiple days throughout multiple years. Through significant investment, Monitor trained people at many levels of the organization—and in every local office—to teach others this material and support them in applying it. The most senior members of the firm had access to expert coaches to ensure they were applying and modeling the skills both internally and with clients. Over time, concepts like the *left-hand column* and the *ladder* and *balancing advocacy (telling) and inquiry (asking)* became part of the common parlance throughout the organization. This allowed everyone to not only keep the skills top of mind personally but to support one another collectively.

To really bake asking into an organization's DNA, it's important to establish feedback rituals that encourage employees to practice and prioritize asking and sharing. One effective strategy that I've used is the 2x2 (two-by-two) method. Twice a year at Transcend, each person in the organization is required to have an individual conversation with every person they work closely with. In these meetings, each participant must share two things the other person is doing well along with two things they could improve upon. They then do the same for themselves. This structure forces people to say what might otherwise remain unspoken by normalizing asking and sharing and reflecting via a collective practice. Otherwise put, the practice relieves employees of the burden of having to make an awkward ask for critical feedback. The practice itself does the asking, and in so doing normalizes and promotes a culture of employees asking each other for feedback more broadly. Invariably, coworkers share things in 2x2s that would likely not have been shared without the prompt. I like to think of it like the ritual of clearing out a closet a few times a year—sometimes we need a committed practice to bring into the open all that has been piling up in the back of our minds.

Strategies to Bake Asking into Your People Practices

- **DO: Hire for curiosity, listening, and reflection.** Don't stop at asking for past examples of these traits—find ways for candidates to demonstrate them authentically in their behaviors during the hiring process. Also, solicit input from references on how well candidates have exhibited these skills in the past.

- **DO: Build these skills into your organization's competency and performance management models**, so people get evaluated on how well they learn from others and get positive reinforcement when they are doing well.
- **DO: Establish feedback rituals that normalize asking as part of the organization's ethos.** Set up annual or biannual 2x2s as a container for employees to ask each other questions that might feel awkward otherwise. Emphasize the value of giving and receiving feedback for everyone in the organization.
- **DO: Train people in asking, listening, and reflection**, all the way to the point of mastery.
- **DON'T: Treat it like a box to check.** Invest in ongoing reinforcement of skills through coaching and feedback practices that help people move the ideas in this book from the page into practice.

Lead Learning Cycles

It is often said that "what gets measured gets managed." This is as true for learning as it is for customer satisfaction or on-time deliveries. Unless organizations formally integrate learning measures into how they evaluate their own performance, learning will remain in the untended arena of the "nice-to-haves," collecting dust in some rusty cabinet instead of acting as a driving force for growth. Further, what we measure reflects what we *value*. By setting learning goals in addition to performance goals, the organization not only improves its chances of learning in a consistent and effective way but also communicates that commitment to employees, customers, and clients.

At Transcend, we operationalize asking through our annual learning cycle, a practice as core to our organization as anything else. In fact, we have an entire process, designed by our chief learning officer, Jenee Henry Wood, dedicated to surfacing, synthesizing, and sharing the collective learnings of our team. The cycle begins by setting a *learning agenda*, in which Jenee's team asks staff from every corner of the organization what topics they are working on and what kinds of information and insights they anticipate developing over the coming year. This step generates a rich list of fodder, which we then prioritize into a set of learning questions we then hope to be able to address over the coming year. Having a learning agenda—a list of *actionable, concise,* and *testable* questions—and a robust process for pursuing insights from everywhere, allows us to develop specific protocols for pursuing answers (who to interview, what statistics to dig up, what kinds of topics to ask about on a survey) in a systematic, manageable way. But this is just the first step.

Throughout the year, Jenee and colleagues facilitate conversations with staff called "table talks" and "project pit stops." These encourage staff members to share what they're seeing—what's working, where they're feeling tensions—and what they're learning from it. Included in these conversations are a combination of people's personal experiences and observations as well as quantitative data we collect about what's happening in each project. Jenee and her team then synthesize the hundreds of amazing nuggets they collect from across the organization into insights that validate, challenge, or complicate Transcend's approach to the work. We reflect on these insights all together as an organization each year, inviting team members to name what *they* see as implications for how we can get better and do better.

The changes that result from this process are not superficial; they have substantially evolved what we do from the ground up. For example, when we started Transcend, we believed that the best way to change education was by developing "breakthrough models" of new school designs, which would then be adopted by schools everywhere. The case for this approach became quickly nuanced when we added it to our learning agenda. We came to realize that we were too narrowly focused on the "supply" side of innovation. But what about the "demand" side of the equation—the communities who would be implementing our models? We began to focus on partnering with communities to learn what they wanted and needed, how they could go about incorporating new designs into their schools, and building models that accounted for those factors. Making teachers, families, and most important, students themselves (the ultimate "customers") *partners* in a local design process led to more successful, sustainable innovation and better outcomes. I believe that if we had only stuck to our initial approach, our organization would not have had nearly the impact we've seen over the years.

Strategies to Lead Learning Cycles

- **DO: Set a learning agenda.** Choose concrete, answerable questions and objectives and prioritize them alongside other top-level performance goals.
- **DO: Build these learning objectives into leaders' job responsibilities** to signal the high-priority level, and equip them with the time and resources to pursue the learning.
- **DO: Ask multiple types of questions.** Make space for asking targeted questions to find information you know you need, as well as more open-ended learning processes, which create a channel for unexpected data, ideas, and feedback to emerge.
- **DO: Create "learning loop" processes**—formal structures and rituals—where teams systematically gather and make meaning of insights from people inside and outside the organization. Consider establishing a team dedicated to organizational asking and learning.
- **DON'T: Forget to report back on the findings.** Keep the organization updated on findings and insights that come out of the learning agenda—including areas that still feel murky and uncertain—and invite their reactions and refinements to what emerges.

Promote Yourself to "Learner in Chief"

I firmly believe that every member of every organization has an opportunity to exert leadership. However, those who are in positions of formal authority have special roles to play. Leaders who emphasize, model, and reward the practices of asking and learning increase the chances that people throughout the organization will do so.

Unfortunately, leaders too rarely do this. In one survey of over twenty-seven thousand people, 42 percent of respondents said their organization never or only rarely "openly shares the challenges facing it," while only 15 percent of respondents reported that their organizations always share their challenges.[6] Leaders can't hope to tap into collective genius if they are unwilling to reveal the questions they are grappling with and what problems need solving. And while many executives intellectually understand the importance of demonstrating and encouraging curiosity in their organizations, the benefits of which have been well documented and taught in business schools for years,[7] few go as far as to actually translate that idea into their own behavior or into the workings of the organization itself.

I have come to believe that the most helpful role a leader can play in fostering learning throughout an organization is to be the "learner in chief." That is, the person who most publicly embodies what it means to be curious, ask questions, and learn from others. By doing this, they send the message that asking and learning is not only allowed but vital—in fact, it is the path toward success.

What I've found in my own experience is that the more I model the behaviors of curiosity, learning, and asking, the more others exhibit them too. One of my favorite mantras is "If you aren't embarrassed by who you were last year, you aren't learning fast enough."[8] As a leader, I try to share and repeat this over and over again to remind people that as awkward as learning in public can be, it won't get you in trouble in our organization. It's our best chance to grow and improve, to make better decisions, and to have meaningful, productive relationships with one another and with the partners we support.

Strategies for Becoming the Learner in Chief

- **DO: Publicly share your own learning and development goals**, needs, dilemmas, and challenges.
- **DO: Foster a culture of openness by modeling vulnerability yourself.** Allow people to see you as a full, complex, flawed human being. To the extent that you can, let people in

on your process—for example, speaking openly about work or personal challenges you have experienced.

- **DO: Seek feedback and input publicly**—don't just invite it but actively go seek it out. Even if you don't receive it publicly, reflect on it publicly by sharing what feedback you have received and how you are making meaning of it.
- **DO: Thank and publicly acknowledge those who gave you input.** Let them know what you plan to do with the input, and why.
- **DON'T: Expect it to feel comfortable.** Asking and learning goes against many norms that suggest leaders need to appear like they have it all figured out. If it's awkward, uncomfortable, and even a little scary, you're doing it right.

Organizations, like leaders (like all of us!), are a work in process. At Transcend, one of our core values is something we call *perpetual beta*. Perpetual beta reflects the idea that we are and will always be a work in progress, meaning that we are always asking what works and what doesn't and growing from what we learn. What's important is not that we've somehow "arrived" or gotten it perfect (this will never happen), but rather that we never forget where genius lives—in the learning that can only happen in ongoing collaboration.

SUMMARY OF KEY POINTS

Essential question: How can you unlock the collective genius of your team?

1. The *Ask* Approach can happen at the level of teams and organizations too. When organizations ask, they are far more successful.
2. To adapt and thrive in our fast-paced and uncertain world, organizations must learn to tap into the collective genius of their stakeholders.

3. How to build organizations that ask:

    - **Tap into the genius of end users** by systematically asking clients and customers about their needs, experiences, opinions, and ideas.
    - **Find wisdom in the front lines** by engaging staff in strategy and decision-making from start to finish.
    - **Build asking into your people practices** by hiring for curiosity and investing in ongoing training in the *Ask* skill set.
    - **Lead learning cycles** by setting a learning agenda and prioritizing learning objectives alongside other key performance indicators.
    - **Become a learner in chief** by being open about the challenges and uncertainties you're dealing with and publicly prioritizing learning. Lead by example.

EXERCISES

9A. Identify a challenging issue or decision that your organization or team is facing. Now, consider:

- What steps are you taking to unlock the collective genius of everyone involved?
- How much are end users, staff members, and other key constituents not only informing your understanding but co-creating the solution?
- If there's room to unlock more collective genius, try one or more of the strategies from this chapter!

9B. Evaluate the people practices of your organization, relative to the *Ask* Approach. To what extent are you:

- Hiring for curious question askers?
- Building these skills into how you manage and reward performance?

- Establishing rituals (such as the 2x2 process) that normalize asking?
- Training people in asking, learning, and reflecting?

Now, choose one of these where there's room for improvement and make a plan to try this out in your team or department.

9C. Promote yourself to learner in chief! Try:

- Publicly sharing your learning and development goals
- Modeling vulnerability and openness (while accounting for the complex realities of culture and identity in your particular context)
- Inviting feedback and input . . . and doing so publicly
- Thanking and publicly acknowledging all who gave you input, and sharing back what you learned

How did it feel to try this? Where and how could you go even further?

Chapter 10

Make It the *Next Generation's* Superpower

Essential question: How can we stop squelching kids' curiosity and unleash their asking?

RHONDA BROUSSARD IS ONE OF THE MOST CURIOUS PEOPLE I know. She has built her life around asking questions. The most recent organization she founded, Beloved Community, partners with companies and nonprofits in a wide variety of industries to increase equity in communities, workplaces, and schools in part by teaching them to ask and learn from their community members. She has designed tools that organizations can use to ask better questions. Before that, she founded and ran the St. Louis Language Immersion School, a free progressive school where students learn to collaborate closely with peers, all while mastering French, Spanish, or Chinese. She literally wrote a curiosity-inspired book called *One Good Question*, which chronicles the ways in which she has used questions to connect and transform throughout her life and career. How did Rhonda become such a curious, creative asker of questions?

Rhonda, like all children, was born full of questions. What does my foot taste like? Where does the moon go every morning? Where do babies come from? But unlike most children, whose question-asking tends to decline throughout childhood and mostly stops by the time they enter adolescence, Rhonda held on to her curiosity throughout childhood and into adulthood. How did this happen?

To understand how Rhonda became an adult who asks, we have to go back in time, to her first day of third grade. Rhonda, along with a handful of other students who had been identified as "gifted," was selected for a program called the "Wonder Y's." The Wonder Y's were sectioned off into a separate classroom and given special T-shirts, bright yellow with a big "Y" emblazoned across the chest like a superhero costume. In the Wonder Y's classroom, school became a place to *wonder*. Teachers asked the students what they thought and what meaning they made of what they were learning, instead of providing the answers themselves. Their classroom was filled with all kinds of books and puzzles and art supplies that they could access as their curiosity led them, moving from cozy reading chairs to clusters of tables to science stations as they liked. The messages she was receiving at school were reflected and reinforced at home by her exceptionally encouraging parents and grandmother. Taken together, these early experiences nurtured Rhonda's innate curiosity and set her up with the love of learning and self-confidence for a lifetime of asking.

Unfortunately, Rhonda's story is the exception, not the rule. Far more often, children's experiences, at school and at home, serve to squash their natural curiosity and question-asking, rather than to foster it. At the other extreme was the experience of Rhonda's uncle, who was only a few months older and grew up in the same home as her. While they received similar encouragement at home, their experiences at school could not have been more different. Rhonda's uncle, who was not part of the Wonder Y's program, spent his days at school sitting at a desk, receiving direct instruction from a teacher who seemed to have all the answers. He wasn't given the space to explore or question or to honor his own curiosity, even though Rhonda knew that he wanted and would enjoy the space to wonder just as much as she did. Rhonda watched him struggle, sensing even from that young age that there was something deeply wrong in the way schools separated their learning environments.

HUMANS ARE BORN CURIOUS, BUT IT DOESN'T LAST

Children are born full of curiosity. Before they can speak, their questions take the form of observation and action. They look intensely at objects and people that are unfamiliar. They experiment with the world around them, putting everything they can find into their mouth. They push things over; they tinker with and take things apart. Their curiosity is voracious, adorable, and, to new parents, a source of endless trouble. By the time they stop eating dirt and crawling dangerously close to the top of the stairs, they have learned a new way to pursue their insatiable desire to know: questions. Specifically, a category of questions called "W-H questions" (what, where, why, when, how).

As research by developmental psychologists has shown, when kids discover they can ask these questions, they go to town. In a landmark study of children's question-asking behavior, Barbara Tizard and Martin Hughes attached tape recorders (the 1984 version of the GoPro) to nursery-aged children so as to listen to their conversations throughout the day.[1] They discovered that, on average, children asked their parents between twenty-five and fifty questions per *hour*. Another study of mothers in the United Kingdom showed that question-asking tends to peak around age four, with children asking their mums an average of 390 questions per day, or about one question every 1 minute 56 seconds![2]

Importantly, the majority of these questions are aimed at gathering information (Why are you doing that? When are we leaving? What sound do clouds make?), rather than, for example, asking permission (May I be excused?). Many of these questions are seeking not just facts but a deeper explanation, indicative of the powerful curiosity at work in the minds of young children as well as their belief that the people around them have answers.[3] And, as research psychologist Susan Engel points out in *The Hungry Mind: The Origins of Curiosity in Childhood*, much of the early question-asking done by children is oriented toward finding things out about other people through other people. Kids, like grown-ups, love to gossip. The near universality of gossip, Engel suggests, reveals something about our "fundamental curiosity about other people's lives."[4] In other words, kids aren't just born curious. They are born with a hefty dose of connective curiosity.

But then a strange thing happens. Right at the moment one might think kids would get even more curious (when they start school), they start asking *fewer* questions. By the time they reach adolescence, most kids have stopped asking questions at all.[5]

Part of this is developmental. As we learned in Chapter 3, our urge for novel information gathering diminishes as we age, which naturally leads us to ask fewer questions than in those early childhood years. But developmental psychology explains only part of the picture. It cannot explain, for example, why, when Tizard and Hughes studied the transcripts of the children at school, they found that the same kids who were asking twenty to fifty questions per hour at home only asked about two questions per hour while they were at school.[6]

The story of Rhonda's uncle completes the puzzle: Most kids are discouraged from asking in school. It is a place where they are taught to *receive* learning instead of actively seeking it. This is not by accident but by design. The so-called factory, or industrial, model of education is over one hundred years old and has persisted despite fundamental changes in economic and social organization in the years since. It was designed to get masses of young people (whether influxes of immigrants or from farms throughout the country) trained, socialized, and ready for work in a factory-based industrial economy. It rewards individual achievement over teamwork, conformity over creativity, and staying quiet over speaking up. It was certainly never designed to produce interpersonally curious, collaborative question askers. And unfortunately, in our education system and beyond, opportunities to express and cultivate curiosity are not distributed equally among children.

Across the United States, cities that have "gifted and talented" programs like Rhonda's are scrambling to address the sad reality that it has led to segregated classrooms, laying bare the widespread educational inequity in the nation. Even students in the same classes, with the same teachers, can have meaningfully different experiences. Race, class, ethnicity, disability, and other dimensions of difference all affect how students are treated: whether their questions are encouraged and answered earnestly; whether their challenges are met with patience or punishment; and worst of all, whether they are made to feel safe and guided toward the discovery of their full potential.

So if we want *all* kids to stay curious and keep asking questions, we can't be passive about it. We actually need to do specific things—both in the home and in schools.

While our education system has a long way to go, many individual administrators and teachers are more aware than ever before that we're failing kids in this regard and are trying to change. If you are a parent or caregiver, I encourage you to ask your teachers and principal what they're doing to foster curious question askers and how you can partner with them to help your children.

In the meantime, through research, practice, and my own experience as a parent, I want to share four key principles for how to help young people remain avid askers into adulthood.

Kindle the Flames of Their Natural Curiosity

In Chapter 6, we met educator and CEO Chong-Hao Fu, whose deep curiosity animates his zest for life. He credits this skill, in part, to his bicultural upbringing. His parents, both native Chinese speakers, left the United States for Singapore when Chong-Hao was still a baby, returning again when he was about five years old. His childhood was both Chinese and American, in language, culture, food, and values. This gave him a unique vantage point. He remembers going to sleepover parties in elementary school and peering into other people's refrigerators, realizing that they were stocked with entirely different foods than his fridge at home. These moments of *observing difference* helped him realize at a young age that everything and everyone is the product of a history and a culture; this set him off on a lifelong journey to understand how people and systems come to be the way they are.

In her book *I Never Thought About It That Way*, Mónica Guzmán argues that *homophily*, the psychological term for our tendency to hang out with those similar to us, is both a basic law of human nature and antithetical to cultivating the kind of connective curiosity that I'm advocating here.[7] If we want to raise kids who are really curious about other people, we have to actively work against this tendency of ours by intentionally exposing them to different types of people, perspectives, and cultures.

For example, Tyler Thigpen, co-founder and head of the Forest School and father of four, invites people of a wide range of backgrounds—ideological, racial, economic, vocational, you name it—to his home for family dinner. Before the dinner, he and his kids brainstorm questions to ask their guests, questions like "What's your favorite thing about your work?" "What makes you laugh?" or "What makes you cry?" In other words, quality questions designed to help them learn something from and about the dinner guest at a human-to-human level. Without fail, these questions spark an interesting and informative conversation. What's more, they allow his children to see how much it is possible to learn by simply asking another person a good question.

Helping kids understand that their reality isn't the only reality is an important curiosity spark—but not the only one. Your kids will provide the sparks themselves, finding a zillion things and people to get curious about. Sometimes, it might show up as moments of confusion, or "Wait, what?" It's easy for them—or for us—to keep moving, to rush past those little sparks of curiosity. But those are the times when it's most important to give oxygen to them, to fan the flames.

Luckily, kids give us many chances, and when they start to really develop a passion or interest, the spark shows up over and over again. For my son, Jacob, it showed up as a growing interest in programming computers. Over time, he started teaching himself coding languages. As my wife and I watched his desire to learn grow, we asked ourselves how we could fan the flames. We had heard about the Recurse Center, a free and unconventional place for people to learn coding, and we encouraged Jacob to apply when he was thirteen. He threw himself into the application process—writing the essays, asking us to give feedback, and taking the online interview very seriously. He was thrilled when he got admitted and spent a week in person for a "retreat" at its facility.

The Recurse Center follows an educational philosophy called "unschooling," which sees the rigid, top-down curriculum in traditional classrooms as the ultimate curiosity killer. At Jacob's retreat, there were no required classes or mandatory anything. Jacob and his fellow participants were given a set of resources and invited to explore, while learning from their new cohort and from the broader Recurse Center community. By the end of his retreat, he got to formally present his work to people of all ages around the world. Even more incredible was that this relatively shy and introverted teenager gained a newfound confidence to speak up and ask questions of everyone around him.

I recently asked Jacob what adults could do to help foster curious question askers. He thought about it for a while and said, "Give them space to figure out what they're interested in. Then let them go learn about that, and don't get in the way."

Strategies to Kindle Their Flames:

- **DO: Offer children stimuli** that will expose them to something new, confusing, or different. Watch their reactions and encourage them to stay with the questions that arise.
- **DO: Give children time and space to play and tinker and explore.** Watch for what they seem most interested in and curious about, and support them to keep exploring.
- **DO: Fan the flames of their sparks** by looking for opportunities for them to keep asking questions, go deeper, explore further in the areas where they express early curiosity.
- **DON'T: Rush them past the moments of confusion or curiosity or exploration.** Rather, sit with them in it.

Model the Behavior You Want to See

One of my favorite quotes about young people and learning comes from James Baldwin, who wisely observed that "Children have never been very good at listening to their elders, but they have never failed to imitate them."[8]

Psychologist Susan Engel was able to demonstrate this wise insight using a classroom experiment at Williams College. She asked one of her college students, Maddie, to lead two groups of children through a science experiment. While working with the first group, Maddie added a surprise step to the experiment midway, telling the kids she had done it because she was curious to see what would happen. With the second group, Maddie also paused midway, but instead of expressing curiosity, she suggested they stop to tidy up a bit. At the end of the lesson, Maddie said she'd be right back and left the room.

What happened next was what Engel was really interested in: Would the small difference in the teacher's behavior influence how the kids behaved once they were left alone? Lo and behold, the students with whom Maddie had demonstrated a moment of curiosity began tinkering with the materials when they were left alone, while those in the tidying-up group just stood there quietly, waiting for the teacher to return. This was just one experiment of many that led Engel to conclude that "one of the most powerful ways teachers can cultivate curiosity in their students is by modeling curiosity."[9]

This holds for parents and caretakers as well. If we want young people to develop connective curiosity, we need to show them *we're* genuinely curious—and in particular, about *them*. Many children are never or only rarely asked questions about themselves. Author and Penn State professor Heather Holleman writes:

> I recently asked my teen daughter how many people at school ever ask questions about her life. It's astonishingly rare. She tells me *maybe one person* out of a thousand students demonstrates genuine interest in her. I then asked my college students the same question, and one student cried, "When I'm out with friends, they *never ask me one question* about myself." The entire class nodded in agreement.... Young adults long for someone to be curious about them, to draw them out and try to connect deeply through good questions, but instead, most people in their lives stay self-absorbed and self-involved.[10]

The younger generations receive a lot of flack for being more self-centered and narcissistic than older generations, but the young learn from watching the adults around them. We have to ask, then, what behavior are we currently modeling for the next generation?

My friend Jonathan Skolnick, a deeply curious and creative thinker, recalls the impact of adults who did this for him. "At least twice a week before dinner, my grandmother would walk into our kitchen, holding grocery bags full of lunch snacks, detergent, cantaloupe, as well as clothing she'd picked up at the thrift store where my grandfather worked," Jonathan recalls. "Before she even put the bags down on the counter, she would give me a kiss and ask me the same question that she'd asked every single other time I'd ever seen her. '*Vos machst du?* (What's happening?)'" His grandmother's choice of Yiddish instead of English in these moments signified to him that she expected more than a perfunctory "fine" or "nothing." She wanted to get real; she wanted details. She wanted to hear his stories, all of which she listened to intently, asking more questions as he shared, modeling the behavior that helped turn Jonathan into the incredible educator he is today.

When we interact with kids, we can do even more to model curiosity than ask and respond to questions, though that's an important start. Like Jonathan's grandma, we can create and even ritualize memorable moments that showcase important asking skills—and resonate for a lifetime. Here are a few examples of easy-to-implement *curiosity rituals*:

"Google" Your Community: Every community is rich in knowledge and experience in ways that we often don't discover unless we ask. A few years before he was interested in coding, my son, Jacob, was obsessed with magnets. One day, he asked me why it was that wrapping a wire around a nail and then sending electricity through the wire would all of a sudden create a magnet? Well, damned if I knew! So I said, "Jacob, that's a great question. I have no idea. But let's think of who we could ask." We remembered that our neighbor down the street, Robert, is a physics teacher. So we put on our jackets, trundled down the street, and knocked on Robert's door. We brought our nail and wire and batteries, and we asked Robert to teach us. It only took him a few minutes to give Jacob the answer he was seeking. My hope was that Jacob's takeaway from this was that the answers we need often reside in the people all around us, if only we ask. Not everyone will know their neighbors well enough to feel safe knocking on their doors, but we all can seek out some form of community where we feel comfortable to ask, whether it be a club, a team, a faith community, or extended family.

Empathy Talk: Throughout her childhood, anytime Emily, my research and writing collaborator on this book, came home from school complaining about a friend who frustrated her or a classmate who said something mean, her mom recognized the chance to expand Emily's understanding. After acknowledging Emily's hard feelings about the situation, she would ask questions like "Why do you think she might have done that? What might she have been thinking? Is it possible she might be feeling some hard things too?" Together, they talked through any assumptions Emily might have made about the other person's intentions and questioned what information she might be missing. At the time, Emily often wished her mom would just take her side, but as she grew older, she began to understand that by talking her through questions like these, her mom instilled in her a mental habit of taking into consideration what other people might be feeling or experiencing when interpreting a given interaction.

Roses, Thorns, Stems, and More: Every Friday evening, my family sits down for Shabbat dinner. Once we're all eating, we start a ritual called "Roses, Thorns, Stems, Buds, and Stars." The exercise originated with the Boy Scouts, and it's been adapted over time. Each of these words is a question prompt. *Roses* prompts you to share something good from your week, perhaps a win or a fun time; *thorns,* something hard or painful; *stars,* something you did that you're proud of; *buds,* something you're looking forward to or a new goal coming up. But my favorite prompt is *stems,* which prompts people to say something they learned or a way they grew during the past week. Sharing stems not only provides children a chance to reflect on their learning, which psychologists call metacognition, but also allows them to see that the adults in their lives similarly experience the surprise, awkwardness, and discomfort that sometimes come with learning. (If this sounds like too much to take on, maybe start with one or two prompts, or let everybody take their pick.)

If we take Baldwin's quote to be true—that children imitate their elders—then narrating our own process of learning from others may be the most powerful way to instill this habit in the children who are always watching us, whether we are aware of it or not.

Strategies to Model the Process of Asking and Learning

- **DO: Admit when you don't know the answer**, even embrace it as a chance to demonstrate enthusiasm at the opportunity for you to learn.
- **DO: Explicitly call out how you use the *Ask* Approach practices** *with* young people to help them see you going through the steps.
- **DO: Share your own reflections** on the process you used and what you learned.
- **DON'T: Cover up your gaps in your knowledge** or feel the need to show you have all the answers.

Teach Them the Skill Set

Even though children are born curious, that doesn't mean they come pre-equipped with all the skills to learn from others. Especially because society and schools can discourage students from building these muscles, they need opportunities to learn and practice them. Thankfully, there are educators and programs on the cutting edge of helping children—in a wide range of contexts and with diverse backgrounds—build the concrete skills of asking and learning from others. Here I want to spotlight two approaches that specifically teach youth how to ask questions of other people, so as to find out something they really want to know.

Shereen El Mallah (the Youth Participatory Action Research psychologist we met in Chapter 7) helps young people become researchers on issues that matter to them. Most traditional research on kids happens *to* them, done by supposedly objective researchers who peer in from the outside. YPAR, instead, puts students in charge of the research. In so doing, it not only generates far more powerful (and practical) insights but also creates a far greater level of agency among young people. They take charge of the research process, meanwhile developing concrete skills around how to learn from one another.

El Mallah starts by teaching students about the mechanics of questions. She asks them to think about what distinguishes a good question from a not-so-good one, something most students have never been asked to think about. She teaches students to ask questions *about* questions, applying those old W-H questions (what, who, where, when, and how) to assess the quality of the question itself. Most of them are familiar with the *what*—what is the question asking?—but what about the rest of the W-Hs? *Who* is doing the asking? Is the question specific to the person being asked? In what context is the question asked (*where* and *when*)? *Why* is the question being asked; what's the motivation behind it? Finally, *how* is the question asked? Is it asked with judgment or without assumptions? With kindness or hostility?

Through this framework, students learn not only how to craft their own high-quality questions but also how to help those around them improve. They develop a sense of agency in this regard, giving feedback to their teachers and peers about the quality of their questions, as well as sharing openly a question's impact on them. As El Mallah explained to me, the goal of this exercise is not to get kids to call out bad questions, but to give them a process through which they can "break down a question into any possible source of disconnection that it could create" so that they can learn to connect more deeply with those around them.

Teaching kids the skills of asking also means teaching them how to *listen* deeply. In this, we can learn a lot from professor of developmental psychology Niobe Way, head of the Science of Human Connection Lab at NYU and founder of the Listening Project along with her colleague and former student Joseph Nelson, who is the head of the Black Studies Department at Swarthmore College. The Listening Project aims to foster curiosity and connection within and across diverse communities by training young people and teachers in something called "transformative interviewing." Transformative interviewing is based on many of the same principles that underlie this book. They consider it a method of "relational intelligence" that involves learning a set of distinct practices of listening with curiosity (e.g., open-ended questions, contrast questions, curated follow-up questions), which allows the interviewer to learn something new about the answer to their question from the experiences of another person. It transforms how interviewers perceive their interviewees and how the interviewers see themselves. Sounds pretty intense, but in Way's extensive experience applying this method in middle and high schools and universities around the world, younger people are better at learning the method than older people, as the former are still connected to their natural curiosity. Early research on the impact of the Listening Project shows that students who participated demonstrated enhanced listening skills, interpersonal curiosity, empathy, connectedness with peers and adults, and a sense of common humanity.[11]

Strategies to Teach the Skill Set

- **DO: Explicitly name, show, and explain the actions** involved so they know what to do.
- **DO: Give them chances to practice** the skills, and support them when they struggle.
- **DO: Offer clear and concrete feedback** so they can refine their approach.
- **DON'T: Give them so much help or direction that they never get to mess up** and learn from their mistakes.

Help Them Experience Immediate Benefits

From a behavioral point of view, one of the best ways to strengthen the learning of a new behavior is to give it immediate positive reinforcement. In the field of education, debates have raged over time about the value and the limitations of what are called "extrinsic rewards" to reinforce learning. I personally subscribe to the research that some forms of extrinsic rewards do have a place in the learning process, but like everything in life, they also have their limits.[12]

My friend Cassandra Sweet shared with me a great example of how her father found a way to demonstrate that connective curiosity has both intrinsic *and* extrinsic rewards. Cassandra's parents, Midge and John Sweet, were fearless, progressive activists in Atlanta. While she was growing up, they took her with them to every meeting and event, where the ethos was to engage and learn from anyone and everyone. They weren't going to let having a daughter stop them from doing their important work, but more important, they believed that exposing Cassandra to their friends and colleagues would be a good influence on her. At the same time, Cassandra's father understood that being the only kid in a room full of grown-ups loses its appeal quickly. And so, he gave her an assignment for each gathering: before they could leave, she would have to tell him about three new people she met that evening and three interesting things she learned about each person. Once she had accomplished the goal, she got the prize: playing with the other kids outside! This game encouraged Cassandra to spend the evening asking questions, and what she learned from people fascinated her.

There's one very obvious intrinsic reward we can give kids for asking: a clear and honest answer that fully satisfies their curiosity. While it's obvious, it isn't always easy. As they say, kids will ask the darnedest things. But your ability to answer their questions in a calm, direct way—even or especially when they're asking about sensitive or taboo topics—goes a long way to encourage future asking.

We need to make ourselves "askable adults." The Askable Adult Campaign, which trains adults to help young people navigate difficult issues in their lives, defines an askable adult as "one who is approachable and easy for children and youth to talk to about anything that is on their mind."[13] Most kids want help dealing with issues like loneliness, drugs and alcohol, bullying, and stress and anxiety, and they report that they wish they had more adults in which they felt they could confide. When kids fear our misunderstanding, dismissal, anger, and, most of all, judgment, they withhold what they have to share as well as the questions they want to ask. By demonstrating that it is safe, satisfying, and way less awkward than they were expecting to ask the questions they want to ask, we can increase the reward and decrease the anticipated punishment associated with asking. This provides children and teens with a safe and welcoming relationship in which to speak openly about their questions and challenges, which in itself is a reward.

Praise is yet another powerful reinforcer. Most of our children go to schools that focus on praising children for getting the right answer rather than for coming up with a valuable question. So when we praise their question-asking, we are helping to overcome forces that suppress their curiosity. One of the best ways to offer this kind of praise is after a child reaches the answer or goal they were seeking, drawing their attention back to a moment in the process when they asked a question that helped propel them forward.[14]

Parents, caregivers, and educators can also advocate for their schools to take on practices that reward behaviors of asking and learning from others. For example, at Tyler Thigpen's Forest School, before each student can graduate, they need to provide evidence of at least one person who can attest to the student's capacity for empathy, someone who feels deeply known and understood by them. Thigpen explained to me that his students, like most adults, tend to point to evidence of what *they've* done—actions they've taken with the intent to help others, times they believe they've been good listeners. However, that isn't enough to fulfill the requirement. Students have to gather the evidence directly from the people in their lives, asking questions that uncover the impact they really have on others. Through this process, students must practice curiosity, vulnerability, and resilience, and, at times, how to receive and reflect upon feedback that might be hard to hear.

Another powerful example comes from a school called Red Bridge, run by Orly Friedman. In most schools, kids are grouped by their age. When you're six, you're in first grade, then at seven you move to second grade, and so on. Some progressive schools resist this linear, age-based sequence, instead allowing students to advance based on their mastery of the material. Red Bridge goes one step further: Students are grouped, and advance in school, based on their demonstration of *readiness for autonomy,* the ability to drive their own learning. For example, to move through Autonomy Level 1, students need to demonstrate the ability to ask clarifying questions. To achieve Level 2, students need to demonstrate the ability to ask adults questions when they feel stuck, and in Level 3, they need to show that they can ask peers when they need help. How many adults in workplaces truly feel comfortable asking peers for help? At Red Bridge, learning how to do this is built into the design of their education.

Strategies to Help Young People Experience Benefits from Asking

- **DO: Offer praise and positive reinforcement when they ask, listen, and learn.** The most natural reinforcement is helping them to actually find out what they are seeking to learn.
- **DO: Help them see and reflect on the connection between their efforts to ask and their success.**
- **DO: Make it fun!** Whether through games like Cassandra's father played with her, or making up your own, keep it playful and not like a chore.
- **DON'T: Undermine children's natural curiosity to ask and learn** by layering on too many extrinsic rewards.

THE AWESOME POTENTIAL OF GENERATION ASK

Recently, my son, Jacob, picked up a fork at the dinner table, examined it for a while, and said, "How do you think this fork is made?" I said, "Great question; what do you think?" My wife laughed and asked, "Is metalwork a new interest?" Jacob replied with four words that let me know we might be doing something right: "I'm interested in everything."

If we can give the next generation the superpowers of learning from others—from curiosity, to asking questions, all the way through reflection—I don't think I'm exaggerating in saying that we might give the human race on planet Earth its best shot at survival. Maybe even more important, our kids will have the tools to build the deep relationships and communities that make life meaningful and satisfying, even during times of great change and challenge.

SUMMARY OF KEY POINTS

Essential question: How can we stop squelching kids' curiosity and unleash their asking?

1. Kids are born curious, but then their question-asking declines.
2. To nurture their desire to know and empower them to learn from those around them:

   - **Kindle the flame of their natural curiosity** by exposing them to a diversity of people, perspectives, and experiences and giving them the time and space to explore what they feel drawn to.
   - **Model the behavior you want to see** by demonstrating your own curiosity. Ask them questions about themselves and really listen. Model vulnerability by being honest when you don't know something.
   - **Teach them the skills of asking** by naming and explaining the practices. Give them chances to practice, and offer them feedback on their efforts.
   - **Help them experience the immediate benefits of asking** by rewarding them for their curiosity. When they ask you a question, do your best to give an honest, thoughtful response. When they make a new discovery, help them trace it back to the questions they initially asked.

EXERCISES

10A. As James Baldwin pointed out, children often repeat the behaviors they see in adults. So, to build self-awareness around how you treat young people, it's useful to think back to your experiences from childhood:

- To whom (if anyone) did you ask the most questions? How did adults in your life respond when you asked questions? Which adults in your life, if any, were "askable adults"?
- To what extent were your questions encouraged or discouraged? In what ways?
- When (if ever) did you stop (or slow down in) asking questions? What cues did you get that encouraged or discouraged your questions?
- What role models (if any) did you have in your life of great question askers? How often (and by whom) were *you* asked questions?

10B. Now, identify a young person in (or around) your life. They could be a child of yours, a niece or a godchild, someone you teach or mentor, or the child of a friend or neighbor.

- Ask them to share something they are curious—or want to learn more—about. How might you fan the flames of their curiosity? Could you help connect them to someone they could ask to learn more?
- Try role modeling the *Ask* Approach in your interactions with them: curiosity, safety, quality questions, listening, reflecting and reconnecting. What did you learn from them? How might you then narrate to them the practices you were using?
- Try teaching them one of the practices from this book that you think they'd especially benefit from learning. Hint: Make it as simple as possible, so consider starting with one of the question suggestions from Chapter 5 or a listening strategy from Chapter 6.

Epilogue

Live the Questions, Repair the World

DANISH-BORN CEO RONNI ABERGEL ONE DAY LOOKED AT THE GROWING division in the world and asked a big question: "How are we to understand each other if we do not have the opportunity to talk to each other?"[1] This question led him to create the Human Library™ (*Menneskebiblioteket* in Danish), a library filled not with books but with people, real individuals who had experienced prejudice or social exclusion and volunteered to share their experiences to be "read" by those who come to learn. When I first heard about the idea, I thought it was brilliant but wondered how many places would actually do such a thing.

Then I learned that eighty-five countries across six continents have now hosted Human Library events, with more every year. The stories from these events are moving, both for the "readers" and for the volunteers who make their lives "open books" for the readers to learn from. Take one event, in the conservative town of Muncie, Indiana, where a woman named Charlize Jamieson volunteered to represent the "book" title *Transgender*. In an interview with the *Muncier Journal*, she reflected that she was initially apprehensive about the reception she would receive as a "book" to be read. Her concern was seemingly borne out when a conservative Christian woman sat down with her, but refused to shake her hand. But after an hour of conversation, in which the woman asked Jamieson questions and listened deeply to her answers, neither wanted to leave the other's company. They finally parted ways with a genuine hug and a deeper understanding of each other as human beings.[2]

At the Human Library, people get to know individuals that they had previously only understood from a distance, as stereotypes. Diane Bottomly, a librarian for Muncie's Human Library, told the *Muncie Journal*, "It has helped me understand people from diverse backgrounds that I probably would never have been exposed to before. And, [I] had lacked . . . understanding because I just had no interaction with anybody like that."[3]

Whether or not you ever have the opportunity to attend a Human Library, nothing is stopping you from stepping into the world with that kind of open spirit. So far in this book, I've focused on the transformations that happen when we give our colleagues, friends, and family the honor of our authentic curiosity. Now, I'd like you to consider what might happen if you brought the *Ask* Approach into every corner of your life—especially those places where you might vehemently disagree with another person or group—using questions, listening, and reflection to access the infinite variety of people in the world all around you.

Even a simple and spontaneous decision to choose curiosity can have profound impact. I once experienced such a moment with an Uber driver. I had called a car to drive me to the airport—then cringed when it pulled up with a recognizable bumper sticker: a black-and-white American flag with a thin blue line running through it. *Oh boy*, I thought, climbing nervously into the back seat. This was not long after the summer that police killed George Floyd and enraged Americans across the country took to the streets to protest police brutality, racism, and injustice. To me, the thin-blue-line bumper stickers represented the pro-police counterprotest.

The driver, a man around my age, had brown eyes and dark hair sticking out from under a baseball cap. When he turned around and introduced himself as Raphael, I saw that his hat bore the same Blue Lives Matter flag as his bumper sticker. As he began to drive, a jumble of judgments flooded my brain. What kind of person would fly a flag that announced their lack of sympathy for the devastating effects of police violence? I felt righteous and indignant. At the same time, I felt uneasy as a Jewish person, since the flag has also been associated with anti-Semitic white supremacy groups.

I sighed and prepared to dissociate into my laptop. As always, my inbox was overflowing, and I was anxious to start chipping away at it. Best to just stay quiet and get some work done. That was my default. But in this moment, I considered a different possibility. If I really believed that questions can ease division and build bridges, perhaps I should muster the courage, and the curiosity, to ask some. I was nervous. How would he respond? Would he be offended? Would he get angry? Would we spend the rest of the forty-five-minute drive arguing or sitting in awkward silence?

I took a deep breath, and with all the genuine curiosity I could drum up, I asked, "I noticed your hat and your sticker with the thin blue line. Are you part of the police force?"

Raphael considered my question before responding in a surprisingly soft and gentle voice. He told me that, yes, he used to be a police officer before deciding to drive for Uber. In fact, several of his family members were also in the force. He then shared with me how gang violence—not an issue that touches me personally in the suburban New York enclave I call home—had led him to enter law enforcement. His cousin had been murdered by gang members on his last day of police academy. His ex-wife, who was also a police officer, and his young daughter had been threatened by gang members. A friend of his—another former officer—who worked in prisons was brutally murdered by inmates whom he had previously arrested. Raphael himself had planned to work in corrections after leaving the force, but reconsidered when he encountered inmates he himself had arrested who threatened violent retaliation against him. As he told these stories, I stepped into a new perspective. I felt shocked at the violence and personal tragedy that he and his friends and family and fellow officers had endured. I could hear his pain and grief, as well as his genuine desire to protect the communities he served.

Taken by his openness and generosity, my questions now flowed more easily. I asked how he felt when people called the police a racist institution or critiqued their use of force. I asked how he felt about those who advocated to defund the police entirely. He considered this and replied that he believed everyone was entitled to their opinions, but that he would want to understand what specifically they wanted to defund, and what alternatives they imagined calling on if their house or store were being broken into.

His own views on this issue were far more nuanced than most others I'd heard, certainly more than my own. He believed the police were a critical social service, but also supported high-quality anti-bias training and reforms that would allow police officers to do their jobs in the service-oriented, respectful spirit that had led him into the job in the first place. He told me about his deep personal commitment to community policing, where officers build personal relationships with people on the streets where they work.

By the time we reached the airport, I had traveled the arc from fear to connection and gratitude. Raphael's willingness to be an open book allowed me to develop and refine my own thinking on the issue in a way I never would have if I hadn't asked and he hadn't shared. Instead of sitting in the back of that car answering emails and feeling self-righteous, I felt empathy for and connected to someone I had been ready to write off as "the problem." Now that I understood Raphael's perspective, I realized I knew less about the issue than I once thought. My formerly strident stance was replaced by a desire to learn more, from a wider variety of sources. I can't know for sure how our conversation affected Raphael, but his receptiveness to my questions suggests that he was grateful to have someone listen to his story.

As valuable as this conversation was for me, these engagements don't come without a cost—everything from emotional labor to real physical risk. Even though being a Jewish person exploring that symbolic flag with Raphael didn't feel 100 percent risk-free, as an able-bodied white male in the back of a taxi, the cost of asking questions felt relatively low and worth the risk. For others, for example a person of color who unavoidably bears both social and physical risk due to racism, the analysis in some situations will be very different. In every circumstance, we each need to weigh the risks of engaging with the potential rewards that come from asking questions. Each person's choices will be unique, depending on circumstances, identity, and safety.

ASKING AS AN ANTIDOTE TO THE DIVISION OF OUR TIME

It's easy to feel like *division*, more than anything else, is the defining characteristic of modern society, not just in the United States but globally. With climbing economic inequality, political polarization, religious and cultural divisions, the rise of hate groups and identity-based violence, it seems like every day there are dozens of news stories that confirm our inability to get along, or to even agree on what is fact versus fiction. We often treat those who hold opposing views or whose identities differ from ours with dismissal, disinterest, and distrust. As Eboo Patel, founder of Interfaith America, put it to me, people too often accept the dangerous idea that "if we disagree on A, then we can't work together on the rest of the alphabet."

We are in a rare and precarious moment in human history. The stakes—and opportunities—have perhaps never been higher. We, as a species, face unprecedented challenges that will *require* us to work together. The climate crisis, wars around the globe, and the continued effects of a pandemic and the looming threat of another (to name just a few issues) demand that we imagine a different way of doing things, a method of cooperation that unleashes the immense power of our collective intelligence. **Asking is the behavior that unlocks everything.**

At the same time, there are powerful forces at work on behalf of division: politicians who benefit from the mobilizing effects of fear and hatred, social media companies who have discovered that radicalizing algorithms are better for business, a culture of materialism and hyper-individualism and self-interest. It is in times like these, when the institutions and culture seem most backward, that it feels most tempting to respond with rage or despair. In our digitally and geographically siloed worlds, it is all too easy to remain comfortable in our indignance and sense of being right (as I initially wanted to in the car with Raphael). These are understandable feelings. But we have another option, one championed by our greatest moral leaders, from Dr. Martin Luther King Jr. to Mahatma Gandhi. We can be the change we wish to see. In a society that pressures us to see our fellow humans as the other, we can instead ask, *What can I learn from this person?*

Imagine a world in which the default was not to criticize those different from us, but to *ask*. How would we treat one another if we cultivated our curiosity about others, if we sought to understand their feelings, thoughts, and experiences instead of judging only what we see on the surface? What if we spent more time listening, and less time telling? What if we really took the time and energy to reflect on what we heard, to allow us to learn from others and maybe even change our thoughts and feelings?

The organization Braver Angels, dedicated to depolarizing politics, plots the path of understanding and connection that inquiry can open up on a continuum, which I have adapted as follows:[4]

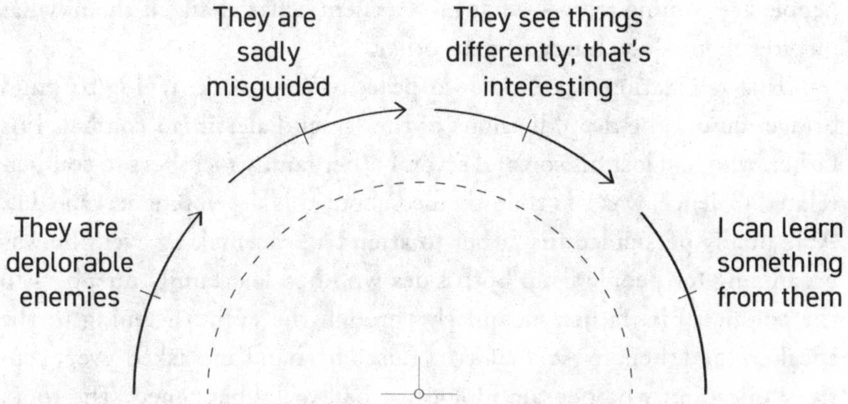

When we don't ask, it's all too easy to get stuck on the left side[5] of the arc. Division and conflict brew on this side, and the possibilities of working together to find creative solutions to our shared problems are basically nil. But when we ask instead, "What can I learn from this person?" we begin to travel toward the right side of the arc, into understanding, empathy, and learning. Here, cooperation, creativity, and community become possible.

Thankfully, such a world does not only exist in our imagination. There are people already leading the charge, even amid some of the world's most devastating, long-standing divisions. Aziz Abu Sarah is one. Growing up in East Jerusalem, Aziz regularly experienced anti-Palestinian violence. When he was ten years old, his brother was killed by Israeli soldiers. He spent his teenage years angry and resentful, dreaming of getting revenge on those on the "other side" who had brought so much senseless suffering to his family and community. But something started to shift in him when he began spending time in West Jerusalem, just a few blocks from his childhood home and a world away from the one he knew, to study Hebrew. Suddenly, the "other side" was not some abstract "them," but actual students in the same classroom as him. As they talked to each other, shared stories about their different experiences growing up on opposite sides of the city, Aziz realized that where he had always seen division, there could actually be connection. As he later reflected, "The moment you start sharing stories and talking to each other and hearing where people are coming from—what moves them, what changed them, what inspires them—you humanize the other."[6]

This realization led Aziz into peacemaking work, trying to build bridges across the deep divisions of the Israeli-Palestinian conflict. His father, who had lost his son and several other family members to conflict-related violence, was less than thrilled about this development. One day, Aziz finally persuaded his father to attend a peacemaking event he was organizing for people from both sides who had lost family members to the conflict. His father sat quietly through the event, listening to the speakers, and then, to Aziz's horror, raised his hand and asked a very sensitive question: whether the Holocaust had really happened. The room fell silent. Aziz braced himself for the inevitable outrage.

But then, one of the Israeli leaders of the event, whose father had been a prisoner in Auschwitz, decided to set his anger aside and answer the question earnestly. "I don't expect you to know something you have never learned about," he said. He offered to have his father, an Auschwitz survivor, take Aziz's father to the Holocaust museum himself and to share his personal story with him. At this point, something incredible happened. Seventy other Palestinians (all of whom, mind you, had had family members killed by Israeli soldiers) raised their hands and asked if they could hear the stories too. They were, they admitted, just as ignorant about the Holocaust.

This moment, in which both sides chose to be curious instead of to condemn, to ask and listen instead of judge, created the possibility of learning where none had existed before. After the group of Palestinians visited the Holocaust museum, Israelis began to express interest in learning about Palestinian history as well. While being interviewed by the organization Braver Angels, Aziz reported that fifteen years after this interaction, groups of Israelis and Palestinians still gather each year to hear each other's stories and learn about each other's cultures and histories.

When we center the question "What can I learn from this person?" in our lives, we begin to see in everyone a wealth of knowledge, experiences, and ideas, even in those who we previously dismissed as wrongheaded, ignorant, or beyond our understanding. It opens the possibility of treating every person we encounter with respect and appreciation, seeing them as our teachers instead of our enemies.

I don't know about you, but I'm ready to move beyond living in a society that spends too much time on the "They are enemies" side of the arc. I want to live in a world rich with interpersonal curiosity and understanding, a world where people ask one another questions and listen deeply to the answers. As Mónica Guzmán, Senior Fellow for Public Practice at Braver Angels and author of the wonderful book *I Never Thought of It That Way*, has written, "What a perfect time to try new ways to listen—to begin with the radical idea that no one is beyond understanding and see what it reveals."[7]

Poet Rainer Maria Rilke once urged a young protégé to "live the questions," allowing them to guide us gently into a different way of relating to ourselves, one another, and the world around us.[8] Ask yourself, what would it look like to *live* this question, again and again, through all your interactions: *What can I learn from this person?*

Only time and intention can answer that question for you. What I can promise is that pursuing it will open previously unimaginable doors of possibility—for you and for all those whom you engage in the adventure.

ACKNOWLEDGMENTS

WHEN I TOLD A FRIEND THAT I WAS WRITING THIS BOOK, HE SAID, "Books seem like one of those things that everyone wants to create until they realize how hard it is to actually do." For me, I only discovered how hard it was to do once I'd committed to doing it.

Writing a book is one of the most humbling professional experiences I've had. But as with the other scary, transformative experiences of my life—namely, having kids and refocusing my career on creating systemic change in society—the rewards of writing this book have far outweighed the challenges. Yet that's only been possible because of the village of mentors, friends, collaborators, teammates, partners, and loved ones who came together in support of this project.

I'm eternally grateful for the many teachers and mentors who have shaped my thinking and whose fingerprints are all over this book. Diana Smith took a chance when she admitted me to her intensive, applied doctoral program on Human Dynamics and Change in Organizations (HDCO). Diana is the quintessential scholar-practitioner and one of the most reflective people I know. Diana put up with my incessant inquisitions, immature and arrogant critiques, and indefatigable hunger for more! She returned it all with grace, humor, and most important, a developmental lens. The three years I spent studying under Diana's tutelage, and the many years of mentorship and friendship that have followed, have profoundly shaped my skills and more important, my orientation to life. I am also grateful to my colleagues in the HDCO program—Emma Barnes Brown, Kathryn Flynn, Erica Ariel Fox, and Neil Pearse—whose friendship and patience sharpened my thinking and helped me to grow, as well as to our many exceptional teachers, including Iris Bagwell, Amy Edmondson, Bill Torbert, Michael Jensen, and many more. And the HDCO program would never have been possible without the creative vision and generosity of Mark Fuller, Joe Fuller, and Alan Kantrow, among many other leaders at Monitor Group.

When I joined Monitor, its recruiting slogan was "A place for optimists to change the world," and for me, it provided exactly that springboard. I spent nearly the first decade of my career growing up professionally at Monitor. At the time, I had no idea just how lucky I was to work in such a thoughtful, creative, curious, and committed environment. It was at Monitor that I met Chris Argyris, whose groundbreaking scholarship is at the heart of this entire book. I will forever treasure our meetings in his office, where he so patiently and generously shared insights, books, and stories with me.

Chris's legacy has been carried on brilliantly by Diana Smith and her colleagues, Phil McArthur and Bob Putnam, the partners of Action Design. Action Design made Chris's brilliant concepts—including the Ladder of Inference, Advocacy and Inquiry, Single- and Double-Loop Learning, and Model I versus Model II operating systems—even more accessible and available to leaders around the world. Their core frameworks and approaches—from the Learning Pathways, to Patterns of Awareness, to the Ladder of Inference, to High-Quality Advocacy and Inquiry, as well as their tradecraft for engaging learners and building competence—are imprinted in my brain and infuse every chapter of this book. I treasure the experiences I've had collaborating, hanging out with, and learning from Bob and Phil over the years. **I also highly recommend working with Action Design and attending the Action Design Institute to anyone who wants to go deeper with the ideas in this book.** You can learn more at www.actiondesign.com. The books and resources coming out of Action Design, including *Action Science* and Diana's books *The Elephant in the Room, Divide or Conquer,* and *Remaking the Space Between Us* are foundational texts for this work.

As if that weren't enough of a candy store to grow up in professionally, I am also grateful for the years I spent at Monitor learning from and working with David Kantor, a luminary in the field of family systems therapy. Even though he had only one working eye, David could see what was happening in a room better than almost anyone—seeing and naming patterns of interpersonal dynamics while also seeing deep into the soul of each person. David applied his profound research on families to teams and leaders in organizations, and the programs he created deeply shaped not only participants but also my practice. His theory of communication domains—meaning, affect, and power—underlies this book's chapter on listening, and so much of my professional work rests on the intellectual foundation he laid for me and the world. Special thanks to Shani Harmon and Neil Pearse, who helped to translate and apply David's work in highly engaging and practical ways.

Monitor invested heavily in bringing the great work of Chris, David, and Action Design to its consultants and clients around the world. Chief among those leading this work were Jamie Higgins and Jim Cutler, both of whom took me under their wings and remain cherished mentors and friends to this day.

Jamie was my manager for many years, as we developed and led a global program called Giving and Receiving Feedback. Jamie intensively taught, coached, and corrected me, all while giving me so much room to run, build, create, and teach others. Her generous and wise mentorship has shaped my career path at multiple turns. She also provided invaluable feedback on this book's every word—combining tremendous encouragement, honest critique, a practitioner's lens, and an English major's eagle-eye editing pen. This book is much stronger for the many ideas and suggestions she shared along the way, both big and small. She did this all while juggling an intense full-time job and a full and busy life.

Jim Cutler invited me into the Human Assets Business Unit (later called Lattice Partners) at Monitor and has been a steadfast mentor ever since. He—together with Mark Fuller—sponsored my efforts to build software that translated much of this work into digital performance support tools, even when the vision outpaced the technology. He also tolerated my immature advice about all the things he could be doing better when building and leading a new business; one of my (and his) favorite moments in our relationship was years later when I called him up, after myself getting some battle scars from leading large teams, to apologize to him for my hubris in critiquing his leadership. I call Jim every time I have a major leadership dilemma or face a career inflection point, and he has never failed to be both generous and insightful with his advice. Jim not only read and commented on every word of every chapter of this manuscript, but he offered up his own examples to share in the book, even when those didn't showcase his proudest professional moments. In so doing, he modeled exactly the kind of learning-oriented, vulnerable leadership that this book espouses.

Monitor gave me the gifts of so many more mentors and friends, far more than I can name here without running out of pages—so I will highlight just a few. Joe Babiec managed me for years on economic development projects, which filled me with moral purpose and steep learning curves. Joe's bar for intellectual rigor is matched by none and served as a boot camp for analysis and framework building. Joe's belief in me and friendship have meant so much to me over the years, and his critical feedback on early drafts of this book made it far stronger. Vanessa Kirsch and Kelly Fitzsimmons, who started New Profit Inc., gave me so many opportunities to grow and have impact throughout my career. This included the chance to apprentice to David Levy, who has become a lifelong friend and mentor. David's breadth of expertise, belief in me, generosity with his time and his network, and willingness to challenge and push have been of immense support over the years.

After working for five years with David, Vanessa, and Kelly to support Teach For America, its founder and CEO at the time, Wendy Kopp, asked me to come and lead a part of the organization. Although I originally planned to take a two-year leave from Monitor, I quickly fell in love with the sector and stayed at TFA for a decade. I'm so grateful to Wendy for taking a chance on me and giving me more responsibility than I deserved but also tremendous resources to do the job. I learned so much from my direct colleagues over the years at TFA, including Susan Asiyanbi, Monique Ayotte-Hoeltzel, Latricia Barksdale, Jemina Bernard, Katie Bowen, Tracy-Elizabeth Clay, Sara Cotner, Lora Cover, Michelle

Culver, Aimee Eubanks Davis, Steven Farr, Charissa Fernandez, Doug Friedlander, Kwame Griffith, Josh Griggs, Erin Gums, Jenee Henry Wood, Maia Heyck-Merlin, Kevin Huffman, Paul Keys, Elisa Kim, Min Kim, Sarah Koegler, Andrew Mandel, Frances Messano, Mike Metzger, Kunjan Narechania, Annie O'Donnell, Matt Petersen, Andrea Pursley, Ted Quinn, Rachel Schankula, Ben Schumacher, Eric Scroggins, Zoe Stemm-Calderon, Katie Tennessen Hooten, Sarah Kirby Tepera, and Omari Todd (of blessed memory), among many others. My manager at TFA for nearly the entire time, Matt Kramer, taught me so much about empowering management, leading with optimism, and rigorous thinking. Elisa Villaneuva Beard, TFA's current CEO, showed me what it means to be *all in*, with fierce commitment to justice, a brave heart, love, persistence, teamwork, and hope. The lessons I learned from generous friends and colleagues at TFA permeate this book and will forever inform my leadership.

Among my favorite colleagues at TFA was Aylon Samouha, with whom I co-led teams there for several years. We had so much fun co-leading that we decided to bring the band back together when we launched Transcend in 2015. Many people told us we were crazy, that co-CEO models never work. Some people even refused to invest in Transcend initially because they didn't believe that this model of leadership could work. But Aylon and I have defied the odds together and truly enjoyed it. I know for certain I never could or would have started and led an organization like Transcend without Aylon's partnership. Someone recently interviewed me about the secrets of co-leadership. She asked me if we have a lot of conflict, and I said, "Of course we do. If we agreed on everything, then what would be the point of having two of us? Our strength is that we bring different perspectives." Aylon and I operate on the philosophy that when we disagree, we likely haven't yet reached the best answer but that, with dialogue, we will either convince each other or find a new, superior way forward. Aylon has been a tremendous champion of this book project, has subjected himself to multiple interviews for the book, and has lovingly held up a mirror on the many occasions where I fail to practice what I preach.

Perhaps most important, Aylon has partnered with me in assembling the most magical team of colleagues whom I've ever had the privilege of knowing and leading, including our original leadership body, which in our aversion at the time to anything that smacked of conventional organizational structures, we called "the Wildcats." This group included Emily Rummo, who was our first-ever hire as chief operating officer and who literally built the place on a foundation of love and commitment to excellence. Jenee Henry Wood has shaped Transcend as a true learning organization, with her trademark depth, wisdom, rigor, and the biggest heart. Lavada Berger has worn almost every hat in the organization, at each turn sprinkling her magical touch, which combines a deep humanity with bold dreaming and impeccable integrity. Jenn Charlot has brought her sky-high bar for excellence, willingness to call bullshit, powerful vulnerability, and commitment to being super-proximate to the work. Every one of these humans has taught me so much, and each of them made unique and valuable contributions to this book.

Co-leading Transcend has been by far the most formative and fulfilling of my professional experiences, and the stories and insights I've gained show up throughout this book. I could fill an entire book with appreciations for all who have made this possible, but for the sake of space, I will limit myself to thanking the funders and investors who believe in us, the board members and advisers who devote collectively hundreds of unpaid hours to championing our mission, the school communities and systems and other organizations with whom we are privileged to partner, and most important, my talented teammates at Transcend who invest their lives to transform education and advance learning opportunities for all. None of the stories or insights that this book lifts up would be possible without them. Four in particular, Jenee Henry Wood, Lavada Berger, Arielle Ritvo Kinder, and Estefany Lopez, went out of their way to not only review drafts of the book but also share on the daily their feedback, experiences, and ideas in ways that taught me so much.

Key concepts in this book were first seeded in my mind in the mid-1990s, with amazing mentorship from two professors I had at Brown University, social psychologists Kari Edwards and Joachim Krueger. Because I'm a glutton for punishment, while I was at Monitor and Teach For America, I spent ten years taking night classes to complete a doctorate at Columbia University Teachers College in the field of adult learning and leadership development. So many of the ideas I learned in that program informed not only my leadership but the thinking in this book. I am eternally grateful to my advisers in the program, Professors Victoria Marsick and Lyle Yorks, for pushing my thinking, exposing me to powerful concepts, and giving me the space to take responsibility for my own learning.

While this book has been germinating in my mind for over two decades, only several years ago did the voice that whispered to me, *It's time to do it,* get loud enough for me to hear. Alex Johnston encouraged me to listen to that voice and helped me find the courage, confidence, and time to go for it. Yet it wasn't a convenient time to write a book—leading a fast-growing organization while raising two adolescents and dealing with some personal health issues, all during a global pandemic, had already taken its toll. Thankfully, I found several brilliant collaborators, without whose partnership this book could never have come about.

I first met Emily Irving on horseback in the foothills of the Absaroka Range in Wyoming. I had come out to Bitterroot Ranch, where Emily was working as a wrangler, while I was on vacation to do a cattle drive with my son, Jacob. Emily and I got to talking, and we asked each other a lot of questions. I learned that prior to moving to Wyoming to work on a remote horse and cattle ranch, she had been pursuing a PhD in organizational behavior and sociology at Harvard. We connected on our shared interest in human behavior and communication. She struck me as a deep thinker and an unusually curious person. At the end of the week, I walked up to the corral where she was busy tacking up horses for the afternoon ride and gave her my business card.

When the wrangling season came to a close, Emily agreed to work with me on the book. She initially provided research support but very soon became a close collaborator on everything from the ideas to the writing. She elicited from me stories and insights that were buried deep in my past. She taught me what it meant to write creative nonfiction and coached me to access my authentic voice. She helped me find the confidence to tell my story unapologetically. She elevated the importance of asking for the sake of human connection, beyond simply the value of information we learn. She helped me work through tricky questions of what it means to be a white man writing a book about interpersonal dynamics and how to do so responsibly.

Emily not only helped me bring the book's concept to life but she quickly turned into a trusted thought-partner and friend. As we together navigated the various twists and turns of any close collaboration, we leaned on the practices of this book—curiously asking questions and listening deeply to each other's experiences. What we learned not only gave us valuable insights but also validated and refined the book's ideas. Undoubtedly, this is a deeper, richer, more just, more heart-centered story thanks to Emily's close collaboration.

What Emily and I developed, Sara Grace took to a whole next level. Sara is a consummate professional—a gifted writer, editor, and collaborator. Sara is a discerning thinker and a true critical friend. She saw the manuscript's potential but also recognized the ways it needed a major lift. She found and fixed the flaws in its logic and the holes in the stories that needed repair. She worked closely with me to take apart some chapters, and she helped put them back together in ways that conveyed the original intent even better. She was never afraid to tell me when my ideas were not so great, but she also welcomed my pushback, and our discussions led us to a better place. Like a master sculptor who chisels away at a stone in order to reveal the angel hidden inside, Sara found the most interesting and compelling parts of what we'd written, and she shined a spotlight on those. She made the book's prose tighter, better paced, and more user-friendly. Perhaps most important for you, dear reader, she cut the chapters down to size so they didn't drag on.

Thank you to Kendal Dooley, the amazing graphic designer behind all the images rendered in this book. It is said that a picture is worth a thousand words, and Kendal's artistic talents helped to take complex concepts and make them easier to understand. It was a joy to collaborate with Kendal.

Thank you to Mark Fuller and Joe Fuller, founders of Monitor Group, where I worked for the first near-decade of my career. On multiple occasions, Mark has taken a bet on me, encouraged me to think big, and immediately shown up whenever I have asked him for counsel and support. Through multiple phone calls and emails, he provided me encouragement and insightful input on this book's content, as well as ideas for how to get the word out. Equal thanks to Joe for being a trusted adviser and brilliant role model and for always being there to provide support. The organization that Mark and Joe built is truly special on so many levels, as are they as leaders and human beings.

Thank you to Professor Amy Edmondson, who, on multiple occasions throughout my career, took my call and showed up with both affirmation and challenge in supremely encouraging and supportive ways. Thank you also to Professor Adam Grant, who shared encouraging feedback on the book's core concepts, while also pointing out important gaps and sharing ideas and sources for how to close those gaps. Both Amy's and Adam's research and thought leadership provide critical intellectual foundation for this book's ideas.

Thank you to Kim Scott for engaging with me on the book's ideas and especially for pushing for the importance of separating the wheat from the chaff. I'm also grateful to Kim for sharing her ideas with our teammates at Transcend, who were enthralled and powerfully affected.

Thank you to Parker Palmer for speaking with me as part of the research on this book and for sharing profoundly helpful insights on listening, learning, and humanity.

Thank you to Professor Niobe Way for engaging deeply on questions of curiosity, connection, and human development and for inviting me into incredible discussions with her research group.

Thank you to Warren Berger, the world's quintessential "questionologist," for taking my call out of the blue, meeting up with me in person, and generously sharing his experience and tips about questions, book writing, and building up a field of thinkers on the topic of questions.

Thank you to everyone—whether named or disguised—whose stories provided helpful illustrations of the key points in this book. What I learned from each of you has deeply enriched my understanding of the *Ask* Approach.

Additionally, I want to acknowledge the many people in my life who showed up in small and big ways to share their time, ideas, and feedback on the book's content and distribution. In addition to those already mentioned above, so many of whom contributed to parts of the book's proposal and/or manuscript, I wish to acknowledge the following people, each of whom made a meaningful contribution to this project:

Nicole Abi-Esber, Jenny Anderson, Susan Asiyanbi, Joe Babiec, Scott Berney, Jen Bird, Rhonda Broussard, Mohit Chandra, Joel Chasnoff, Jim Collins, Hanne Collins, Sara Cotner, David Daniels, Stephen Dubner, Melanie Dukes, Amelia Dunlop, Shereen El Mallah, Susan Engel, Kareem Farah, Benjamin Finzi, Kathryn Flynn, Orly Friedman, Chong-Hao Fu, Bill George, Thaly Germain, Steve Goldbach, Maia Heyck-Merlin, Debby Irving, Barbara Koltuv, Phil McArthur, Max Koltuv, David Levy, Divya Mani, Jamie McKee, Mike Metzger, Fred Muench, Adam Neaman, Richard Nyankori, Dana O'Donavan, Michael Passero, Eboo Patel, Bruce Patton, Amanda Ripley, Irene Rosenfeld, Jenn Rothberg, Emily Rummo, Jon Schwartz, Mijail Serruya, Adam Simon, Tom St. Hilaire, Shay Stewart-Bouley, Yutaka Tamura, Tyler Thigpen, Ari Wallach, Andy Wetzler, Lauren Wetzler.

The book is stronger for all their contributions, yet all errors, omissions, and shortcomings are my own.

Thank you also to all my friends and colleagues (you know who you are) who responded so supportively when I told you I was undertaking this crazy project. When you said, "This is the perfect book for you to write," it gave me so much courage and strength and confidence.

I am eternally grateful to my agent, Howard Yoon, of WME Agency. Looking back, it's amazing that Howard even took a call with me. I showed up to him with a messy two-pager and a writing style that sounded like a management consultant—hardly the makings of a page-turner, let alone something that would net a major book deal. Yet Howard saw something in the idea and stuck with me. He helped me to reframe the initial concept and gave me page after page of feedback and coached me to dramatically improve my writing. In the end, when we did what he calls the "barn-raising" of putting all the pieces of the proposal into a single document, I was stunned by what he helped me create.

Similarly, huge thanks to my editor, Dan Ambrosio, of Hachette Book Group, who saw the value of this book and the various audiences it could influence. From the start, Dan has been unwaveringly positive and enthusiastic. He partnered with me through every aspect of the publishing process and struck a helpful balance in giving me room to create while making highly targeted suggestions to improve the book's readability and practical utility for readers.

Last but not least, I wish to thank my family. My parents, John and Pat Wetzler, were the first to nurture my love of learning. They embraced my many questions, made countless sacrifices, and advocated for me to have a quality education. My wife, Jennifer Goldman-Wetzler, has supported me with this project from day one. Having already written a book herself, she knew the immense work and sacrifice it takes to do this, but as she always has in life, she encouraged me to follow my passion. She also provided powerful thought partnership to sharpen the ideas and a keen editing pen to strengthen the prose. My children, Jacob and Eden, are incredible bundles of curiosity and joy, whose questions and passion inspire me every day. They both provided feedback on the book's content and graphics, and Jacob built the technology for the *Ask* Assessment, which you can find at www.AskApproach.com. And a final thanks to our puppy, Breeze, who modeled curiosity in her own way, but even more important, kept me company on the couch for hours on end during my early-morning and late-night writing sessions. I love you all.

NOTES

FOREWORD

1. Amy Edmondson, *Right Kind of Wrong: The Science of Failing Well* (New York: Atria Books, 2023).

INTRODUCTION: INVITATION TO A SUPERPOWER

1. The year 2011 survey conducted by MaristPoll. Interestingly, for many groups, including non-whites, women, and Gen-Xers, *mind reading* was the clear favorite.
2. Glen Levy, "Forget Flying: Americans Want to Read Minds and Travel Through Time," *Time*, February 10, 2011, https://maristpoll.marist.edu/wp-content/misc/usapolls/US101115/Super%20Powers/Super%20Power%20Preference.htm.
3. Nicholas Epley, *Mindwise: How We Understand What Others Think, Believe, Feel, and Want* (New York: Knopf, 2014).
4. Epley, *Mindwise*.
5. Epley, *Mindwise*. As one piece of evidence that we vastly overestimate our ability to read body language, Epley points to the extremely low success rate of the TSA's SPOT program (less than 1 percent). See "Michael S. Schmidt and Eric Lichtblau, "Racial Profiling Rife at Airport, U.S. Officers Say," *New York Times*, August 12, 2012, https://www.nytimes.com/2012/08/12/us/racial-profiling-at-boston-airport-officials-say.html.
6. Tal Eyal, Mary Steffel, and Nicholas Epley, "Perspective Mistaking: Accurately Understanding the Mind of Another Requires Getting Perspective, Not Taking Perspective," *Journal of Personality and Social Psychology* 114 (2018): 547–571, https://doi.org/10.1037/pspa0000115.
7. This quote comes from an interview of Epley by Michelle McQuaid, "Can You Mind Read? With Nick Epley," *Making Positive Psychology Work*, podcast, 2018.
8. Elaine D. Eaker and Margaret Kelly-Hayes, "Self-Silencing and the Risk of Heart Disease and Death in Women: The Framingham Offspring Study," in

Silencing the Self Across Cultures: Depression and Gender in the Social World, ed. Dana C. Jack and Alisha Ali (New York: Oxford University Press, 2010), 399–414, https://doi.org/10.1093/acprof:oso/9780195398090.003.0020.

9. See, for example, Denise M. Sloan, "Self-Disclosure and Psychological Well-Being," in *Social Psychological Foundations of Clinical Psychology*, ed. James E. Maddux and June Price (New York: Guilford Press, 2010), 212–225. See also Dorota Weziak-Bialowolska, Piotr Bialowolski, and Ryan M. Niemiec, "Being Good, Doing Good: The Role of Honesty and Integrity for Health," *Social Science & Medicine* 291 (December 2021): 114494, https://doi.org/10.1016/j.socscimed.2021.114494.
10. Morrison said this during a speech delivered at the 1981 annual meeting of the Ohio Arts Council.

CHAPTER 1: WHAT STAYS UNSPOKEN

1. If this methodology is interesting to you and you want to go deeper on the ideas in this book, I encourage you to check out www.actiondesign.com. Action Design has translated Chris Argyris's ideas into powerful methods for interpersonal learning and reflection, and their founders are among my most important mentors in learning this work.
2. Frances J. Milliken, Elizabeth W. Morrison, and Patricia F. Hewlin, "An Exploratory Study of Employee Silence: Issues That Employees Don't Communicate Upward and Why*," *Journal of Management Studies* 40, no. (2003): 1453–1476, https://onlinelibrary.wiley.com/doi/abs/10.1111/1467-6486.00387.
3. Milliken, Morrison, and Hewlin, "An Exploratory Study of Employee Silence."

CHAPTER 2: WHY THEY WITHHOLD

1. Nicole Abi-Esber et al., "'Just Letting You Know…' Underestimating Others' Desire for Constructive Feedback," *Journal of Personality and Social Psychology* 123, no. 6 (2022): 1362–1385, https://doi.org/10.1037/pspi0000393.
2. Abi-Esber et al., "'Just Letting You Know.'"
3. Whenever I coach someone who is contemplating whether to share something with someone else, the first thing I say to them is: "If the roles were reversed and they had something to share with you but worried it would hurt your feelings, would you want them to tell you?" Most often, the other person says, "Of course I would," despite the fact that they were leaning toward "protecting" someone else from the same information.
4. Lauren Vogel, "Why Do Patients Often Lie to Their Doctors?," *Canadian Medical Association Journal* 191, no. 4 (2019): E115, https://doi.org/10.1503/cmaj.109-5705.
5. Shay Stewart-Bouley and Debby Irving cohost a talk series titled *Tell Me the Truth: Exploring the Heart of Cross-Racial Conversation* in which they model difficult conversations on a variety of topics live, onstage or virtually. Shay

Stewart-Bouley is a Black anti-racism speaker and educator and the executive director of Community Change Inc. and founding disruptor at *Black Girl in Maine Media*. Debby Irving is a white anti-racism educator and author of the book *Waking Up White, and Finding Myself in the Story of Race* (Cambridge, MA: Elephant Room Press, 2014). The ideas in this paragraph stemmed from an interview conducted with both Stewart-Bouley and Irving.

6. David A. Thomas, "Race Matters," *Harvard Business Review*, April 1, 2001, https://hbr.org/2001/04/race-matters.
7. Shelley J. Correll and Caroline Simard, "Research: Vague Feedback Is Holding Women Back," *Harvard Business Review*, April 29, 2016, https://hbr.org/2016/04/research-vague-feedback-is-holding-women-back.
8. Thomas, "Race Matters."
9. Ned T. Sahin et al., "Sequential Processing of Lexical, Grammatical, and Phonological Information Within Broca's Area," *Science* 326, no. 5951 (2009): 445–449, https://doi.org/10.1126/science.1174481. The data in this study reflect the brain's processing speed in milliseconds. I found the translation into words per minute and interpretation of this data in Oscar Trimboli, *How to Listen: Discover the Hidden Key to Better Communication* (Vancouver, BC: Page Two Books, 2022), 35.
10. Daphna Motro et al., "The 'Angry Black Woman' Stereotype at Work," *Harvard Business Review*, January 31, 2022, https://hbr.org/2022/01/the-angry-black-woman-stereotype-at-work.
11. Maura Cheeks, "How Black Women Describe Navigating Race and Gender in the Workplace," *Harvard Business Review*, March 26, 2018, https://hbr.org/2018/03/how-black-women-describe-navigating-race-and-gender-in-the-workplace.
12. In her book *Let Me Tell You What I Mean* (New York: Knopf, 2021), Joan Didion reflected, "I write entirely to find out what I'm thinking, what I'm looking at, what I see and what it means." Additionally, the quote "I write to discover what I know" is attributed to Flannery O'Connor, while the quote "I write to find out what I think" has been widely attributed to Stephen King.
13. This story was relayed from a confidential source who was in the room with Kissinger when he said this.
14. Susan Cain, *Quiet: The Power of Introverts in a World That Can't Stop Talking* (New York: Broadway Paperbacks, 2013), 22 (digital version).
15. "Workplace Burnout Survey | Deloitte US," Deloitte United States, n.d., accessed March 9, 2023, https://www2.deloitte.com/us/en/pages/about-deloitte/articles/burnout-survey.html.
16. "The Impact of Discrimination," Apa.org, 2015, accessed April 21, 2023, https://www.apa.org/news/press/releases/stress/2015/impact.
17. Marissa Shandell and Michael Parke, "The Paradoxical Relationship Between Employee Burnout and Voice on Well-Being," *Academy of Management Proceedings* 2022, no. 1 (2022): 16933, https://doi.org/10.5465/AMBPP.2022.16933abstract.

18. The term "impostor syndrome" was originally coined in 1978 by psychologists Pauline Rose Clane and Suzanne Imes to describe the experiences of the high-achieving women they studied. It has since been broadened to describe the psychological experience of "persistent doubt concerning one's abilities or accomplishments accompanied by the fear of being exposed as a fraud despite evidence of one's ongoing success," (*Merriam-Webster*).
19. Victoria L. Brescoll, "Who Takes the Floor and Why," *Administrative Science Quarterly*, February 2012, https://doi.org/10.1177/0001839212439994.

CHAPTER 3: CHOOSE CURIOSITY

1. Tara Brach references this anonymous quote in "The Power of Deep Listening: Part I," *The Power of Deep Listening*, Tara Brach.com, 2021, podcast, https://www.tarabrach.com/deep-listening-pt-1/?cn-reloaded=1.
2. George Loewenstein, "The Psychology of Curiosity: A Review and Reinterpretation," *Psychological Bulletin* 116 (1994): 75–98, https://doi.org/10.1037/0033-2909.116.1.75.
3. Matthias J. Gruber, Bernard D. Gelman, and Charan Ranganath, "States of Curiosity Modulate Hippocampus-Dependent Learning via the Dopaminergic Circuit," *Neuron* 84, no. 2 (2014): 486–496, https://doi.org/10.1016/j.neuron.2014.08.060.
4. A related concept often used in social science is interpersonal curiosity, which Jordan Litman and Mark Pezzo define as "the desire for new information about people." Jordan A. Litman and Mark V. Pezzo, "Dimensionality of Interpersonal Curiosity," *Personality and Individual Differences* 43 (2007): 1448–1459, https://doi.org/10.1016/j.paid.2007.04.021.
5. These definitions for "diversive" and "epistemic curiosity" come from Ian Leslie, *Curious: The Desire to Know and Why Your Future Depends on It* (New York: Basic Books, 2015), 17–20 (digital version).
6. Hanne K. Collins et al., "Underestimating Counterparts' Learning Goals Impairs Conflictual Conversations," *Psychological Science* 33, no. 10 (2022): 1732–1752, https://doi.org/10.1177/09567976221085494.
7. Celeste Kidd and Benjamin Y. Hayden, "The Psychology and Neuroscience of Curiosity," *Neuron* 88, no. 3 (2015): 449–460, https://doi.org/10.1016/j.neuron.2015.09.010.
8. For more on *choosing* curiosity, I strongly recommend listening to the radio show and podcast *Choose to Be Curious* by Lynn Borton, https://lynnborton.com.
9. This quote comes from Viktor E. Frankl (1905–1997), *Man's Search for Meaning: An Introduction to Logotherapy* (Boston: Beacon Press, 1962). Thank you to Marilee Adams's seminal and excellent book *Change Your Questions, Change Your Life* (New York: MJF Books, 2009), both for emphasizing the importance of choosing a path of learning and questions rather than judgment, and for pointing out Viktor Frankl's words on this topic.

10. I first learned the phrase "strong ideas, loosely held" from Phil McArthur of Action Design. A related phrase, "Strong ideas, weakly held," is originally attributed to future forecaster Paul Saffo and is explained by him in the blog https://saffo.com/02008/07/26/strong-opinions-weakly-held/.
11. Chris Argyris first developed the "Ladder of Inference" as a tool for what he called "Double Loop Learning" (discussed in Chapter 8 of this book), a type of learning that produces not only behavioral change but also a deeper shift in the learner's beliefs and values. The Ladder of Inference is detailed in the book *Action Science: Concepts, Methods, and Skills for Research and Intervention* (San Francisco: Jossey-Bass, 1985), which Chris coauthored with Robert Putnam and Diana Smith, as well as in this article: https://hbr.org/1977/09/double-loop-learning-in-organizations. The concept was further popularized by MIT professor Peter Senge's book *The Fifth Discipline* (New York, Doubleday Business, 1990). For more information, visit https://actiondesign.com/resources/readings/ladder-of-inference.
12. Daniel Kahneman, *Thinking, Fast and Slow*. (New York: Farrar, Straus and Giroux, 2013).
13. R. S. Nickerson, "Confirmation Bias: A Ubiquitous Phenomenon in Many Guises," *Review of General Psychology* 2, no. 2 (1998): 175–220, https://doi.org/10.1037/1089-2680.2.2.175.
14. Action Design's "Learning Pathways" framework, from which this is adapted, refers to "our stuff" as our "Model."
15. Edward Jones and Richard Nisbett, *The Actor and the Observer: Divergent Perceptions of the Causes of Behavior* (New York: General Learning Press, 1971).
16. L. Ross, "The Intuitive Psychologist and His Shortcomings: Distortions in the Attribution Process," in *Advances in Experimental Social Psychology*, vol. 10, ed. L. Berkowitz (New York: Academic Press, 1997), 173–220.
17. *Empathy: The Human Connection to Patient Care*, Cleveland Clinic, 2013, https://www.youtube.com/watch?v=cDDWvj_q-o8.
18. Shankar Vedantam, "How to Really Know Another Person," *Hidden Brain*, 2022, podcast, https://hiddenbrain.org/podcast/how-to-really-know-another-person/.
19. Note: The full framework, called "Patterns of Awareness," also makes explicit the mirror image: what we can see that others cannot (e.g., what we are up against, our intentions, how they come across, and their impact on us). It is just as important for us to become aware of what the other person cannot see, for this, too, is a blind spot we often forget and fill in with erroneous stories and assumptions.
20. The term "amygdala hijack" was first coined by Daniel Goleman in his book *Emotional Intelligence: Why It Can Matter More Than IQ*, 10th ann. trade pbk. ed. (New York: Bantam Books, 2005), to describe an immediate and overwhelming emotional response that is disproportionate to the actual event at hand.

21. Senior McKinsey researcher Jacqueline Brassey discusses this vicious cycle in her TED Talk at TEDxINSEAD, presented in July 2018, https://www.ted.com/talks/jacqueline_brassey_authentic_confidence_through_emotional_flexibility.
22. Tricia Hersey, *Rest Is Resistance: A Manifesto* (New York: Little, Brown Spark, 2022), 14.
23. Holly MacCormick, "How Stress Affects Your Brain and How to Reverse It," *Scope* (blog), October 7, 2020, https://scopeblog.stanford.edu/2020/10/07/how-stress-affects-your-brain-and-how-to-reverse-it/.

CHAPTER 4: MAKE IT SAFE

1. NeuroLeadership Institute, *Asked for Vs. Unasked for Feedback*, 2018, https://vimeo.com/291804051.
2. Amy C. Edmondson, "Learning from Mistakes Is Easier Said Than Done: Group and Organizational Influences on the Detection and Correction of Human Error," *Journal of Applied Behavioral Science* 32, no. 1 (1996): 5–28, https://doi.org/10.1177/0021886396321001.
3. Our society owes a debt of gratitude to Brené Brown for not just normalizing but highlighting the strength and value that comes from vulnerability.
4. Leslie Perlow, *When You Say Yes but Mean No: How Silencing Conflict Wrecks Relationships and Companies* (New York: Crown Business, 2003).
5. Thank you to Wharton professor Adam Grant for pointing out the importance of this.
6. J. Lee Cunningham et al., "Seeing Oneself as a Valued Contributor: Social Worth Affirmation Improves Team Information Sharing," *Academy of Management Journal* (2020), ISSN 0001-4273.
7. NeuroLeadership Institute, *Asked for Vs. Unasked for Feedback*.
8. Scott Barry Kauffman, "Adam Grant: Think Again," *Psychology Podcast*, 2021, https://podcasts.apple.com/us/podcast/adam-grant-think-again/id942777522?i=1000507702458.

CHAPTER 5: POSE QUALITY QUESTIONS

1. A poll conducted by Mu Sigma of their consulting clients. Tom Pohlmann and Neethi Mary Thomas, "Relearning the Art of Asking Questions," *Harvard Business Review*, March 27, 2015, https://hbr.org/2015/03/relearning-the-art-of-asking-questions.
2. For example, see page 46 of Eliza Bisbee Duffey's "The Ladies' and Gentlemen's Etiquette" (Philadelphia: Porter and Coates, 1877)—"Never ask impertinent questions; and under this head may be included nearly all questions. Some authorities in etiquette go so far as to say that *all* questions are strictly tabooed. Thus, if you wished to inquire after the health of the brother of your friend, you would say, "I hope your brother is well,' not 'How is your brother's health?'"

3. Einav Hart, Eric M. VanEpps, and Maurice E. Schweitzer, "The (Better Than Expected) Consequences of Asking Sensitive Questions," *Organizational Behavior and Human Decision Processes* 162 (January 2021): 136–154, https://doi.org/10.1016/j.obhdp.2020.10.014.
4. Margaret J. Wheatley, *Turning to One Another: Simple Conversations to Restore Hope to the Future*, expanded 2nd ed. (Oakland, CA: Berrett-Koehler Publishers, 2009).
5. Roger Fisher, William L. Ury, and Bruce Patton, *Getting to Yes: Negotiating Agreement Without Giving In* (New York: Penguin, 2011), 58–59.
6. In Fisher, Ury, and Patton's *Getting to Yes*, these are called "positions," which are distinct from underlying interests and concerns.
7. Jerome Bruner, "Life as Narrative," *Social Research* 54, no. 1 (1987): 11–32.

CHAPTER 6: LISTEN TO LEARN

1. Atul Gawande, "Curiosity and What Equality Really Means," *New Yorker*, n.d., accessed March 24, 2023, https://www.newyorker.com/news/news-desk/curiosity-and-the-prisoner.
2. Gawande, "Curiosity and What Equality Really Means."
3. "Accenture Research Finds Listening More Difficult in Today's Digital Workplace," Accenture, n.d., accessed March 24, 2023, https://newsroom.accenture.com/news/accenture-research-finds-listening-more-difficult-in-todays-digital-workplace.htm.
4. Bob Thompson and Hugh Sullivan, "Now Hear This! Most People Stink at Listening [excerpt]," *Scientific American*, May 3, 2013, accessed March 24, 2023, https://www.scientificamerican.com/article/plateau-effect-digital-gadget-distraction-attention/.
5. Kenneth Savitsky et al., "The Closeness-Communication Bias: Increased Egocentrism Among Friends Versus Strangers," *Journal of Experimental Social Psychology* 47, no. 1 (2011): 269–273, https://doi.org/10.1016/j.jesp.2010.09.005.
6. Susan Cain, *Quiet: The Power of Introverts in a World That Can't Stop Talking* (New York: Crown Publishers, 2012).
7. "Listening as a Spiritual Practice," *Friends Journal*, September 13, 2020, https://www.friendsjournal.org/listening-as-a-spiritual-practice/.
8. Shohola is the Eastern Algonquin word for "place of peace" and comes from the Lenni Lenape, the Indigenous inhabitants of the land on which Camp Shohola now resides.
9. As quoted in M. M. Owen, "The Psychologist Carl Rogers and the Art of Active Listening," Aeon, n.d., accessed April 22, 2023, https://aeon.co/essays/the-psychologist-carl-rogers-and-the-art-of-active-listening.
10. Kate Murphy, *You're Not Listening: What You're Missing and Why It Matters* (New York: Celadon Books, 2020), 1.
11. David Kantor called these three channels "meaning," "affect," and "power"—I've changed the names for ease of remembering. His work builds on pioneering

work on listening by Carl Rogers, who emphasized that true listening—or "active listening," as he called it—required paying attention not only to the words themselves but also to the emotion and meaning underlying those words, a practice of deep attention that requires both empathy and concentration. For more on this topic and on David's work more broadly, I recommend his book *Reading the Room: Group Dynamics for Coaches and Leaders* (San Francisco: Jossey-Bass, 2012).

12. Adrian F. Ward et al., "Brain Drain: The Mere Presence of One's Own Smartphone Reduces Available Cognitive Capacity," *Journal of the Association for Consumer Research* 2, no. 2 (2017): 140–154, https://doi.org/10.1086/691462.
13. Oscar Trimboli, *How to Listen: Discover the Hidden Key to Better Communication* (Vancouver, BC: Page Two Books, 2022), 164–165, Kindle version.
14. Tara Brach, *The Power of Deep Listening I,* Tara Brach.com (podcast), 2021, https://www.tarabrach.com/deep-listening-pt-1/?cn-reloaded=1.
15. As quoted in a podcast interview with Ezra Klein, "The Tao of Rick Rubin," *The Ezra Klein Show,* 2023, https://podcasts.apple.com/us/podcast/the-tao-of-rick-rubin/id1548604447?i=1000599009150.
16. The phrase "wait time" was originally coined by education scientist Mary Budd Rowe in 1972 to describe the duration of time between a teacher's question and a student's response. In her research, Rowe discovered that when teachers waited silently for at least three seconds after asking a question, students demonstrated greater creativity and learning. The concept was later expanded by Robert Stahl in 1985 to include the reflection and processing that occurs for teacher and student during this pause. See also Mary Budd Rowe, "Wait Time: Slowing Down May Be a Way of Speeding Up!," *Journal of Teacher Education* 37 no. 1 (1986): 43–50, https://doi.org/10.1177/002248718603700110.
17. Richard Davis, "Tactics for Asking Good Follow-Up Questions," *Harvard Business Review,* November 7, 2014, https://hbr.org/2014/11/tactics-for-asking-good-follow-up-questions.
18. Hanne K. Collins, "When Listening Is Spoken," *Current Opinion in Psychology* 47 (October 2022): 101402, https://doi.org/10.1016/j.copsyc.2022.101402.
19. Dotan R. Castro et al., "Mere Listening Effect on Creativity and the Mediating Role of Psychological Safety," *Psychology of Aesthetics, Creativity, and the Arts* 12, no. 4 (2018): 489–502, https://doi.org/10.1037/aca0000177.
20. Michael Bungay Stanier, *The Coaching Habit: Say Less, Ask More & Change the Way You Lead Forever* (Box of Crayons Press, 2016), 57–58, Kindle ed.
21. Debby, who came up with this idea with her husband, Bruce, called it "Back to Me" (BTM) listening, and I adapted it from their concept.

CHAPTER 7: REFLECT AND RECONNECT

1. From Pirkei Avot 5:22.
2. Note: This reflective process is adapted from a reflective process developed by Chris Argyris and Donald Schön called "single-loop" and "double-loop"

learning, and from a framework developed by Diana Smith and Action Design called the Learning Pathways. Double-loop learning produces not only behavioral change but also a deeper shift in the individual's or organization's beliefs and values that changes the outcome sought in the future. The concepts of single- and double-loop learning were originally employed by cybernetic theorist W. R. Ashby, who likened single-loop learning to a thermostat that turns the heat on or off as it hovers around a set point, whereas double-loop learning involves changing the set point altogether. Argyris and Schön applied this model to organizations, defining double-loop learning as "behavioral learning that changes the governing variables (values, norms, goals) of one's theory-in-use, the theory of action that can be inferred from behavior." https://actiondesign.com/resources/readings/double-loop-learning. See also C. Argyris and D. A. Schön, *Theory in Practice: Increasing Professional Effectiveness* (San Francisco: Jossey-Bass, 1974).

3. Jon Kabat-Zinn, *Wherever You Go, There You Are: Mindfulness Meditation in Everyday Life* (New York: Hyperion, 2005).
4. Brené Brown first coined the term "vulnerability hangover" in her book *I Thought It Was Just Me (but It Isn't): Making the Journey from "What Will People Think?" to "I Am Enough"* (New York: Avery, 2008), Kindle location: 3668.
5. "Gratitude Definition | What Is Gratitude," Greater Good, n.d., accessed March 28, 2023, https://greatergood.berkeley.edu/topic/gratitude/definition.
6. See, for example, Sara B. Algoe, Laura E. Kurtz, and Nicole M. Hilaire, "Putting the 'You' in 'Thank You': Examining Other-Praising Behavior as the Active Relational Ingredient in Expressed Gratitude," *Social Psychological and Personality Science* 7, no. 7 (2016): 658–666, https://doi.org/10.1177/1948550616651681.

CHAPTER 8: MAKE IT YOUR SUPERPOWER

1. The mastery spiral is adapted from a version that was included in a textbook from 1960 called *Management of Training Programs*, and referenced in Paul R. Curtiss and Phillip W. Warren, *The Dynamics of Life Skills Coaching* (Prince Albert, Saskatchewan: Training Research and Development Station, 1973). It was also used by Gordon Training International. It also draws inspiration from the spiral dynamics model of evolutionary development by Don Edward Beck and Christopher Cowan, based on the work of Clare Graves. For more, see Don Edward Beck and Christopher C. Cowan, *Spiral Dynamics: Mastering Values, Leadership, and Change* (Oxford, England: Blackwell Publishing, 1996).
2. Adam Gopnik, *The Real Work: On the Mystery of Mastery* (New York: Liveright, 2023), 8.

CHAPTER 9: MAKE IT YOUR ORGANIZATION'S SUPERPOWER

1. Alexander Newman, Ross Donohue, and Nathan Eva, "Psychological Safety: A Systematic Review of the Literature," *Human Resource Management Review* 27, no. 3 (2017): 521–535, https://doi.org/10.1016/j.hrmr.2017.01.001.
2. Filip Lievens et al., "Killing the Cat? A Review of Curiosity at Work," *Academy of Management Annals* 16, no. 1 (2022): 179–216, https://doi.org/10.5465/annals.2020.0203.
3. Daniel Jiménez-Jiménez and Raquel Sanz-Valle, "Innovation, Organizational Learning, and Performance," *Journal of Business Research* 64, no. 4 (2011): 408–417, https://doi.org/10.1016/j.jbusres.2010.09.010.
4. The term "collective genius" was coined and popularized by Harvard Business School professor Linda Hill and her colleagues Greg Brandeau, Emily Truelove, and Kent Lineback in their book *Collective Genius: The Art and Practice of Leading Innovation* (Boston: Harvard Business Review Press, 2014). While this book uses it in a slightly different way, it draws upon fundamentally similar notions.
5. "Glossier and Customer Centricity in the Digital Age—Consumer Products, Marketing & Strategy, Weekly Column Executive Search," MBS Group, February 17, 2023, https://www.thembsgroup.co.uk/internal/glossier-beautiful-on-the-inside-too/.
6. Importantly, of the latter group, 63 percent said their organization would strongly recommend it as a great place to work, while only 6 percent of those in the former category said they would do the same. Mark Murphy, "This Study Shows the Huge Benefits When Leaders Are Vulnerable," *Forbes*, April 4, 2021, accessed April 21, 2023, https://www.forbes.com/sites/markmurphy/2019/04/21/this-study-shows-the-huge-benefits-when-leaders-are-vulnerable/.
7. Lievens et al., "Killing the Cat?"
8. Adapted from Alain de Botton, who said, "Anyone who isn't embarrassed of who they were last year probably isn't learning enough."

CHAPTER 10: MAKE IT THE NEXT GENERATION'S SUPERPOWER

1. Barbara Tizard and Martin Hughes, *Young Children Learning* (Oxford, England: Blackwell Publishing, 2008).
2. "Mums Asked Nearly 300 Questions a Day by Kids," *Business Standard*, March 29, 2013, https://www.business-standard.com/article/pti-stories/mums-asked-nearly-300-questions-a-day-by-kids-113032900197_1.html.
3. According to Harvard developmental psychologist Paul Harris, "If you look more closely at the kinds of questions they ask, about 70 percent of them are seeking information as opposed to things like, for example, asking permission. And then when you look at those questions, 20 to 25 percent of them go beyond asking for bare facts like 'Where are my socks?' Children ask for explanations, like 'Why is my brother crying?' If a child spends one hour a day

between the ages of 2 and 5 with a caregiver who is talking to them and interacting with them, they will ask 40,000 questions in which they are asking for some kind of explanation. That's an enormous number of questions." "'Why Won't You Answer Me?'" Salon.com, May 20, 2012, accessed April 21, 2023, https://www.salon.com/2012/05/20/why_wont_you_answer_me/.

4. Susan L. Engel, *The Hungry Mind: The Origins of Curiosity in Childhood* (Cambridge, MA: Harvard University Press, 2015), 132.
5. Po Bronson and Ashley Merryman, "The Creativity Crisis," *Newsweek*, July 10, 2010, https://www.newsweek.com/creativity-crisis-74665. However, recent research suggests that interpersonal curiosity continues to play an important role in social and emotional development during adolescence. See Jinjoo Han et al., "Interpersonal Curiosity and Its Association with Social and Emotional Skills and Well-Being During Adolescence," *Journal of Adolescent Research*, April 2023, https://doi.org/10.1177/07435584231162572.
6. Tizard and Hughes, *Young Children Learning.*
7. Mónica Guzmán, *I Never Thought of It That Way: How to Have Fearlessly Curious Conversations in Dangerously Divided Times* (Dallas: BenBella Books, Inc., 2022).
8. James Baldwin, *Nobody Knows My Name: More Notes of a Native Son* (New York: Vintage Books, 1993).
9. This quote and the research study referenced are from a talk Engel gave at Williams College in 2011, in which she discussed many of the ideas and research covered in her book *The Hungry Mind: The Origins of Curiosity*, https://www.youtube.com/watch?v=Wh4WAdw-oq8.
10. "Teaching Teens the Art of Interpersonal Curiosity" (blog post), Rooted Ministry, January 19, 2021, https://rootedministry.com/teaching-teens-the-art-of-interpersonal-curiosity/.
11. Niobe Way and Joseph D. Nelson, "The Listening Project: Fostering Curiosity and Connection in Middle Schools," in *The Crisis of Connection: Roots, Consequences, and Solutions* (New York: New York University Press, 2018), 274–298.
12. See, for example, work on self-determination theory in education and learning, such as Edward Deci et al., "Motivation and Education: The Self-Determination Perspective," *Educational Psychologist* 26, nos. 3–4 (1991): 325–346, https://doi.org/10.1080/00461520.1991.9653137. For a review of the relative effects of intrinsic versus extrinsic rewards on learning outcomes, see Edward L. Deci, Richard Koestner, and Richard M. Ryan, "Extrinsic Rewards and Intrinsic Motivation in Education: Reconsidered Once Again," *Review of Educational Research* 71, no. 1 (2001): 1–27, https://doi.org/10.3102/00346543071001001.
13. "Askable Adult Campaign—Vermont Network," n.d., accessed April 21, 2023, https://www.vtnetwork.org/askableadult/.

14. MIT professor Hal Gregersen refers to this strategy as "noting the question that produced the answer." Hal B. Gregersen, *Questions Are the Answer: A Breakthrough Approach to Your Most Vexing Problems at Work and in Life* (New York: HarperBusiness, 2018), 164–165 (Kindle edition).

EPILOGUE: LIVE THE QUESTIONS, REPAIR THE WORLD

1. "Ronni Abergel, Inventor of the Human Library™," Human Library Organization, March 30, 2023, https://humanlibrary.org/dt_testimonials/ronni-abergel-inventor-of-the-human-library/.
2. Mike Rhodes, "Human Library Aims to Erase Prejudices" (blog post), *Muncie Journal*, July 10, 2021, https://www.munciejournal.com/2021/07/human-library-aims-to-erase-prejudices/.
3. Rhodes, "Human Library Aims to Erase Prejudices."
4. This figure is adapted from the Braver Angels framework "The Emotional and Intellectual Transformation of De-Polarization," which can be viewed at https://braverangels.org/our-story/.
5. Note: This continuum has nothing to do with political "left" and "right."
6. This quote and story comes from an interview of Aziz Abu Sarah, by Randy Lioz, "Want to Fight Polarization? Take a Vacation!" The *Braver Angels Podcast,* 2023, https://podcasts.apple.com/us/podcast/what-curiosity-can-teach-us-monica-guzman-with-ciaran/id1457136401?i=1000584016020.
7. Mónica Guzmán, *I Never Thought of It That Way: How to Have Fearlessly Curious Conversations in Dangerously Divided Times* (Dallas: BenBella Books, Inc., 2022), 234.
8. Rainer Maria Rilke and Mary D. Herter Norton, *Letters to a Young Poet,* rev. ed. (New York: W. W. Norton, 1993).

WORKS CONSULTED

Abel, Jennifer E., Preeti Vani, Nicole Abi-Esber, Hayley Blunden, and Juliana Schroeder. "Kindness in Short Supply: Evidence for Inadequate Prosocial Input." *Current Opinion in Psychology* 48 (December 2022): 101458. https://doi.org/10.1016/j.copsyc.2022.101458.

Abi-Esber, Nicole, Jennifer E. Abel, Juliana Schroeder, and Francesca Gino. "'Just Letting You Know…' Underestimating Others' Desire for Constructive Feedback." *Journal of Personality and Social Psychology* 123, no. 6 (2022): 1362–1385. https://doi.org/10.1037/pspi0000393.

"Accenture Research Finds Listening More Difficult in Today's Digital Workplace." n.d. Accessed March 24, 2023. https://newsroom.accenture.com/news/accenture-research-finds-listening-more-difficult-in-todays-digital-workplace.htm.

Adams, Marilee G. *Change Your Questions, Change Your Life: 12 Powerful Tools for Leadership, Coaching, and Results*. 4th ed. Oakland, CA: Berrett-Koehler Publishers, 2022.

Alexander, Elizabeth. *American Sublime: Poems*. St. Paul, MN: Graywolf Press, 2005.

Algoe, Sara B., Laura E. Kurtz, and Nicole M. Hilaire. "Putting the 'You' in 'Thank You': Examining Other-Praising Behavior as the Active Relational Ingredient in Expressed Gratitude." *Social Psychological and Personality Science* 7, no. 7 (2016): 658–666. https://doi.org/10.1177/1948550616651681.

Argyris, Chris. "Good Communication That Blocks Learning." *Harvard Business Review*, July 1, 1994. https://hbr.org/1994/07/good-communication-that-blocks-learning.

———. *Overcoming Organizational Defenses: Facilitating Organizational Learning*. Boston: Allyn and Bacon, 1990.

———. "Skilled Incompetence." *Harvard Business Review*, September 1, 1986. https://hbr.org/1986/09/skilled-incompetence.

———. "Teaching Smart People How to Learn." *Harvard Business Review*, May 1, 1991. https://hbr.org/1991/05/teaching-smart-people-how-to-learn.

———. *Teaching Smart People How to Learn*. Harvard Business Review Classics Series. Boston: Harvard Business Press, 2008.

Argyris, Chris, Robert Putnam, and Diana McLain Smith. *Action Science*. The Jossey-Bass Social and Behavioral Science Series. San Francisco: Jossey-Bass, 1985.

Argyris, Chris, and Donald A. Schön. *Organizational Learning II: Theory, Method, and Practice*. Addison-Wesley OD Series. Reading, MA: Addison-Wesley, 1998.

———. *Theory in Practice: Increasing Professional Effectiveness*. Jossey-Bass Higher and Adult Education Series. San Francisco: Jossey-Bass, 1992.

Asch, S. "Effects of Group Pressure upon the Modification and Distortion of Judgments." In *Groups, Leadership and Men; Research in Human Relations*, 177–190. Oxford, England: Carnegie Press, 1951.

Ashcroft, Paul, Simon Brown, and Garrick Jones. *The Curious Advantage*. Laïki Publishing, 2020.

"Askable Adult Campaign—Vermont Network." n.d. Accessed April 21, 2023. https://www.vtnetwork.org/askableadult/.

"Atul Gawande: Curiosity and What Equality Really Means." *New Yorker*. n.d. Accessed March 24, 2023. https://www.newyorker.com/news/news-desk/curiosity-and-the-prisoner.

Baldwin, James. *Nobody Knows My Name: More Notes of a Native Son*. New York: Vintage Books, 1993.

Beck, Don Edward, and Christopher C. Cowan. *Spiral Dynamics: Mastering Values, Leadership, and Change; Exploring the New Science of Memetics*. Oxford, England: Blackwell Publishing, 2009.

Berger, Warren. *The Book of Beautiful Questions: The Powerful Questions That Will Help You Decide, Create, Connect, and Lead*. New York: Bloomsbury USA, 2018.

———. *A More Beautiful Question: The Power of Inquiry to Spark Breakthrough Ideas*. New York: Bloomsbury USA, 2014.

"BioLINCC: Framingham Heart Study (FHS) Offspring (OS) and OMNI 1 Cohorts." n.d. Accessed April 1, 2023. https://biolincc.nhlbi.nih.gov/studies/framoffspring/.

Brach, Tara. *The Power of Deep Listening I*. Tara Brach.com, 2021. Podcast. https://www.tarabrach.com/deep-listening-pt-1/?cn-reloaded=1.

———. *Radical Compassion: Learning to Love Yourself and Your World with the Practice of RAIN*. New York: Viking, 2019.

Brescoll, Victoria L. "Who Takes the Floor and Why." *Administrative Science Quarterly*, February 2012. https://doi.org/10.1177/0001839212439994.

Bronson, Po, and Ashley Merryman. "The Creativity Crisis." *Newsweek*, July 10, 2010. https://www.newsweek.com/creativity-crisis-74665.

Broussard, Rhonda. *One Good Question: How Countries Prepare Youth to Lead*. US ed. New York: TBR Books, 2021.

Brown, Brené. *Dare to Lead: Brave Work, Tough Conversations, Whole Hearts*. New York: Random House, 2018.

———. *I Thought It Was Just Me (but It Isn't): Making the Journey from "What Will People Think?" to "I Am Enough."* New York: Avery, 2008.

Bruner, Jerome. "Life as Narrative." *Social Research* 54, no 1 (1987): 11–32.

Cain, Susan. *Quiet: The Power of Introverts in a World That Can't Stop Talking*. New York: Crown Publishers, 2012.

Castro, Dotan R., Frederik Anseel, Avraham N. Kluger, Karina J. Lloyd, and Yaara Turjeman-Levi. "Mere Listening Effect on Creativity and the Mediating Role of Psychological Safety." *Psychology of Aesthetics, Creativity, and the Arts* 12, no. 4 (2018): 489–502. https://doi.org/10.1037/aca0000177.

Cheeks, Maura. "How Black Women Describe Navigating Race and Gender in the Workplace." *Harvard Business Review*, March 26, 2018. https://hbr.org/2018/03/how-black-women-describe-navigating-race-and-gender-in-the-workplace.

Clance, Pauline Rose, and Suzanne Ament Imes. "The Imposter Phenomenon in High Achieving Women: Dynamics and Therapeutic Intervention." *Psychotherapy: Theory, Research & Practice* 15 (1978): 241–247. https://doi.org/10.1037/h0086006.

Coghlan, David, and Mary Brydon-Miller, eds. *The Sage Encyclopedia of Action Research*. Thousand Oaks, CA: SAGE Publications, 2014.

Collins, Hanne K. "When Listening Is Spoken." *Current Opinion in Psychology* 47 (October 2022): 101402. https://doi.org/10.1016/j.copsyc.2022.101402.

Collins, Hanne K., Charles A. Dorison, Francesca Gino, and Julia A. Minson. "Underestimating Counterparts' Learning Goals Impairs Conflictual Conversations." *Psychological Science* 33, no. 10 (2022): 1732–1752. https://doi.org/10.1177/09567976221085494.

Correll, Shelley J., and Caroline Simard. "Research: Vague Feedback Is Holding Women Back." *Harvard Business Review*, April 29, 2016. https://hbr.org/2016/04/research-vague-feedback-is-holding-women-back.

Creelman, David. "Interview: Robert Putnam, Applying Argyris." October 2003. https://actiondesign.com/resources/readings/applying-argyris.

Cunningham, J. Lee, Julia, Francesca Gino, Dan M. Cable, and Bradley R. Staats. "Seeing Oneself as a Valued Contributor: Social Worth Affirmation

Improves Team Information Sharing." *Academy of Management Journal* 64, no. 6 (2021): 1816–1841. https://doi.org/10.5465/amj.2018.0790.

Davis, Richard. "Tactics for Asking Good Follow-Up Questions." *Harvard Business Review,* November 7, 2014. https://hbr.org/2014/11/tactics-for-asking-good-follow-up-questions.

Deci, Edward L., Richard Koestner, and Richard M. Ryan. "Extrinsic Rewards and Intrinsic Motivation in Education: Reconsidered Once Again." *Review of Educational Research* 71, no. 1 (2001): 1–27. https://doi.org/10.3102/00346543071001001.

Deci, Edward L., Robert J. Vallerand, Luc G. Pelletier, and Richard M. Ryan. "Motivation and Education: The Self-Determination Perspective." *Educational Psychologist* 26, nos. 3–4 (1991): 325–346. https://doi.org/10.1080/00461520.1991.9653137.

Didion, Joan. *Let Me Tell You What I Mean*. New York: Knopf, 2021.

Dubner, Stephen J. "Can I Ask You a Ridiculously Personal Question?" *Freakonomics Radio,* 2021. Podcast. https://freakonomics.com/podcast/can-i-ask-you-a-ridiculously-personal-question-ep-451/.

Duffey, Eliza Bisbee. *The Ladies' and Gentlemen's Etiquette: A Complete Manual of the Manners and Dress of American Society*. Philadelphia: Porter and Coates, 1877.

Dunlop, Amelia. *Elevating the Human Experience: Three Paths to Love & Worth at Work*. Hoboken, NJ: Wiley, 2022.

Eaker, Elaine D., and Margaret Kelly-Hayes. "Self-Silencing and the Risk of Heart Disease and Death in Women: The Framingham Offspring Study." In *Silencing the Self Across Cultures: Depression and Gender in the Social World,* ed. Dana C. Jack and Alisha Ali. New York: Oxford University Press, 2010. https://doi.org/10.1093/acprof:oso/9780195398090.003.0020.

Edmondson, Amy C. *The Fearless Organization: Creating Psychological Safety in the Workplace for Learning, Innovation, and Growth*. Hoboken, NJ: Wiley, 2019.

———. "Learning from Mistakes Is Easier Said Than Done: Group and Organizational Influences on the Detection and Correction of Human Error." *Journal of Applied Behavioral Science* 32, no. 1 (1996): 5–28. https://doi.org/10.1177/0021886396321001.

Edmondson, Amy C., and Diana McLain Smith. "Too Hot to Handle? How to Manage Relationship Conflict." *California Management Review* 49, no. 1 (2006): 6.

Empathy: The Human Connection to Patient Care. Cleveland Clinic. 2013. https://www.youtube.com/watch?v=cDDWvj_q-o8.

Engel, Susan L. *The Hungry Mind: The Origins of Curiosity in Childhood*. Cambridge, MA: Harvard University Press, 2015.

Epley, Nicholas. *Mindwise: How We Understand What Others Think, Believe, Feel, and Want*. New York: Knopf, 2014.

Eyal, Tal, Mary Steffel, and Nicholas Epley. "Perspective Mistaking: Accurately Understanding the Mind of Another Requires Getting Perspective, Not Taking Perspective." *Journal of Personality and Social Psychology* 114 (2018): 547–571. https://doi.org/10.1037/pspa0000115.

Fisher, Roger, William Ury, and Bruce Patton. *Getting to Yes: Negotiating Agreement Without Giving In*. 2nd ed., Business Books. London: Random House, 2007.

Fosslien, Liz, and Molly West Duffy. *Big Feelings: How to Be Okay When Things Are Not Okay*. London: Canongate Books, 2022.

Glaser, Judith E. *Conversational Intelligence: How Great Leaders Build Trust and Get Extraordinary Results*. New York: Abingdon, 2016.

"Glossier and Customer Centricity in the Digital Age—Consumer Products, Marketing & Strategy, Weekly Column Executive Search." MBS Group. February 17, 2023. https://www.thembsgroup.co.uk/internal/glossier-beautiful-on-the-inside-too/.

Goleman, Daniel. *Emotional Intelligence: Why It Can Matter More Than IQ*. 10th ann. trade pbk. ed. New York: Bantam Books, 2005.

Gopnik, Adam. *The Real Work: On the Mystery of Mastery*. New York: Liveright, 2023.

Grant, Adam M. *Think Again: The Power of Knowing What You Don't Know*. New York: Viking, 2021.

"Gratitude Definition | What Is Gratitude." Greater Good. n.d. Accessed March 28, 2023. https://greatergood.berkeley.edu/topic/gratitude/definition.

Greene, Robert, and Joost Elffers. *The 48 Laws of Power*. New York: Penguin Books, 2000.

Gregersen, Hal B. *Questions Are the Answer: A Breakthrough Approach to Your Most Vexing Problems at Work and in Life*. New York: HarperBusiness, 2018.

Gruber, Matthias J., Bernard D. Gelman, and Charan Ranganath. "States of Curiosity Modulate Hippocampus-Dependent Learning via the Dopaminergic Circuit." *Neuron* 84, no. 2 (2014): 486–496. https://doi.org/10.1016/j.neuron.2014.08.060.

Guzmán, Mónica. *I Never Thought of It That Way: How to Have Fearlessly Curious Conversations in Dangerously Divided Times*. Dallas: BenBella Books, Inc., 2022.

———. "What Curiosity Can Teach Us." *The Braver Angels*, 2022. Podcast. https://podcasts.apple.com/us/podcast/what-curiosity-can-teach-us-monica-guzman-with-ciaran/id1457136401?i=1000584016020.

Hall, Edward T. *The Silent Language*. New York: Anchor Books, 1990.

Hari, Johann. *Stolen Focus: Why You Can't Pay Attention*. New York: Crown, 2021.

Hart, Einav, Eric M. VanEpps, and Maurice E. Schweitzer. "The (Better Than Expected) Consequences of Asking Sensitive Questions." *Organizational Behavior and Human Decision Processes* 162 (January 2021): 136–154. https://doi.org/10.1016/j.obhdp.2020.10.014.

Healy, Patrick. "A Phone Call with Angela Lansbury Changed Me." *New York Times*, October 15, 2022. https://www.nytimes.com/2022/10/15/opinion/angela-lansbury-memory-dead.html.

Hersey, Tricia. *Rest Is Resistance: A Manifesto*. New York: Little, Brown Spark, 2022.

Hill, Linda A. *Collective Genius: The Art and Practice of Leading Innovation*. Boston: Harvard Business Review Press, 2014.

"The Impact of Discrimination." Apa.org, 2015. Accessed April 21, 2023. https://www.apa.org/news/press/releases/stress/2015/impact.

Jiménez-Jiménez, Daniel, and Raquel Sanz-Valle. "Innovation, Organizational Learning, and Performance." *Journal of Business Research* 64, no. 4 (2011): 408–417. https://doi.org/10.1016/j.jbusres.2010.09.010.

Joiner, Bill, and Stephen Josephs. *Leadership Agility: Five Levels of Mastery for Anticipating and Initiating Change*. San Francisco: Jossey-Bass, 2007.

Jones, Edward, and Richard Nisbett. *The Actor and the Observer: Divergent Perceptions of the Causes of Behavior*. New York: General Learning Press, 1971.

Kabat-Zinn, Jon. *Wherever You Go, There You Are: Mindfulness Meditation in Everyday Life*. New York: Hyperion, 2005.

Kahneman, Daniel. *Thinking, Fast and Slow*. New York: Farrar, Straus and Giroux, 2011.

Kantor, David. *Reading the Room: Group Dynamics for Coaches and Leaders*. San Francisco: Jossey-Bass, 2012.

Kashdan, Todd B. *The Art of Insubordination: How to Dissent and Defy Effectively*. New York: Avery, 2022.

———. *Curious? Discover the Missing Ingredient to a Fulfilling Life*. New York: Harper, 2010.

Kauffman, Scott Barry. "Adam Grant: Think Again." *Psychology Podcast*, 2021. https://podcasts.apple.com/us/podcast/adam-grant-think-again/id942777522?i=1000507702458.

Kidd, Celeste, and Benjamin Y. Hayden. "The Psychology and Neuroscience of Curiosity." *Neuron* 88, no. 3 (2015): 449–460. https://doi.org/10.1016/j.neuron.2015.09.010.

Kimball, Robert. "COMMENTARY: Thinking of Life: Dealing in Certainties—UPI Archives." UPI, January 1, 2001. https://www.upi.com/Archives/2001/01/01/COMMENTARY-Thinking-of-Life-Dealing-in-certainties/4154978325200/.

Klein, Ezra. "The Tao of Rick Rubin." *The Ezra Klein Show*, 2023. Podcast. https://podcasts.apple.com/us/podcast/the-tao-of-rick-rubin/id1548604447?i=1000599009150.

"The Ladder of Inference | Resources." Action Design. n.d. Accessed March 28, 2023. https://actiondesign.com/resources/readings/ladder-of-inference.

Leslie, Ian. *Curious: The Desire to Know and Why Your Future Depends on It*. New York: Basic Books, 2015.

Levy, Glen. "Forget Flying: Americans Want to Read Minds and Travel Through Time." *Time*, February 10, 2011. https://newsfeed.time.com/2011/02/10/forget-flying-americans-want-to-time-travel-and-read-minds/.

Lievens, Filip, Spencer H. Harrison, Patrick Mussel, and Jordan A. Litman. "Killing the Cat? A Review of Curiosity at Work." *Academy of Management Annals* 16, no. 1 (2022): 179–216. https://doi.org/10.5465/annals.2020.0203.

Lioz, Randy. "Want to Fight Polarization? Take a Vacation!" *The Braver Angels*, 2023. Podcast. https://podcasts.apple.com/us/podcast/what-curiosity-can-teach-us-monica-guzman-with-ciaran/id1457136401?i=1000584016020.

"Listening as a Spiritual Practice." *Friends Journal*, September 13, 2020. https://www.friendsjournal.org/listening-as-a-spiritual-practice/.

Loewenstein, George. "The Psychology of Curiosity: A Review and Reinterpretation." *Psychological Bulletin* 116 (1994): 75–98. https://doi.org/10.1037/0033-2909.116.1.75.

Lydon-Staley, David. *Choose to Be Curious*. n.d. Podcast.

MacCormick, Holly. "How Stress Affects Your Brain and How to Reverse It." *Scope* (blog), October 7, 2020. https://scopeblog.stanford.edu/2020/10/07/how-stress-affects-your-brain-and-how-to-reverse-it/.

Machiavelli, Niccolò. *The Prince*. Trans. George Bull. New York: Penguin Classics, 2003.

Marquardt, Michael J. *Leading with Questions: How Leaders Find the Right Solutions by Knowing What to Ask*. Rev. and updated ed. San Francisco: Jossey-Bass, 2014.

McQuaid, Michelle. "Can You Mind Read? With Nick Epley." *Making Positive Psychology Work*, 2018. Podcast.

Mehrabian, Albert. "Communication Without Words." In *Communication Theory*, ed. C. David Mortensen, 2nd ed. Routledge, 2008.

Milliken, Frances J., Elizabeth W. Morrison, and Patricia F. Hewlin. "An Exploratory Study of Employee Silence: Issues That Employees Don't Communicate Upward and Why*." *Journal of Management Studies* 40, no. 6 (2003): 1453–1476. https://doi.org/10.1111/1467-6486.00387.

Motro, Daphna, Jonathan B. Evans, Aleksander P. J. Ellis, and Lehman Benson III. "The 'Angry Black Woman' Stereotype at Work." *Harvard Business Review*, January 31, 2022. https://hbr.org/2022/01/the-angry-black-woman-stereotype-at-work.

Murphy, Kate. *You're Not Listening: What You're Missing and Why It Matters*. New York: Celadon Books, 2020.

Murphy, Mark. "This Study Shows the Huge Benefits When Leaders Are Vulnerable." *Forbes*, April 21, 2019. Accessed April 21, 2023. https://www.forbes.com/sites/markmurphy/2019/04/21/this-study-shows-the-huge-benefits-when-leaders-are-vulnerable/.

NeuroLeadership Institute. *Asked for Vs. Unasked for Feedback*. 2018. https://vimeo.com/291804051.

Newman, Alexander, Ross Donohue, and Nathan Eva. "Psychological Safety: A Systematic Review of the Literature." *Human Resource Management Review* 27, no. 3 (2017): 521–535. https://doi.org/10.1016/j.hrmr.2017.01.001.

Nickerson, Raymond S. "Confirmation Bias: A Ubiquitous Phenomenon in Many Guises." *Review of General Psychology* 2, no. 2 (1998): 175–220. https://doi.org/10.1037/1089-2680.2.2.175.

"Our Story." *The Braver Angels*, n.d. Podcast. Accessed April 24, 2023. https://braverangels.org/our-story/.

Owen, M. M. "The Psychologist Carl Rogers and the Art of Active Listening | Aeon Essays." Aeon, n.d. Accessed April 22, 2023. https://aeon.co/essays/the-psychologist-carl-rogers-and-the-art-of-active-listening.

Pence, Lara. *Dr. Cart Hart: On Being and Seeing the Human*. Curious Minds, 2021.

Perlow, Leslie A. *When You Say Yes but Mean No: How Silencing Conflict Wrecks Relationships and Companies, and What You Can Do About It*. New York: Crown Business, 2003.

Pohlmann, Tom, and Neethi Mary Thomas. "Relearning the Art of Asking Questions." *Harvard Business Review*, March 27, 2015. https://hbr.org/2015/03/relearning-the-art-of-asking-questions.

"Research: Vague Feedback Is Holding Women Back." *Harvard Business Review*, April 29, 2016. Accessed March 9, 2023. https://hbr.org/2016/04/research-vague-feedback-is-holding-women-back.

Rhodes, Mike. "Human Library Aims to Erase Prejudices." *Muncie Journal* (blog), July 10, 2021. https://www.munciejournal.com/2021/07/human-library-aims-to-erase-prejudices/.

Rilke, Rainer Maria, and Mary D. Herter Norton. *Letters to a Young Poet*. Rev. ed. New York: W. W. Norton, 1993.

Ripley, Amanda. *High Conflict: Why We Get Trapped and How We Get Out*. New York: Simon & Schuster, 2021.

Rogers, Carl R., and Richard Farson. *Active Listening.* Mansfield Centre, CT: Martino Publishing, 2015.

"Ronni Abergel, Inventor of the Human Library™," Human Library Organization. March 30, 2023. https://humanlibrary.org/dt_testimonials/ronni-abergel-inventor-of-the-human-library/.

Rooted Ministry. "Teaching Teens the Art of Interpersonal Curiosity" (blog), January 19, 2021. https://rootedministry.com/teaching-teens-the-art-of-interpersonal-curiosity/.

Ross, Lee. "The Intuitive Psychologist and His Shortcomings: Distortions in the Attribution Process." In *Advances in Experimental Social Psychology*, ed. Leonard Berkowitz: 173–220. New York: Academic Press, 1997.

Rowe, Mary Budd. "Wait Time: Slowing Down May Be a Way of Speeding Up!," *Journal of Teacher Education* 37, no. 1 (1986): 43–50. https://doi.org/10.1177/002248718603700110.

Rudolph, Jenny, Steve Taylor, and Erica Foldy. "Collaborative Off-Line Reflection: A Way to Develop Skill in Action Science and Action Inquiry." In *Handbook of Action Research*. Thousand Oaks, CA: SAGE Publications, 2000.

Sahin, Ned T., Steven Pinker, Sydney S. Cash, Donald Schomer, and Eric Halgren. "Sequential Processing of Lexical, Grammatical, and Phonological Information Within Broca's Area." *Science* 326, no. 5951 (2009): 445–449. https://doi.org/10.1126/science.1174481.

Savitsky, Kenneth, Boaz Keysar, Nicholas Epley, Travis Carter, and Ashley Swanson. "The Closeness-Communication Bias: Increased Egocentrism Among Friends Versus Strangers." *Journal of Experimental Social Psychology* 47, no. 1 (2001): 269–273. https://doi.org/10.1016/j.jesp.2010.09.005.

Schein, Edgar H. *Humble Inquiry: The Gentle Art of Asking Instead of Telling*. San Francisco: Berrett-Koehler Publishers, 2013.

Schmidt, Michael S., and Eric Lichtblau. "Racial Profiling Rife at Airport, U.S. Officers Say." *New York Times*, August 12, 2012. https://www.nytimes.com/2012/08/12/us/racial-profiling-at-boston-airport-officials-say.html.

Schön, Donald A., ed. *The Reflective Turn: Case Studies in and on Educational Practice*. New York: Teachers College Press, 1991.

Scott, Kim. *Just Work: Get Sh*t Done, Fast & Fair*. New York: St. Martin's Press, 2021.

———. *Radical Candor: How to Get What You Want by Saying What You Mean*. Fully rev. and updated ed. London: Pan Books, 2019.

Sesno, Frank. *Ask More: The Power of Questions to Open Doors, Uncover Solutions, and Spark Change*. New York: AMACOM, 2017.

Shandell, Marissa, and Michael Parke. "The Paradoxical Relationship Between Employee Burnout and Voice on Well-Being." *Academy of Management Proceedings*, no. 1 (2022): 16933. https://doi.org/10.5465/AMBPP.2022.16933abstract.

Sloan, Denise M. "Self-Disclosure and Psychological Well-Being." In *Social Psychological Foundations of Clinical Psychology*, 212–225. New York: Guilford Press, 2010.

Smith, Diana McLain. *Divide or Conquer: How Great Teams Turn Conflict into Strength*. New York: Portfolio, 2008.

———. *Elephant in the Room: How Relationships Make or Break the Success of Leaders and Organizations*. San Francisco: Jossey-Bass, 2011.

———. "Keeping a Strategic Dialogue Moving." In *Corporate Communication: A Strategic Approach to Building Reputation.*, ed. Peggy Simcic Brønn and Roberta Wiig Berg. Oslo, Norway: Gyldendal Norsk Forlag, 2002.

Sobel, Andrew, and Jerold Panas. *Power Questions: Build Relationships, Win New Business, and Influence Others*. Hoboken, NJ: Wiley, 2012.

Solin, Daniel. *Ask: How to Relate to Anyone*. Silvercloud Publishing, 2020.

Standard, Business. "Mums Asked Nearly 300 Questions a Day by Kids." March 29, 2013. https://www.business-standard.com/article/pti-stories/mums-asked-nearly-300-questions-a-day-by-kids-113032900197_1.html.

Stanier, Michael Bungay. *The Coaching Habit: Say Less, Ask More & Change the Way You Lead Forever*. Box of Crayons Press, 2016.

Stone, Douglas, Bruce Patton, and Sheila Heen. *Difficult Conversations: How to Discuss What Matters Most; [Updated with Answers to the 10 Most Frequently Asked Questions about Difficult Conversation]*. 10th. ann. ed. of 2nd ed. New York, London: Penguin Books, 2010.

Thomas, David A. "Race Matters." *Harvard Business Review*, April 1, 2001. https://hbr.org/2001/04/race-matters.

Thompson, Andrea. "Speed of Thought-to-Speech Traced in Brain." Live Science. October 15, 2009. https://www.livescience.com/5780-speed-thought-speech-traced-brain.html.

Thompson, Bob, and Hugh Sullivan. "Now Hear This! Most People Stink at Listening [excerpt]." *Scientific American*. n.d. Accessed March 24, 2023. https://www.scientificamerican.com/article/plateau-effect-digital-gadget-distraction-attention/.

Thompson, Sherwood. *Encyclopedia of Diversity and Social Justice*. Lanham, MD: Rowman & Littlefield, 2015.

Tizard, Barbara, and Martin Hughes. *Young Children Learning*. Oxford, England: Blackwell Publishing, 2008.

Trimboli, Oscar. *How to Listen: Discover the Hidden Key to Better Communication*. Vancouver, BC: Page Two Books, 2002.

Vedantam, Shankar. "How to Really Know Another Person." *Hidden Brain*, 2022. Podcast. https://hiddenbrain.org/podcast/how-to-really-know-another-person/.

Vogel, Lauren. "Why Do Patients Often Lie to Their Doctors?" *Canadian Medical Association Journal* 191, no. 4 (2019): E115–E115. https://doi.org/10.1503/cmaj.109-5705.

Wallace, David Foster. *This Is Water: Some Thoughts, Delivered on a Significant Occasion About Living a Compassionate Life*. New York: Little, Brown, 2009.

Ward, Adrian F., Kristen Duke, Ayelet Gneezy, and Maarten W. Bos. "Brain Drain: The Mere Presence of One's Own Smartphone Reduces Available Cognitive Capacity." *Journal of the Association for Consumer Research* 2, no. 2 (2017): 140–154. https://doi.org/10.1086/691462.

"Water Cooler Chat & Why to Encourage Water Cooler Conversation." Axero Solutions (blog), August 28, 2020. https://axerosolutions.com/blog/water-cooler-chat-11-smart-reasons-to-encourage-it.

Way, Niobe, and Joseph D. Nelson. "The Listening Project: Fostering Curiosity and Connection in Middle Schools." In *The Crisis of Connection: Roots, Consequences, and Solutions*, ed. Niobe Way, Alisha Ali, Carol Gilligan, and Pedro Noguera, 274–298. New York: New York University Press, 2018.

Weziak-Bialowolska, Dorota, Piotr Bialowolski, and Ryan M. Niemiec. "Being Good, Doing Good: The Role of Honesty and Integrity for Health." *Social Science & Medicine* 291 (December 2021): 114494. https://doi.org/10.1016/j.socscimed.2021.114494.

Wheatley, Margaret J. *Turning to One Another: Simple Conversations to Restore Hope to the Future*. Expanded 2nd ed. A BK Life Book. Oakland, CA: Berrett-Koehler Publishers, 2009.

"'Why Won't You Answer Me?'" Salon.com, May 20, 2012. Accessed April 21, 2023. https://www.salon.com/2012/05/20/why_wont_you_answer_me/.

Williams College. *The Hungry Mind: The Origins of Curiosity*. 2011. https://www.youtube.com/watch?v=Wh4WAdw-oq8.

Wise, Will, and Chad Littlefield. *Ask Powerful Questions: Create Conversations That Matter*. 2nd ed. CreateSpace Independent Publishing Platform, 2017.

"Workplace Burnout Survey," Deloitte United States. n.d. Accessed March 9, 2023. https://www2.deloitte.com/us/en/pages/about-deloitte/articles/burnout-survey.html.

Zurn, Perry, and Danielle S. Bassett. *Curious Minds: The Power of Connection*. Cambridge, MA: MIT Press, 2022.

INDEX